D1599134

STATES OF CONFUSION

States of Confusion

*How Our Voter ID Laws Fail Democracy
and What to Do About It*

Don Waisanen, Sonia R. Jarvis, *and*
Nicole A. Gordon

NEW YORK UNIVERSITY PRESS
New York

NEW YORK UNIVERSITY PRESS
New York
www.nyupress.org

Please contact the Library of Congress for Cataloging-in-Publication data.

ISBN: 9781479807918 (hardback)
ISBN: 9781479807925 (paperback)
ISBN: 9781479807963 (library ebook)
ISBN: 9781479807949 (consumer ebook)

New York University Press books are printed on acid-free paper, and their binding materials are chosen for strength and durability. We strive to use environmentally responsible suppliers and materials to the greatest extent possible in publishing our books.

Manufactured in the United States of America

10 9 8 7 6 5 4 3 2 1

Also available as an ebook

CONTENTS

In a recent election year, Lila Cockrell went to the polls to cast a vote in her city's mayoral runoffs. As the first female mayor of San Antonio, you can imagine her shock when election officials told her that she could not vote without a form of authorized identification.[1] As an elderly person who no longer drives and has no need for an ID, Cockrell could have had this situation easily addressed through a provision in Texas law that had been repealed. The state's ID requirements had only become harsher in recent years. "It was uncomfortable for the election officials to tell her, 'No.' Obviously, they knew who she was," said one of the administrators in her county.[2] At a time when the stakes for many elections could not be higher, outraged citizens like Cockrell have been finding themselves subject to new, frustrating barriers to voting across the United States.

The last decade has seen an exponential growth in voter documentation requirements, affecting around twenty-five million eligible voters and their constitutional right to cast a vote.[3] Many of the states with the strictest voter ID requirements also happen to be swing states that matter the most in general elections. During the US general election in 2020, the voter registration efforts that reduced these barriers made headlines, especially in shattering expectations for turnout among minorities, from Asian American and Black voters in Georgia to Navajo and Latino voters in Arizona.[4] Former Georgia House Democratic minority leader and voting rights activist Stacey Abrams and community organizations led on-the-ground voter registration drives that not only supported the election of a new president but flipped the state from red to blue—and the US Senate majority with it.[5] In response to these successes, hundreds of new, stricter voting laws continue to be proposed and passed in state legislatures across the nation.[6] Following these and other pressing developments, such as renewed attention to voter identification requirements due to an increase in the use of mail-in ballots during the COVID-19 pandemic, in this book we chart the state of voter

ID requirements and the maddening difficulties that they are creating for people, and we offer solutions for this growing challenge that is failing democracy in the United States.

States of Confusion surveys ten states with especially strict documentation requirements for registration and for voting. The type of broad research we conducted—the first of its kind on this issue—is the basis for a series of practical recommendations arising from our communication with citizens, state agencies, and nonprofit groups working on voter engagement and assisting eligible citizens to obtain necessary documentation. We explain the recent history of voter ID laws and offer several perspectives on the challenges voters face in complying with these requirements.

Ultimately, we find that many citizens are confused by documentation requirements and frustrated by the barriers to voter registration and voting that have been put in place in many states, particularly over the past decade. As a result, large numbers of people are being excluded by our voting system. We also find that voters in different states have vastly different experiences, raising the question of why citizens in one state should confront radically different requirements than citizens in another state.

We thus call on policymakers to adopt uniform, national voter ID standards that are simple, accessible, and cost-free. In the absence of sweeping policy changes, however, we provide interim solutions for assisting eligible citizens with voter documentation requirements through the nonprofit and community organizations closest to, and most capable of helping, those most affected by these new laws. This change would address unreasonable barriers that are preventing eligible voters from voting and provide for more equitable experiences with the voting process.

That any person faces difficulties in getting what they need to vote should be cause for alarm. Tackling new voter ID requirements is an urgent matter that will shape public participation in this country for a generation and the health of our democracy.

* * *

While we were finishing this book, the COVID-19 pandemic broke out, affecting just about every person on the planet. In the United States, we observed the challenges that voters face multiply during a presidential election year. Every issue connected to citizens' opportunities to vote underwent a political magnification, particularly with regard to mail-in voting. With the virus's very public, deep, and wide effects, it became difficult to keep political intentions private. The political parties had opposite aims: it was believed that Democrats would be aided by increased voter turnout, and that Republicans would be aided by decreased voter turnout. Amid the COVID outbreak in Wisconsin, for example, attempts to relax mail-in voting rules for a primary election were thwarted, forcing tens of thousands of voters to the polls at risk of exposure to the virus.[7] In Alabama the choice between protecting one's health and voting (especially for those with disabilities, the elderly, and people of color) was brought to the fore through lawsuits pointing to the significance of ID requirements: "Absentee voters are currently required to submit photocopies of their photo identification as well as sign the absentee ballot before a notary or two witnesses," impossible expectations during the pandemic.[8] In Kentucky, too, the issue of ID came forcefully into view when lawmakers overrode their governor's veto of a bill limiting voting only to those with a particular type of government-issued photo ID. Those who opposed the bill argued that the measure would have suppressive effects on certain voters, and they raised the question of how people could be expected to procure such an ID during a time when the government offices that supply them were closed.[9] Choosing to cast a vote became a matter of life and risking death.

Former US president Donald Trump and his followers asserted during the pandemic election season that voting from home would intensify election vulnerabilities, cheating, and other problems.[10] Continuing a running theme from across his years as president, Trump created a megaphone for claims that the election was stolen due to ballot insecurities and similar charges,[11] laying a foundation for everything from a violent insurrection at the US Capitol on January 6, 2021, to an insistence that audit upon audit take place in battleground states, to the establishment of even more limiting and exclusionary voter ID laws across the country.[12]

On the other side, advocates cited long-standing successes with mail-in voting, virtually no evidence of election integrity violations, and the vast numbers of eligible voters who already stood to be disenfranchised by consequences of the pandemic.[13] Responding to claims by Trump and his followers, judges and officials (including Trump's own appointees) and election staff at every level of government concluded that, despite the challenges of COVID, this "was one of the most secure elections in our history."[14] Through the lens of ID requirements, we address these and related issues throughout this book, at a time when they have never mattered more in the United States. We find that connected problems point toward larger issues arising from our voting systems, their inequitable processes, and the consequent disenfranchisement of many US citizens.

We believe in election integrity. What became apparent in the course of our project is that many citizens feel similarly. No one wants an election to be run by anything other than the highest standards and processes for accountability, to make sure that every vote cast is valid and counted. We know that at first glance strict voter documentation requirements can seem to exist simply to enforce the law by making sure that each person will only have one vote. Yet, in practice, these laws function to exclude many citizens from this basic right by making voting far more complicated and challenging than it needs to be.

For reasons we will detail, in the absence of federal oversight, and in part arising from constitutional complexities,[15] states have been determining what forms of ID work for voting, reflecting arbitrary and sharply partisan preferences. Since generally speaking election processes are governed and implemented by states, it is the states that allow these inequities to increase. Technicalities have been designed to create disproportionate, racial imbalances in voting accessibility. As one report highlights, Texas doesn't allow student ID cards but does accept concealed weapons permits for the purposes of voting.[16] Underscoring the potential impact of this law, "More than 80 percent of handgun licenses issued to Texans in 2018 went to [W]hite Texans, while more than half of the students in the University of Texas system are racial or ethnic minorities."[17] Millions of eligible voters, or those previously eligible to vote, continue to come up against these types of obstacles constructed by policymakers who have learned that changing state-level election laws can tip the balance of power in their favor, maximizing the impact of some voting blocs while minimizing others. These developments have led the Reverend William Barber II to conclude, "Jim Crow did not retire: he went to law school and launched a second career. Meet James Crow, Esquire."[18]

Voter documentation requirements are thoroughly politicized and racialized policies designed to excise the votes of marginalized communities and partisan political enemies in the guise of protecting election integrity. These requirements follow a long and ugly history of voter suppression in the United States. Until the exclusionary effects of voter documentation requirements and many other, connected forms of suppression are overcome, it will not be possible to claim that any national or even local election is truly representative of US citizens. These are the stakes.

We hope that readers of this book do not lose sight of our main point: voting should be easy. We want readers to see and feel the infuriating frustrations that many voters continue to experience, in the hope that the crisis in voter identification requirements can be addressed and the electorate expanded through the community-informed, research-based solutions identified in this project. Everyone learning from this book can find ways to oppose voter disenfranchisement and ensure that every citizen's vote and voice count.

Introduction

Voting Made Difficult

College students don't always have their birth certificates on them, something they have at their parents' home. Not everyone has their driver's license . . . so there should be more options. Going to the DMV [Department of Motor Vehicles] is time-consuming and there is a cost, like twenty-two dollars. I myself don't currently have that to spare. Some are trying to vote to change that but can't. It feels like no one cares about me or cares for what I have to say because I can't get there. I pay taxes and everything yet can't be heard like everyone else. I feel like that's why people think their votes don't matter, because it takes so much effort and it's such a hassle that not everyone can handle to get it done. For places where it is harder for some people, they should have accommodations for everybody.
—Focus group participant, Ohio

Imagine you're a citizen who has never had problems casting your vote in an election. You consider it your duty to show up at the voting booth each Election Day, and feel proud of performing your most essential act as a participant in the life of this country. Like most people, regardless of your party or candidate preferences, you believe that every citizen deserves the right to vote and should have equal access to doing so. You also know that for many groups securing the ability to vote has historically been a hard-won right.

However, with a recent change in employment and personal circumstances, you've just moved to a different state for a new job, and the national election is around the corner next month. You hop online to find your local county election office, some thirty miles away, and realize that it's open only during business hours Tuesday through Fridays, so you'll need to ask your new boss, with some trepidation, for time off to go register to vote. Your boss lets you head out, and you arrive at the office, equipped with an ID that always worked for election purposes in your last state. You stand in a long line for an hour and pull out your ID for the clerk, who tells you that only state photo IDs will work for voter registration, and that you'll need to bring two documents to the transportation commission to begin that process, some forty miles away in the other direction.

These documents could include a birth certificate and a utility bill with your new address on it. Although some documents you possess would present no difficulties, such as your previous state's driver license, your birth certificate was destroyed in a small basement flood last year, and you have not had enough time to get another one. You learn that a duplicate certificate costs thirty-three dollars and that the utility bill or other documents may need to be notarized (the clerk can't remember), because you also recently changed your last name due to a divorce. You make little income from your new job as is, and then there's the additional gas cost of all the driving you need to do. Exhausted and confused by this maze of requirements, and with the kids needing to be picked up from daycare soon anyway, you give up, head home, and simply decide to sit out this election cycle.

Although this may be an extreme case, stories like it are not uncommon. Even one or two of the obstacles described can easily discourage attempts to get the documentation needed to vote. Throughout the United States, many citizens face substantial challenges to registering to vote, often through a dizzying array of new documentation requirements that have arisen in many states across the past decade. Historically, one's eligibility to vote in the United States was determined at registration, with no form of identification required in any state. That changed in 1950 when South Carolina began requiring people to show ID when voting. In the 1970s, Texas, Hawaii, and Florida added the requirement, and by the year 2000, fourteen states had voter ID laws. Yet all these policies had a "fallback mechanism" if a document could not be produced, such as using a bank statement with a name and address or signing a statement attesting to one's identity under penalty of perjury.[1]

A turning point that led to a new era in voter restrictions occurred in 2006. Policymakers discovered new ways to restrict voting with the innovation of the photo ID, with Indiana becoming one of the first states to enact an especially "strict photo ID law" as a condition to voting, a requirement that was challenged but upheld by the US Supreme Court two years later.[2] Numerous states followed suit in developing strict voter ID legislation, making it difficult for many previously registered or eligible citizens to practice one of their most basic rights. If the two actions of getting people to want to register to vote and then vote have historically been a challenge in US elections, an additional preregistration set of hurdles has now been added: asking citizens to compile multiple, selective forms of documentation to meet their state's policies for voter registration. Like the example mentioned earlier, one state may require collecting a birth certificate, a driver's license, and other forms of ID, or may require many such documents to obtain a "free voter ID."[3] In 2021, "A total of 36 states have laws requesting or requiring voters to show some form of identification at the polls," with many proposals for stricter laws in the pipeline.[4]

With some quiet yet monumental changes to state and federal election procedures in the past two decades, propped up by many shaky premises and outright false narratives about US elections, voter documentation requirements for registering to vote have been engineered to change the rules of voting and win elections along politicized and racialized lines. The advancement of new voter ID laws has taken place in electorally competitive and racially heterogeneous states where those on the political right "preside over an electoral coalition that is declining in size," as a means of maintaining control and diminishing the opposition.[5] The impact of these often below-the-radar policies can already be seen on a vast scale. If nothing is done to change the direction of these problematic laws and connected forms of voter suppression, it may not matter how many people get out and try to vote, if the system has been reconstructed to make sure that only some votes count.

National Frustrations

Each of us writing this book came to this project as "pracademics" whose past work has focused on maximizing opportunities for citizens to connect with civic life and the building of robust political systems. Some of us have worked on improving public discourse, examining what it will take for people to meaningfully participate in society from the ground up, while others have extensive backgrounds working on big-picture policy, legal, and administrative challenges in national and local government. Like many individuals and organizations around the country, we are most interested in the question: "What does it take to make democracy work as it should?"[6]

The more we looked into this issue, the more we became both frustrated by what we discovered and energized to do something about it. We quickly converged around a need to undertake a deep exploration of voter documentation requirements for a simple reason: we all believe that a first step toward building democracies is making sure that there are minimal burdens to accessibility in our elections and voting systems. Obstructions to voting accessibility hinder all the other means of promoting civic engagement and the most inclusive and responsive political processes possible.

After searching through literature on voter documentation requirements and related issues, we began a conversation at the City University of New York involving community stakeholders and people from different fields about this national issue. A number of studies and organizations doing fieldwork have captured snapshots of the crisis that many people face in getting what they need to vote. At the same time, many legal and policy-focused organizations are fighting battles to overturn states' strict voter ID laws.

Building on this developing scholarly and practitioner work, we decided that a national study of voter documentation requirements, with a particular emphasis on the stories of what it is like to face these challenges in everyday life, could contribute a valuable resource, new directions, and calls to action for this critical conversation.[7] Numerical evidence certainly provides an important perspective on the topic (and we advance our own statistical research through a number of means in this project), but the crisis of voter documentation requirements becomes most apparent in citizens' experiences with voting in different state contexts. Linda Alcoff has pointed scholars toward "the problem of speaking for others." In this spirit, we attempt at every opportunity to conduct analyses that bring others' voices to the fore.[8]

While there are many people working on the legal front to address these challenges, we focus on the role that nonprofits and community organizations might play in helping those who are eligible get what they need to vote. This accords with expert calls highlighting that "fighting voter ID laws in the courts isn't enough. We need boots on the ground."[9] We wanted to map the problems of voter documentation requirements and to discover what research-informed solutions local community organizations that have direct contact with citizens could suggest for addressing the challenges.

From a variety of perspectives and methods, we researched voter documentation nationally to try to understand what is happening in communities, election systems, and people's lives as a result of these laws. In the course of our yearlong study of the problem, we found much more than anticipated, especially regarding the inconsistent or unavailable information and chaotic processes involved in contemporary voting across the United States. We discovered how voter ID challenges are connected with other forms of suppression that look innocuous on their face until their reach and impacts on elections are observed. These related challenges to voting include the alienation of citizens from government, changing and inaccessible polling sites, redistricting, and more. We have chosen to cast a spotlight on voter ID requirements because of the devastation they are wreaking across the US voting system. Yet in replicating citizens' experiences with voter ID, readers will get to see how this stand-alone burden must be considered in the context of many other roadblocks.

We began this project as a nonpartisan study of voter documentation requirements. The results of our research, however, revealed highly partisan reasons for why voting difficulties, relative to our focus on voter ID, are largely based on successful partisan attempts to suppress certain demographics and to thwart the possibilities of success for Democratic Party candidates. Following a lengthy history of voter suppression in the United States, it became clear that voter documentation requirements are wolves in sheep's clothing, so to speak; they support oppressive government regulations that achieve their effects in the guise of avoiding voter fraud, of which there is no meaningful or substantial evidence.

As important as it is to tell people to get out and vote, that means very little if all along politicians have been busy changing the eligible voter base and wiping out the voices of millions of Americans by skewing the rules through both policy and practice.[10]

Our main argument in this book is that many citizens are confused by documentation requirements and frustrated by the barriers to voter registration and voting that have been put in place by many states, particularly over the past decade. As a result, millions of qualified voters are being lost—or, perhaps more accurately, thrust—through the cracks of our voting system. According to VoteRiders, a nonprofit dedicated to helping people get what they need to vote, more than twenty-five million Americans are affected by voter documentation requirements.[11] These citizens need all the help they can get to navigate the perplexing challenges that these laws now pose across the United States.

Confusion should not be a reason why people are kept away from the ballot box. Choosing one's political representatives is essential to democracy. For many people, however, confusion is the starting and ending point in their election process participation. But there are paths for moving forward.

Multiple Viewpoints on the Citizen Experience

At the foundation of every public policy lie stories about what the world is like and how it works.[12] Baseless claims about voter fraud have been used to frame and sustain the disenfranchising voter documentation requirements we explore in this project.[13] Indeed, a sitting US president made it his cause célèbre to do so in claiming the following via Twitter: "All over the country . . . voter fraud is rampant. Must be stopped. Strong voter ID!"[14] It's critical to research and advance accurate narratives that can serve as a basis for good policy and implementation. This book briefly treats the purported public policy justifications for voter ID as a foil for the surprising stories from all kinds of people with a stake in voting, and provides analytic work on voter documentation requirements as a social, political, and racial challenge. Our research design and recommendations reflect our commitment to helping people facing voter documentation problems and constructed so that the evidence we have uncovered can elevate conversations about voting reforms, establish new interventions, and most of all change these pernicious policies and their disenfranchising effects across the nation.

To provide a context for this book, chapter 1 maps the current state of voter ID laws. Chapter 2 lays out our research design and process implemented nationally, involving data collection from recognized practitioners and experts on voting requirements to affected community members in some of the strictest voter ID states.

In chapter 3, we provide three broad perspectives on voter documentation requirements through statistical snapshots of how this issue affects citizens in the United States. The first perspective comes from surveys of forty-four civically engaged nonprofits, exploring what these community organizations across the United States are doing to help citizens with voter documentation requirements, registration, and voting. We learned about the difficulties these organizations and their constituents face and the strategies many of them are using. The second, eye-opening perspective emerged from our calls to 150 election offices in the strict voter ID states to understand what it is like to be a previously registered or eligible voter trying to find out what is needed to vote. The third perspective stems from a broad sample of over two hundred community members from the strict voter ID states across the United States.

In chapter 4, we move to the disconnections between citizens and systems, focusing on the breakdowns and opportunities for work on voter documentation requirements nationally. Drawing from thirty-eight in-depth interviews across the United States with experts, practitioners, and nonprofit staff, we analyze the fractures that individuals and groups face relative to governments and elections. With an eye toward what might be done to best address these issues, we construct themes that contribute to this project's overall framework.

In chapter 5, we focus more deeply on what it is like to navigate voter documentation requirements in everyday life. Through focus groups carried out in Ohio and Mississippi, we learned from approximately sixty local citizens what their own and others' experiences have been with voter ID and related challenges. From these candid and energized community conversations, it became clear that, absent significant changes in state and federal voting laws, a context-sensitive approach to addressing voter documentation requirements is necessary for building solutions both nationally and locally.

In chapter 6, we summarize the results of this project and put forth specific recommendations for a national intervention to make voter identification easy, accessible, cost-free, and ultimately, uniform. In the absence of that kind of sweeping change, we advance specific, actionable ideas for providing eligible voters with realistic local assistance in the interim.

In the conclusion, we again pose a question raised by this entire project: Why do many eligible voters in different states have vastly different experiences? Given the United States' state-level control of elections, it makes no sense that any citizen in one state should have a much different experience from a citizen in another state. The current norm is a chaotic "state of confusion." We address the emerging challenges of REAL ID, absentee (or mail-in) voting in the context and aftermath of COVID-19, what other countries do with voting, and other topics of importance for closing the gaps between citizens and systems in US elections. Integrating our findings with work across a number of disciplines, we propose solutions for improving voting and elections in the face of current ideological divides.

New Challenges, Old Intentions

Before we move to the next chapter, it's worth zooming out to see how voter documentation requirements align with some very old intentions. The history of the United States provides a grim litany of local laws, regulations, and their implementation that have suppressed votes. These include property ownership requirements, literacy tests, poll taxes, segregated primaries, gerrymandering, fearmongering, grandfather clauses, voter intimidation, overly punitive policies that disenfranchise former felons, redlining, malapportionment, purging voters from voter rolls (especially after periods of inaction), and creating practical barriers to vote, such as through limiting polling places, the days and times for voting, and absentee ballots.[15]

Even with the most generous regulations and templates for best practices, the actual effect of administrative actions, such as requiring voter ID or limiting absentee balloting—even if well-intentioned, which often they are not—is to undermine the implementation of processes that should be simple and accessible to all citizens. As Stacey Abrams says, this all comes down to "registration access, ballot access, and ballot counting."[16] There are enough issues in US politics with the latter two hurdles, but if a person can't even get past the first obstacle, they won't get near the others.

In this spirit, our work affirms and adds to critical recent works by Gilda Daniels, Carol Anderson, and many others, establishing that voter suppression isn't simply a minor feature but a systemic function of the US political system as is.[17] In the face of these disenfranchising measures, none of us should allow our elections to continue in a regressive direction. As Daniels underscores, suppression measures such as voter ID laws always come about "after periods of minority electoral success" and "as a country, we have slept through the continuous assault on access to the ballot box in the name of stricter voting requirements, meritless claims of rigged elections, and baseless voter-fraud proclamations. These laws . . . have created a crisis . . . not only seek[ing] to abolish members of a political party but, with the same result, to eliminate voters of color."[18]

The US Supreme Court has referred to voting as a "fundamental right."[19] In recent years, however, laws intended to protect marginalized communities have been diluted, which leads one to question lawmakers' respect for that view. And although both Democrats and Republicans will say unequivocally that all citizens have a "right to vote," we are seeing more and more overt statements that contradict this professed claim.[20]

Ironically, it's the Supreme Court itself that has most often broken its promise by laying a foundation for destabilizing voter ID laws in recent years. The Voting Rights Act of 1965 (VRA) required a federal review of changes in states' voting systems before changes could be implemented ("preclearance"). In 2013, the Supreme Court invalidated the VRA formula used to identify the jurisdictions that must preclear voting changes. The Court held that the formula was insufficiently supported by current conditions and effectively nullified the preclearance mechanism itself.

The Supreme Court reached its conclusions notwithstanding that it was, in the late Justice Ginsburg's words, "a remedy Congress designed both to catch discrimination before it causes harm, and to guard against return to old ways. . . . Throwing out preclearance when it has worked and is continuing to work to stop discriminatory changes is like throwing away your umbrella in a rainstorm because you are not getting wet."[21] Congress thereafter failed to make the necessary findings to re-enact "preclearance" in a way that would satisfy the Court.

On a separate front, state policymakers have increasingly created election mazes that penalize individual constituents for failing to register or vote. Historian Heather Ann Thompson argues that journalists in particular need to stop using the claim that low voter turnout is due to apathy and instead should call "attention to the myriad barriers that have been placed there [by governments] to stop them from showing up."[22] So it's critical that governments are held accountable for their actions instead of putting the onus on citizens to hop through the challenges created by policymakers and election systems in the first place.

Most fundamentally, voter documentation requirements make a mockery of the promises of the Thirteenth, Fourteenth, and Fifteenth Amendments, abolishing slavery and establishing citizenship and the right to vote for formerly enslaved people. What's most concerning is how quiet and hidden forms of voter suppression, like voter documentation requirements, are in achieving voter disenfranchisement.[23] These newer requirements are grounded in assumptions about postracialism and state sovereignty, and are different from overt forms of suppression (but certainly made more explicit in the aftermath of the US general election in 2020).

We must bring a moral megaphone to overcome these retrogressive developments. Before turning to the framework for this project, to set some context, let's next take a deeper look at how voter documentation requirements arose, what we know about their impact, the role they have played in US politics, and their current application in and across various states.

1

On the Ground

The Reality of Voter ID Requirements

I was at an event yesterday, working with people who have
some sort of disability and they are living in this complex,
so they can get full-time assistance and not all of them have
a driver's license or state ID. They don't drive. The complex
didn't have a birth certificate on file for everyone who was
there, so this became a hurdle for those people who wanted
to register to vote there, eligible to register to vote, but do
not have that proof of citizenship documentation with them,
and would have difficulties getting them from the appropriate agency. It's a problem . . . and we want to make sure that
everybody who wants to register to vote, can get registered
to vote. It is a problem.
—Community relations director for a county record office
and election department, Arizona

A week's worth of groceries. That's equivalent to what it costs many
people trying to meet new voter ID requirements in their state.[1] Everyone knows that voter turnout matters because it determines election
outcomes. Elected officials give attention to and provide resources
for their constituents.[2] But in a perverse twist, politicians who create
and sustain voter ID laws across the United States exact costs on those
they are supposed to serve. Instead of doing the hard work of governing
with the needs and interests of all in mind, the legislators creating these
laws in effect seek to include supporters and exclude opponents from
voting.

These developments may be surprising for many readers. Indeed,
one of the most common and reasonable reactions people across the
political spectrum have to voter ID is that, since an ID is needed for

everything from getting on a plane to procuring some over-the-counter medications, it can't be much of a burden to require it for voting as well. If it were that simple, we'd agree. But the reality is that strict ID laws for voting are not analogous to these other experiences. Take the case of Sean Reynolds, a military veteran who went to vote at his local polling place in Wisconsin.[3] Because Wisconsin allows same-day registration, he showed up on Election Day with his driver's license (that could easily be shown for a variety of purposes such as driving or purchasing alcohol across US states) but was denied the right to vote because he had an Illinois license. Having served in Afghanistan and Iraq, Sean left the navy and moved to Wisconsin in 2015 to pursue a degree from a nearby university in Illinois. He told a reporter, "'I was a little incredulous that they wouldn't accept another state's driver's license. I didn't understand why it was not a valid form of ID.' Reynolds said he had been working 50-hour weeks, receiving hourly pay, and could not afford to take time off from his job in security management to visit a local DMV and transfer his license from Illinois."[4] And there you have it, no vote. When it comes to strict voting ID laws, the devil is in the details.

In the 1990s and early 2000s, most US states did all they could to make it easier for citizens to vote through initiatives such as early voting and voting by mail.[5] Now, many states require that eligible voters provide proof of documentation before they can register to vote. Although enacted with the professed intention to ensure that election processes remain fair and just, these requirements work toward the opposite end.

Before moving to further background on the development of voter documentation requirements, their measured effects to date, and the controversies and issues that they continue to evoke across the United States, a word on terminology is in order. For this book's purposes, we will use the terms "voter documentation" and "voter identification" (or "voter ID") interchangeably to describe the documentary requirements a state may have for registering or voting. Voter documentation requirements concern the documents that one is required to show to register to vote (e.g., a birth certificate, a driver's license), which are forms of voter ID.

Yet there are two different times when voter documentation or ID can be required in some states. One is to register to vote, and the other is to present to vote at the polls, as in the prior story. In the latter case, some states have strict photo ID requirements that one must show to poll workers, for instance. In this book, we'll focus most on the pre-registration requirement for assembling and showing documentation to register to vote, a major challenge for many citizens to overcome. At the same time, we'll observe how the additional step of needing to show ID at the polls also comes into play.

How Did Voter Documentation Requirements Develop?

The types of voter documentation requirements now present all over the nation can partly be traced to the the US general election in 2000, in which George W. Bush appeared to have won the presidency, by a machine count, by 537 (out of nearly 6 million) highly contested votes in Florida.[6] Notwithstanding dozens of pending lawsuits that challenged the outcome, it was effectively let stand by the US Supreme Court in the infamous case of *Bush v. Gore*.[7] What happened in Florida during that election ignited a firestorm of interest in inadequate and unfair voting processes nationally with, by one count, for example, 14.4 percent of Black voters having their ballots rejected, compared with only 1.6 percent of non-Black voters in the state. In addition to fears about a presidential election being so closely contested, these events cast doubt on the result. Post-2000 election concerns about potential voting irregularities combined with an obsession among policymakers for identity and security measures nationwide after the events of 9/11. For many citizens, "instead of enlarging the vote, exercising the franchise became more cumbersome and restrictive" as legislatures created new obstacles via ID requirements and similar regulations.[8]

Signature verification had long been the norm for voting, but the Help America Vote Act (HAVA) of 2002 required that first-time voters now provide a wide range of acceptable forms of ID for registering to vote. Many states went beyond HAVA in mandating that all voters have ID, and also specific types of ID.[9] With some nineteen million potential voters across the United States lacking state IDs or driver's licenses (primarily Black, elderly, poor, and youth voters), the impact has been far-reaching.[10] In the following years, previously unthinkable restrictions around voting (and legal tussles over them) began emerging across the United States. But with federal oversight for state voting changes through the Voting Rights Act of 1965 (VRA) still in place, the Pandora's box wasn't yet completely open. That monumental change came in 2013.

As mentioned in the introduction, the most dramatic result of shifts in federal oversight took place when the US Supreme Court effectively nullified the "preclearance" requirements in Section 4 of the VRA in *Shelby County v. Holder.*[11] It's worth diving into further detail on the 2013 case's features and impacts, since they provide one backdrop for what's "new" about voter ID requirements, what has happened in recent elections, and where the United States is heading with voting.

The VRA had required a federal preclearance of any changes in voting practices in states identified, in the preclearance process, as having a history of discriminatory practices.[12] In 2013, the Supreme Court voided the provision of the VRA that governed the manner of identifying which states were subject to preclearance. The Court did so on the basis that the formula for making a determination on the need for preclearance in a state was no longer necessary to protect minority voters. Dismissing the concerns of their liberal colleagues, the conservative majority on the US Supreme Court in *Shelby* effectively ruled that Congress had not shown that the preclearance protections of the VRA were necessary to protect minority voters. It is worthy of note that more than three thousand forms of voting discrimination had been blocked under preclearance by federal courts and the Justice Department between 1965 and 2013.[13] But ever since, starting with *Shelby*, states have been subject to minimal oversight.

In the years since *Shelby*, states have closed down thousands of polling locations, pulled back on voter registration drives in areas with large minority populations, limited early voting, and made third-party registration more difficult. They have purged voters from rolls (e.g., because of the slightest discrepancies such as omitted hyphens or the use of initials instead of full middle names); closed offices in local jurisdictions; and created selective, politicized, and racialized lists of what is sufficient for registration, invalidating even some forms of government ID.[14]

Favoring IDs such as driver's licenses may seem like a simple matter until one realizes that in places like Alabama, "71 percent of those in public housing are African American," and for many, public-housing IDs are the only form of identification they have. A former Alabama governor closed Department of Motor Vehicle facilities in Black counties in one of the states with the fewest public transportation options, among a population often without cars. These "quiet bureaucratic mechanisms" serve the same purposes as more overtly discriminatory forms of suppression from the past.[15]

In 2016, the United States had its first presidential election in a half century without the VRA's preclearance protections.[16] As states made voting harder for many citizens, effectively redefining the voting population of the United States, many offending laws wound their way through various court systems, notwithstanding some "wins." One win was the Fish v. Schwab ruling invalidating "Kansas' documentary proof-of-citizenship law that requires people, when they register to vote, to show documents to prove their citizenship."[17] According to the American Civil Liberties Union (ACLU), the law violated "the National Voter Registration Act, a federal law designed to make it easier for Americans to register to vote and maintain their registrations."[18] Yet the Supreme Court continues to eviscerate the VRA's protections.[19] To fully understand the consequences of this recent US history, we must look beyond legal battles. The practical effects of these laws warrant closer examination.

The Effects of Voter Documentation Requirements

How much are US citizens affected by these laws? Research shows that the laws' impact falls disproportionately on certain parts of the population. In a widely cited early study of voter documentation requirements, the Brennan Center for Justice at New York University found that "as many as 11 percent of United States citizens—more than 21 million individuals—do not have government-issued photo identification," and that the effects of voter ID laws have unreasonably disadvantaged the elderly, poor, and minority voters.[20] An updated report shows how studies confirm that about one in ten eligible voters do not have the precise government documents these shifting laws require.[21] Many elderly people do not have birth certificates, including Native Americans on reservations and African Americans who have faced discrimination.[22] One example is illustrative:

> Mrs. Smith has lived in Milwaukee since 2003. She was born at home, in
> Missouri, in 1916. In her long life she has survived two husbands, and she

has left many of the typical traces of her life in public records. But, like many older African Americans born in the South, she does not have a birth certificate or other documents that would definitively prove her date and place of birth. After Wisconsin's voter ID law took effect, she needed a photo ID to vote. So she entered the ID Petition Process (IDPP) at the Wisconsin Department of Motor Vehicles (DMV) to get a Wisconsin ID. DMV employees were able to find Mrs. Smith's record in the 1930 census, but despite their sustained efforts, they could not link Mrs. Smith to a Missouri birth record, so they did not issue her a Wisconsin ID. She is unquestionably a qualified Wisconsin elector, and yet she could not vote in 2016. Because she was born in the South, barely 50 years after slavery, her story is particularly compelling. But it is not unique.[23]

These challenges do not affect people equally. In the United States, White individuals have the highest rates of identification ownership (with only about 5 percent of White people lacking ID), while approximately 10 percent of Latinos and 13 percent of Blacks do not possess photo ID.[24] In terms of incomes, 12 percent of those making less than $25,000 annually do not have a photo ID, as contrasted with only 2 percent of those making over $150,000 a year. Although many elderly people face voter ID challenges, some 15 percent of seventeen- and twenty-year-olds and 11 percent of twenty-one- and twenty-four-year-olds also do not possess a photo ID.[25]

Across the nation, Latinos often lack ID or the ability to acquire documentation to register to vote and ensure that their ballots will be cast and counted.[26] Voter documentation requirements further affect populations of women and others who have had their names changed after getting married or for other reasons. Even people with a number of government IDs who never dreamed of running into difficulties with proving their citizenship status have shared stories online of moving from one state to another and encountering substantial problems related to documentation.[27]

The finding that large numbers of eligible citizens do not have the necessary forms of ID for registering or voting is a constant throughout emerging scholarly literature.[28] Even small impediments to voting can have outsized effects on the voters who are least likely to vote.[29] Richard Hasen, author of The Voting Wars, says that "there's no question that in a very close election, they [the US population affected by ID requirements] could be enough to make a difference in the outcome."[30] Indeed, out of approximately 136 million ballots cast in the 2016 presidential election, the election result was decided by a mere 77,744 votes spread across Wisconsin, Pennsylvania, and Michigan.[31] And in many US states, small segments of the population have come to matter a great deal, with congressional elections easily turning on several thousand votes.[32]

Additional support for these conclusions comes from a Brennan Center for Justice report noting that voter ID requirements can substantially affect Americans' voting access, especially in states such as Kansas and Arizona.[33] For example, some 14 percent of new registrants in Kansas (or thirty-five thousand people) were blocked by new voter documentation requirements between 2013 and 2015, which affected mainly young people and those unaffiliated with a political party, with only one-quarter of this group able to register to vote even two years later.[34] In general, voter ID laws tend to decrease turnout among lower-income and less-educated groups.[35] It is a form of disenfranchisement that runs parallel to economic inequalities across the nation.

Most telling is how these laws play out in different states. In the face of Arizona's proof-of-citizenship-to-register law, in the state's three most populated counties, in the new law's first five months one-third of applicants were thrown out for documentary requirements, acting as a preregistration barrier despite voting eligibility.[36] In Wisconsin in 2016, too, the state's voter ID law apparently deterred 11.2 percent of eligible registrants, with about 6 percent of nonvoters being unable to vote due to lacking ID or citing ID requirements as the reason they did not vote. Many citizens reported that they were confused about these laws and what was required.[37] Another study in Wisconsin found a reverse form of confusion at play. Many people thought they did not have the ID they needed to vote, when in fact they did. The findings suggest that low levels of knowledge about acceptable forms of ID correlate with a greater likelihood of being affected by these laws.[38]

In recent years, Georgia has become emblematic of voting battles. The state even faced corporate backlash when a series of new laws around voting were passed after the 2020 general election.[39] One Georgia study found that a new photo ID law suppressed votes among people lacking specific IDs.[40] This study followed previous analyses finding that states having "voter ID laws have a significant, negative relationship with voter turnout compared to states without voter ID laws."[41] These conclusions align with research underscoring that as monetary and nonmonetary voting costs increase, voter turnout decreases—even incremental cost increases can make a big difference in turnout rates.[42]

Some work poses the question whether it is possible to administer voter ID laws in a race-neutral manner. Zoltan Hajnal, Najita Lajevardi, and Lindsay Nielson found that voter documentation challenges break down along racial and ethnic lines. They write, "There are substantial drops in minority turnout in strict voter ID states and no real changes in [W]hite turnout. Latino turnout is 7.1 percentage points lower in strict voter ID states than it is in other states in general elections and 5.3 points lower in primary elections," and "For [B]lacks, the gap is negligible in general elections but a full 4.6 percentage points in primaries. For Asian Americans, the difference is 5.4 points and 6.2 points."[43] No additional characteristics used in the authors' model, such as religiosity, education, and income variables changed the basic findings of this analysis. Given voting patterns that follow racial and ethnic lines, it is clear that one consequence is that those on the political right simply get to outvote those on the political left when strict photo ID laws are in effect.[44]

Despite the landmark status of this study, some called its conclusions into question, following the mixed findings in some scholarship with regard to registration and turnout.[45] Comparisons across studies have often been meaningless in light of extensive variation in process across and, more important, within jurisdictions, where terms can have different meanings and updates to these laws continue to be made. Mixed findings strengthen the need to understand voter ID but also to take the approach we follow in this book: to look under the hood after policy implementation. And the general direction of findings has pointed toward impacts that cannot be ignored. For example, follow-up work to the Hajnal, Lajevardi, and Nielson study in 2020 using official turnout data rather than survey results found that discriminatory turnout gaps between more and less racially diverse counties were larger in strict photo ID law states than elsewhere.[46] Looking at nationally representative data across nine election years, Jennifer Darrah-Okike, Nathalie Rita, and John R. Logan further found that "voter ID policies, and especially 'strict photo ID policies,' have a suppressive effect on participation. Voter ID requirements can reduce the probability of self-reported voting by as much as four percentage points, enough to swing a national election," with disproportionately suppressive effects on Latinos.[47]

Other work has shown that Black and Latino voters get asked for ID more than White voters, accounting for other factors.[48] Some researchers hence position these laws as vestiges of an "American Jim Crow belief system" still in operation.[49] Overall, the need for broader and deeper analyses of these issues remains critical amid these laws' widespread and continuing rise.

The US Government Accountability Office undertook one of the most comprehensive efforts to capture these laws' effects to date. As is the case with some research on this topic, the report relied on early data that did not reach beyond the 2012 election and the effects of stricter versions of these laws in recent years. Still, the report concluded that "of the 10 studies we reviewed, 5 found that state voter ID requirements had no statistically significant effects on voter turnout nationwide, and 5 studies found that changes in voter ID requirements had statistically significant effects on voter turnout."[50] Other research, however, found that turnout was largely reduced among African American registrants in the states of Kansas and Tennessee.[51] In comparison to Alabama, Arkansas, Delaware, and Maine, both Kansas and Tennessee showed decreases in voter turnout in the general elections from 2008 to 2012, which the authors cite as "attributable to changes in the two states' voter ID requirements."[52]

The logistical challenges citizens face and the substantial barriers to voting have only increased since earlier research was completed. Although these studies make important contributions to mapping the voter ID territory and its effects, they have operated from a high-level view. The on-the-ground experiences of people involved with this issue remain vital to untangling how these voting dynamics work and what can be done to address them. Many of the qualitative impacts on citizens' lives need to be better understood, and there's a case that, even if these laws' effects were less influential than research highlights, societies would still have a moral obligation to remove obstacles to the ballot for those who are eligible to vote. Glimpses of the known barriers that people have faced over time demonstrate that ethical and policy problems about disenfranchisement have intensified.

Documentation Barriers to Voter Registration

In strict voter ID states, some obstacles to obtaining voter ID include (1) a physical lack of access to offices that can provide a state ID (some five hundred thousand eligible voters in strict ID states lack access to a vehicle and live more than ten miles from a state ID office that opens more than twice a week, while ten million live more than ten miles from such an office in general); (2) costs and access to state offices for documentation (such as fees for birth certificates, the limited business hours of many state ID issuing offices, etc.); and (3) a lack of reliable information from government offices about what documents are needed. The strict voter ID states tend to lack public transportation, making travel to government offices that are open only during weekday working hours more difficult, a problem heightened in rural communities.[53]

One high school student sued the state of Alabama in 2015 because she needed a state voter ID provided by the DMV. But the closest DMV was open only one day a month, and there were no public transportation options to another DMV that would require a 40-mile round trip.[54] Raising these stakes, in Texas some voters would have to travel 176 miles roundtrip to obtain ID from the proper offices.[55] On the other hand, those in urban areas are also more likely to use public transportation and thus are less likely to possess a driver's license as a specific form of ID that a state may require for voting.[56]

Citizens remain frustrated and confused, but apparently, so do actual administrators. Voting rights lawyer Chad Dunn notes, "Sometimes government officials don't know what the law requires. . . . People take a day off work to go down to get the so-called free birth certificates. People who are poor, with no car and no Internet access, get up, take the bus, transfer a couple of times, stand in line for an hour and then are told they don't have the right documents or it will cost them money they don't have. . . . A lot of them just give up."[57] These policy implementation problems have raised concerns. For example, when contacted directly, some Georgia county offices provided incorrect information about documentation requirements; in other offices, election staff in the state answering phone calls replied that they did not know much about free voter IDs.[58]

All this assumes that "street-level bureaucrats" are well-intentioned or aware of their biases in implementing policies. Sometimes they are not. One study of more than seven thousand election officials across forty-eight states found that "officials provide different information to potential voters of different putative ethnicities," raising concerns about the power of local administrative gatekeepers across the election system.[59] Another study revealed that poll workers discriminate by using surnames as prompts for asking people for voter ID, particularly among Latinos, showing how voters of different attributes can receive unequal treatment in how laws are applied on the front lines of election work.[60]

Attorney and activist Molly McGrath further finds that when states cherry-pick the forms of ID required for voting, they almost always engage in exclusionary acts. McGrath spent one Election Day driving a ninety-nine-year old World War II veteran, Fred Leidel, to the DMV in a Wisconsin county. Leidel, who didn't have a car and rode his bicycle to the polls at a local elementary school to vote that day, did not have one of the state's acceptable IDs. The poll workers knew the man—as he was a volunteer at the school who read to kindergartners twice a week—but could do nothing under the new state ID law. They couldn't even accept his faculty ID for teaching at the University of Wisconsin that he had previously used to vote. Although McGrath was able to get the right paperwork so that Leidel could receive an ID and cast a ballot, she notes, "In my line of work, stories like Fred's are not uncommon . . . unfortunately they do not all end with a vote being counted."[61] Even military veterans have run into substantial challenges related to ID.[62] Without uniform policies nationally, voting rights activists are left to take up the cause locally, helping people get what they need to vote on a case-by-case basis.

Richard Sobel at Harvard Law School undertook an extensive analysis of the time, travel, and other expenses involved in getting a "free" voter ID in relevant states, breaking down the exact costs to eligible voters. He concluded that the instructions for how to get a free voter ID are frequently distorted, incomplete, and difficult to find. Sobel found the burdens placed on voters whom these laws most affect striking.[63] When legal help is required to get documentation together, costs can be as high as $1,500, and "when aggregating the overall costs to individuals for 'free' IDs in all voter ID states, plus the costs to state government for providing 'free' IDs, the expenses can accumulate into the $10s of millions per state and into the multiple $100s of millions nationwide."[64]

If there's any trend arising from efforts to make voting more accessible in the United States, it's that many policymakers quickly engineer obstacles to block any gains made. In Florida, after a bipartisan 2019 constitutional amendment was passed by referendum to end a lifetime voting ban for those who had served their sentences for felony convictions, lawmakers created an additional, extraordinary legislative requirement that legal debts such as fees, fines, and restitution be paid before these individuals (who had served their time) could vote—making the payment of court costs a condition for voting.[65] This type of maneuver connects voter documentation challenges with the thicket of other barriers to voting that people face. Navigating the voting system is a confusing journey through multiple issues for millions of people. Complicating an already complicated picture, however, there's another consideration to add to what's known about these requirements: how they reflect the nation's polarized political climate.

The Politics of Voter ID Laws

Voter ID laws cannot be separated from the political polarization that is rampant in the United States. Like many other political issues affected by the well-documented divisions found throughout the country,[66] distinct perspectives on voter documentation requirements break down largely along party lines.

Conservatives are concerned about the potential for voter fraud and expect that restrictive ID laws will ensure the integrity of election systems. Liberals focus on the potential for these laws to suppress and disenfranchise many eligible citizens. Those on the right tend to rely on historical anecdotes in support of their claims, often citing the corruption of the Tammany Hall era when ballot boxes were rigged and the very rare cases of voting interference that do exist, while those on the left highlight the legacies of the Jim Crow South and its violent suppression of Black people.[67] Yet no other narrative has captured conservatives' imaginations, policy designs, and current approaches to electioneering more than stories about "voter fraud."

Voter fraud allegations have a long history in US politics.[68] Hans von Spakovsky of the Heritage Foundation describes the main issues of concern for conservative lawmakers, including fictitious voter registrations, impersonation fraud, double voting by those registered in different states, and voting by noncitizens.[69] Citing instances of voter fraud and abuse in his and other states, Kansas's former secretary of state, Kris Kobach, notes, "You can't cash a check, board a plane, or even buy full-strength Sudafed over the counter without ID. Why should voting be different?"[70] From the other side, the ACLU finds a lack of evidence of any significant voter fraud, noting that these laws are discriminatory and deprive many citizens of the right to vote.[71] Similarly, Supreme Court justice Ruth Bader Ginsberg called Texas's voter ID laws "purposely discriminatory," while former US attorney general Eric Holder likened voter ID laws to poll taxes.[72]

Even though voter fraud in the form of individual voter impersonation is exceedingly rare, the hard data have not obviated conservatives' stated fears. Nowhere did this come to the fore more than in the period following the 2020 general election, when despite recounts, audits, and more, at least half of Republicans still believed baseless claims that voter fraud had a significant impact on the results.[73]

The data over many years contradict voter fraud claims. Across a fourteen-year period, "a comprehensive investigation of voter impersonation [found] 31 credible incidents out of one billion ballots cast throughout the United States."[74] The News21 journalism consortium related that there has been only one case of voter fraud found per 14.6 million voters, making it more than twelve times less probable than being hit by lightning.[75] A running theme in work examining claims of voter fraud is that policymakers and others extrapolate from such rare examples wildly exaggerated conclusions that the evidence cannot support.[76] This illustrates what social scientists call a "third-person effect,"[77] where the issue may not affect oneself (i.e., with this issue, those claiming voter fraud don't necessarily know anyone or any election office locally who has engaged in voter fraud) but is seen as impacting all kinds of unidentified election offices and voting jurisdictions "out there."

Election expert Ian Vandewalker writes in summary that "everyone agrees election integrity is important, and the rules must be enforced. At the same time, protections against noncitizens registering to vote should be proportionate to the threat," since "it is extremely rare for noncitizens to attempt to register, and when they do it is typically because of 'mistaken understandings of the eligibility requirements' rather than intent to commit fraud."[78] Charles Stewart III, describing a case in New Jersey involving a council vice president and three others, points out that where clear cases of fraud do exist, they almost always involve local elections where the miscreants manipulate a small numbers of ballots—and get caught. In contrast, it would not be possible to manipulate sufficient numbers of ballots in a statewide or general election, involving hundreds of thousands or millions of ballots. The number of coconspirators alone needed to accomplish an upset win would by itself make success impossible.[79] Contrary to the assertions of some politicians, mail-in balloting, in particular, is a relatively secure procedure that has multiple steps and guardrails built in to protect each person's vote.[80] Voter fraud rarely happens, and, when it is put to the test, recent investigations have come up with vanishingly thin support.[81] Some journalists have therefore called assertions about voter ID fraud "a solution in search of a problem."[82]

Researchers find that party identification conditions the connection between confidence in state elections and photo ID laws, with Democrats in strict photo ID states less confident and Republicans more confident about their respective states' elections.[83] Since the US general election in 2000, conservative administrations have "prioritized prosecutions of voter fraud over investigations into voter disenfranchisement."[84] Some Republican partisans have even publicly asserted that strict voter ID laws help their party.[85] Others point out that there's a type of "projection" occurring in claims of voter fraud and similar political positioning, as often Republicans are found guilty of actual voter fraud, despite the rarity of these events.[86] But one consideration for moving forward is that most voters, both Republicans and Democrats, appear to support some version of these laws for their expected potential to keep elections fair and valid.[87] We will return to this important point in subsequent chapters.

It's critical to take all rationales into account to help eligible or previously registered voters get what they need to vote. To understand the development of voter ID laws, let's briefly turn to our present moment.

The Current State of Voter ID Laws

Although voter ID laws continue to make news, what's less obvious is that these laws have both tightened and loosened in different states. While many states have enacted and sustained voter ID laws that have made it more difficult for many eligible voters to gather documentation to vote, some have undergone legal challenges that have had the effect of turning formerly strict ID states into lenient ones. Texas, for example, has been a state where voter ID laws have shifted from strict to lenient and back again over time. During the course of our research, stricter voter ID requirements returned with force to the political agenda in North Carolina, while some of the strictest requirements of a law in Kansas were invalidated.[88] While we were gathering data for this project, the US Supreme Court also let a North Dakota court decision stand, requiring citizens to possess proof of residential street addresses for eligibility to vote in the midterm elections, disproportionately affecting Native Americans living on tribal lands where residential addresses are not the norm.[89] South Dakota lawmakers have also rejected tribal IDs for voter registration, the very same IDs that are acceptable by federal agencies for everything from going through airport security to voting.[90] Amid these laws' fluctuations, however, the trend is toward strict voter ID laws.[91] The Brennan Center has useful interactive maps showing the increase in strict voter ID states and laws that we encourage readers to view.[92] The maps provide a bird's-eye view of how different states have aggressively sought to both limit and expand access to voting after the 2020 US general election.[93] Even those states with less strict laws continue to present citizens with substantial barriers to getting the documentation that they need to vote.[94] For comparative purposes, states that do not currently have voter ID laws usually have "nondocumentary" ID provisions that allow voters to verify their identity through, for example, signing poll books or affidavits, or by providing addresses or birth dates.[95] In contrast to these easier processes, documentary forms of ID can impose substantially different costs in money and time for voters. For instance, birth certificates can run between $15 and $30. New or updated passports cost more than $110, and it costs $345 for a certificate of citizenship or replacement naturalization certificate. The costs for document delivery services must be added to these numbers.[96] In states such as Pennsylvania, the costs for non-driver photo ID rose by 104 percent in a single year as a result of legislative change.[97] The monetary and nonmonetary barriers presented by documentary requirements do not even begin to reflect many of the additional concerns discussed later in this book, such as the time it takes for government agencies to process information that can put citizens up against voter registration deadlines, nor do they include the many people who will not have these documents readily at hand for voter registration drives.[98] Indeed, any "policies that impose a financial hardship, create confusion, limit access to the ballot, dilute the vote geographically, or use subjective measures of eligibility" contribute to the disenfranchisement disproportionately experienced by marginalized communities.[99] Yet it appears that there is no established routine for alerting many voters to less demanding ways of registering to vote.

A real-life example is telling. Anthony Settles, a retired engineer, lived in Texas and had an expired ID card, a Social Security card, and a past student ID from time spent at the University of Houston decades ago. Yet the only document he could use to satisfy the requirement to vote in a presidential election was an up-to-date Texas photo ID. To receive one, a name matching his birth certificate was required, but when he was fourteen years old his mother changed his last name after marrying. So when Texas established a new ID law, Settles was asked for a 1964 name-change form to get an ID to vote. He had to enlist the assistance of lawyers to search Washington, DC, courthouses for the certificate, but came up short. Settles was basically asked to find a way to prove his name of fifty-one years, for a process that would cost more than $250, which he was understandably unwilling to pay. As he summarized, "It has been a bureaucratic nightmare. . . . I feel like I am not wanted in this state."[100]

The state-level challenges that people such as Settles face are compounded by a number of additional factors. An often insurmountable problem for getting documentation and meeting voting deadlines is that "90 million eligible voters—45 percent of the population—moves every five years," with many assuming, incorrectly, that they do not need to re-register to vote in their new states (or request to have their names taken off voter lists for their previous address).[101] And, while all states that require voter ID do accept local driver's licenses, "no two states have the same overall requirements."[102]

On a more hopeful note, no law needs to remain static. As a report on the costs of voting makes clear, improving even one policy for voting can have the effect of "increasing access to the ballot in a state." For example, "Virginia moved from its position as 49th most difficult state all the way up to 12th between 2016 and 2020" due to new legislation that eliminated in-person registration deadlines.[103]

The National Conference of State Legislatures (NCSL) has tracked shifts in voter ID requirements over time, and at the beginning of our data collection, we followed the NCSL's report showing the strictest voter ID states.[104] We selected ten states for our research that all fell within the NCSL's "strict photo ID" category. There were states that required an ID like a driver's license. At the time, these included Georgia, Indiana, Kansas, Mississippi, Tennessee, Virginia, and Wisconsin. We examined "strict non-photo ID" states that at that time required an item such as a utility bill. These included Arizona, North Dakota, and Ohio.[105] (See appendix A for the NCSL's details for in-effect documentation requirements, indicating what voters need in each of these states). Taken together, these states constitute a major portion of the Electoral College votes in US elections.

Voter Documentation Assistance

Examining the exclusionary effects of voter documentation requirements raises the question: What organizations exist that can assist eligible voters with the documentation that they need to vote? Many analyses focus the issues of distance, cost, and the uphill battles that many citizens face in obtaining voter IDs in counties and states where voter ID laws apply.[106] Other than the descriptive and effects-based accounts of voter ID laws, we found only two reports concerning how to help US citizens with voter documentation requirements.

One study revealed that mailed get-out-the-vote messages with details about an ID requirement and how to get help appear more impactful than messages that speak only to the need to bring proof of ID for voting, and even influence turnout among others in one's household.[107] Another report by Tova Andrea Wang, prepared at the inception of many of these states' documentation laws, involved interviews with organizations in Wisconsin, Tennessee, and Colorado. This research urges future efforts at understanding and addressing voter ID challenges to create a broad coalition of organizations, work with government agencies, identify affected voters through community outreach strategies, address transportation issues, and find sources that can help voters offset costs.[108] Wang concludes that "one approach to identifying voters in need is to widely publicize the efforts of the NGOs that are helping voters obtain photo ID,"[109] a line of thinking that we build upon in this book.

Momentum for this type of effort is already underway, with nonprofits such as Spread the Vote, a 501(c)(3) organization created in 2017, pairing volunteers with those in need of IDs in states such as Virginia, Georgia, Tennessee, Florida, and Texas—especially people who are homeless, poor, or recently released from prison. Spread the Vote staff and volunteers go to food banks, churches, and housing projects in search of would-be voters.[110] To get a flavor for how this assistance works, it's worth highlighting one of the nonprofit's success stories:

> Leon Thomas is a 26-year veteran of the US Air Force. Four years ago, a stroke left him paralyzed on his left side. He currently resides with 3 other veterans under the supervision of the Department of Veterans Affairs (VA) with 24-hour care. Mr. Thomas' driver's license expired 1 year ago. He had already renewed online for his previous driver's license, so he was required to visit his local tax collector to receive his state ID. He bore the burden of getting to the tax collector, since public transportation for an individual in a wheelchair is only available for medical appointments. The cost for securing transportation to the tax collector 5.5 miles from his residence was $110.00 round trip. He also needed a private nurse who knew how to address his needs while out. Spread The Vote covered the cost of both the transportation and the private nurse. Mr. Thomas was ready to get a van from the VA. But in order to receive, register, and insure his van, he needed a state ID and his family members do not have vehicles that can accommodate his wheelchair, which meant it was unfeasible/unaffordable for him to leave the house for social visits, to attend church, and the like. We're proud to say that is no longer the case. IDs change lives.[111]

This example of what it took to assist one individual with documentation requirements shows in microcosm both the problems and the opportunities for helping citizens in need of ID. But the costs and effort to help this one individual need to be scaled to millions of others, requiring major commitments in funding and other resources.

Many current efforts are helping eligible voters get what they need to vote. To this point, however, research has largely conceived of this problem in terms of legal and policy challenges, rather than focusing on the resources needed to reach a much larger population and open up the franchise to everyone who is entitled to exercise it.

In this book, we concentrate less on the legal and policy challenges in which many organizations are already engaged.[112] Instead, we focus on citizens' experiences in navigating voter documentation requirements, from broad and deep perspectives. As anecdotes about these requirements attest, geography, psychology, sociology, culture, and the complexities of communication all play roles in these matters. Integrating our findings with insights from relevant disciplines, we address how best to motivate and *help* people get the documentation they need.[113] At the same time, we use these findings to build toward a national call and a road map for change. While we certainly call on policymakers to create sweeping changes in the US voting system, we construct realistic ways for nonprofits and other community institutions to address voter documentation requirements on the ground, as a means to build greater trust and legitimacy with clients, to broaden their audiences and partnerships for funding, and signal their commitment to civic engagement and overall missions of serving the public interest. In the next chapter, we turn to how we mapped voter identification challenges nationally, in pursuit of any and all ways forward on this election-defining issue.

2

Understanding the Problem

What We Need to Know

Every single state, it's like a different country. And they all
present their requirements differently. . . . This is the system
we have. The system demands ID in a country that doesn't
provide it.
—Staff member at a foundation working with voter
engagement

The irony of voting challenges was not lost on the first author of this
book (Don Waisanen) during the US general election season in 2020.
In the fall, he and his spouse moved out of the state of New Jersey, and
while in limbo and with voter registration criteria and deadlines for
another potential state of residency too soon to meet, both filled out a
change of address form so that New Jersey could send mail-in ballots to
the home of a relative with whom they were staying for a short period.
While Don was happy to receive his mail-in ballot upon arriving at their
relative's house, his wife's never came. She frantically called the county
elections office and found out there was some glitch that had stalled the
process, likely due to understaffing at the agency because of COVID-19.
She filled out another form and waited for her ballot to arrive. Time
passed and they became increasingly worried that she would have to
sit out one of the most important elections of their lifetimes. There was
always the option of voting on Election Day if all else failed, but that
would have required driving back across states to fulfill New Jersey's
requirements.

Luckily, after much persistence, her ballot arrived, and she was able
to cast her vote. Although Don and his spouse were both registered to
vote, the lesson that it only takes one small complication to make voting difficult, especially in dealing with cross-state complexities, became

shockingly clear while we were completing this book. For those not registered to vote or those who are part of marginalized and other communities being targeted with further obstacles to voting put in place by state legislatures, these hardships are compounded.

For interested readers, this chapter will cover the *how* of this project, detailing the key questions, launching points, and design for examining these state-by-state intricacies. With an eye toward capturing the voter documentation requirements across the United States that are especially making the very first stage of becoming a voter more difficult, we looked across the national landscape. Like a camera with both wide and narrow frames for capturing the tenor and hues of different scenes, we wanted to provide a number of angles on voter ID across contexts. Ultimately, we sought to figure out the roles that community organizations such as nonprofits and the government itself could play in helping citizens get the documents that they need to vote.[1] We wanted to identify how to reduce the barriers to getting documentation for voting, and current efforts that might be considered "bright spots" in tackling this issue.[2]

Some voter education campaigns have been created to help potential voters ensure that they have the appropriate documentation. These include voter awareness campaigns covering documentation requirements in Wisconsin and Texas, although they appear to have had mixed results.[3] One initiative sent reminder postcards about voter ID requirements to voters in Tennessee and Virginia and found that messaging with helpful information and a warning about the ID requirement did increase voter turnout.[4]

Not all organizations have relied solely on educational methods to help potential voters deal with documentation issues. Nonprofits such as Spread the Vote (spreadthevote.org) and VoteRiders (voteriders.org), and voting rights advocates and activists like Molly McGrath (voter-molly.com) have done extensive work in identifying barriers and actually assisting citizens with the logistics of obtaining needed documentation.

One success story has been the Key to Community Voter Involvement Project that used a marketing-based approach to reach California voters.[5] The project offered insights about involving communities in voter engagement efforts and effective messaging concepts, moving beyond assumptions that people do not vote for many of the reasons commonly described in media explanations (e.g., apathy). The research with eligible nonvoters and lapsed voters revealed that these voters rejected phrases like "voter education" because they did not see themselves as voters to begin with. The project also found that many of the common excuses for not voting relate to information needs and low self-efficacy (or a perceived ability to act and make a difference) as well as "performance anxiety."[6] Our research design builds upon these important findings to address the multidimensional nature of this issue.

Without significant legal and policy changes on the horizon nationally, we see the advancement of unique "midstream" interventions as critical. Midstream interventions focus on the institutions that can help "downstream" clients or constituents directly.[7] These interventions would engage nonprofits and community organizations in several voter ID states to assist previously registered to vote or other eligible citizens in gathering, paying for, and using necessary documentation. We worked with nonprofits and community organizations in this study because they have a wealth of information and experience. They are in every state, have a convenience sample of people we wanted to reach, and are locally positioned to adapt strategies to their clients' lives and their states' contexts in ways that outside researchers and practitioners may fail to envision.

We collaborated with the national civic engagement organization Nonprofit VOTE, a 501(c)(3) organization that "partners with America's nonprofits to help the people they serve participate and vote" and that works as "the leading source of nonpartisan resources to help nonprofits integrate voter engagement into their ongoing activities and services."[8] Nonprofit VOTE's national network helped us to establish relationships and conduct research with nonprofits in several states with voter documentation challenges. We learned from Nonprofit VOTE that most nonprofits have no voting-related functions, so we built a road map for how nonprofits and other community organizations generally can make a difference in their constituents' lives by taking on voter documentation and similar challenges in mission-driven and program-aligned ways.

Our Questions

Following what's been written about voter ID requirements since policymakers began implementing them (and particularly after they ramped up exponentially since the *Shelby v. Holder* ruling in 2013), we examined prior and continuing efforts to address voter documentation issues, while looking to contribute to practitioner and academic work in the elections arena. Several specific questions emerged for our project design. These included:

- What do citizens in voter ID states know about the current documentation requirements in their respective states?
- What are the key barriers and incentives for voters related to documentation requirements?
- How do nonprofits and other organizations currently work with potential voters to assist with documentation requirements?
- Which states/counties with voter ID laws (and elections offices and similar organizations within those states/counties) are effective at helping voters with documentation requirements? How are they succeeding?
- What are the most effective interventions, places, and promotional methods and models that nonprofits and other organizations can use to assist voters in meeting voter documentation requirements in voter ID states?
- Should a new national nonprofit or similar entity or entities be created to help local nonprofits (e.g., by administering small grants) in assisting previously registered or eligible voters to meet the provisions of voter ID states with documentation requirements?

Given our review of works on voter documentation and the preceding questions, we identified the following four publics as likely sources of information and insight:

- Executive directors and key staff in community outreach or voter engagement programs working in nonprofit organizations that serve communities having a high percentage of potential voters with documentation challenges.
- Community members in voter ID states who match the demographics of those less likely to have a voter ID: senior citizens, young people, racial and ethnic minorities, and low-income populations. Casting our net widely, we were also open to a secondary audience of those who are currently registered to vote in each voter ID state (i.e., people who are *not* less likely to have voter ID) to find out what they know about their

respective states' voter documentation requirements and whether their understanding matches the actual requirements.

- Experts and practitioners in the field of elections who could speak to current trends and strategies for assisting voters with documentation requirements.
- Staff working in county election offices, state-level election divisions, or secretary of state offices who are in contact with citizens regarding voting documentation and registration requirements.

To explore these different audiences' insights,[9] we created a five-part research design to examine from as many angles as possible what challenges and opportunities lay ahead for voting in the United States.

Online Survey of Nonprofits

To engage with nonprofits in strict voter ID states, we worked with the civic engagement organization Nonprofit VOTE based in Cambridge, Massachusetts, which has "over 114 national and state partners, representing more than 65,210 nonprofits nationally."[10] The goal of Nonprofit VOTE is to build the capacity of human service agency nonprofits to conduct voter engagement with the people they serve, as opposed to any direct advocacy or policy work. This fit well with a primary purpose of our research: to explore the potential for nonprofits and community organizations generally to support voting. The organization's vast library of nonpartisan resources, including fact sheets, checklists, and webinars, reaches over fourteen thousand nonprofit professionals nationwide. It has collaborated with national nonprofits, including the YMCA of the USA, Goodwill Industries, Habitat for Humanity, and Feeding America, to engage their respective affiliates in voting and election activities.

We reasoned that surveying nonprofit staff would help us find out about the main barriers citizens in local communities face with voter documentation requirements. Nonprofit staff are attuned to specific local issues through the clients they serve, and they can speak to the geographic, psychological, sociocultural, communication, and other dimensions of voter ID. Nonprofits would be knowledgeable about what motivates their constituents and how they might best be assisted.

Nonprofit VOTE provided email introductions to its organizational partners in each of the states with strict voter ID laws (see appendix C for our protocol and instruments). Nonprofit VOTE has built these partnerships by looking for organizing nonprofits and partners interested in promoting "nonpartisan voter engagement to their affiliates, members, constituents, and peers," as "leaders in advocating for the importance of voter participation and its value to both the nonprofit sector and our communities," and who have participated in or been part of events like National Voter Registration Day. Partners typically have advanced voting through their websites, communication, and social media while seeking to use the online resources, trainings, print materials, and more provided by Nonprofit VOTE to build the civic capacity of the entire sector.[11] Overall, this provided us with a sample of nonprofits and community organizations highly engaged with voting issues.[12] Most have other topics that are their primary focus but have dipped their toes into voting as part of their overall missions.

Nonprofit VOTE emailed its network of state conveners to discuss their willingness to participate in distributing our online survey and make introductions to their nonprofit service provider partners. The survey of nonprofits collected information about each organization's mission, whom they serve, how the organization is currently involved in voter registration efforts, whether and how they address voter documentation issues, and if their executive director or another key staff member would be willing to participate in a further telephone interview with our research team. After having sent the initial email with the survey link, those who had not yet responded received a follow-up email reminder from Nonprofit VOTE. Since the request to complete the survey came from the convener organization, which has credibility with its service providers, the likelihood of a good response rate for this initial step was high, even without offering an initial incentive to the nonprofits.[13]

Online Survey of Community Members

To collect quantitative data about potential voters living in states with strict voter ID requirements, we conducted an online survey of individuals recruited through Amazon's Mechanical Turk (MTurk) platform.[14] The online survey included questions about demographics, voter registration status, knowledge of voter ID requirements in the relevant state, whether the participant or others they knew had been personally affected by voter ID requirements, voter registration status, and voting-related attitudes and behaviors. It also concentrated on perceived benefits and barriers to obtaining voter ID and voting, help-seeking behaviors and receipt of assistance in obtaining voter ID from or with the help of nonprofit or government organizations, and attitudes about the use of nonprofits to help people with documentation requirements (see appendix C).

While the literature to this point shows that MTurk workers tend to follow directions and provide high-quality responses, we also followed emerging evidence for how to design and use several features in online surveys to increase the probability that they would be taken seriously.[15] After conducting this part of the research, the survey data were analyzed to better understand the respondents and identify differences between states, demographic groups, levels of knowledge, and other key factors.

Audit of County Voter Registration Staff Procedures

Given anecdotes in the literature about people being told the wrong information regarding state voter ID requirements—sometimes from the government itself—we explored this issue in further depth to see what the experience of finding out about these requirements might be like for citizens in the strict voter ID states. Our research team called the relevant county and state government elections offices in these states to better understand the system citizens encounter. We asked questions to find out what is needed in each jurisdiction and to assess whether the information provided by the government staff related to documentation requirements was accurate and consistent, and to identify any service issues or other observations that may affect citizen interactions with the government on this issue.[16]

Interviews with Nonprofit Staff, Experts, and Practitioners

We conducted phone interviews with nonprofit staff who took the online surveys in the first step described earlier and had indicated that they would be willing to speak with us further about voter documentation requirements in their work with community members. We wanted to better understand their experiences with state voter documentation requirements to register and vote, and to gain insight into the communities they served. These calls also functioned to explore the question of whether and how visits from our research team could be carried out (i.e., to conduct focus groups or interviews with community members that these nonprofits served).

Nonprofits that had not previously engaged in voter outreach but had indicated intent to do so by partnering with Nonprofit VOTE's conveners were also included. Our interviews lasted approximately twenty to thirty minutes and were recorded for reference. Interviewers followed an interview guide that provided the key questions to be asked, with an ability to probe and follow up on responses and pursue new avenues of inquiry as appropriate.

Some of the interview topics included the background of the nonprofit staff member's organization and constituents; their work related to voter registration and documentation, if any; their knowledge and attitudes toward voter ID laws in their states; specific experiences with voter documentation issues among their constituents; what their states/counties were doing to help voters secure a voter ID (or that hindered potential voters from doing so); their perceptions of the incentives and barriers for their constituents related to voter registration and documentation; and where, when, and how to best reach their constituents on this topic.

We also asked these participants their thoughts about the need for a new national nonprofit or similar entity specifically to address voter documentation requirements, or how existing nonprofits could be supported to work on this topic. We focused especially on the kinds of incentives that would most motivate each nonprofit to undertake this type of work as an addition to extant programming. We explored the nonprofits' interest in partnering with us on research, which would include recruitment and logistics for focus groups or in-depth interviews with their constituents. Recordings were transcribed and coded for common themes across these data.

In addition to the nonprofit staff we were able to speak to, we interviewed an extensive snowball sample of experts in the voter ID area (i.e., after interviewing one expert, we asked them about others who we should contact and continued that process outward) to find out more about their current knowledge on the issue. These included policy experts engaged on this topic, those who have written reports on it in previous years at organizations such as New York University's Brennan Center, and more. Since political parties and religious organizations engage in voter registration and voter ID assistance work, we also sought to interview practitioners in these types of spaces. Many individuals and organizations have a strong incentive to do this work and to get it right, and are therefore likely to devote resources to the effort, including galvanizing many volunteers. Overall, we stood to learn a lot from such groups.[17]

Despite the polarized nature of voter ID and its asserted connections to voter fraud and supported connections to voter suppression, we tried to frame these interviews to elicit responses from those having the most experience with the subject, without posing questions through any partisan lens. We attempted to interview people from both major political parties and any others who could illuminate this topic in greater depth. We first surmised that political campaigns—bound by short timelines, win/lose stakes, and focused on high- and mid-propensity voters— might be unlikely to invest significant resources into a low-propensity voter who lacks ID. Different organizations could also be expected to vary significantly in the kind of help they provide. The question was not so much who was providing such help, but more what we could learn from anybody who was doing it, especially if done on a large scale. We didn't want to discover that, because our study was mostly about the citizen experience, we missed out on some important strategies or experiences from organizations that could inform our conclusions.

We began our snowball sample of experts and practitioners by working through our existing networks, asking those we interviewed at each step of the way if they knew others who could also help us understand US voter documentation requirements. We further used online searches of people and organizations to identify participants who might be willing to interview with us, thus increasing our sample. For example, we worked with a list maintained by Guidestar showing all the nonprofits in the United States that work on voter education and registration.[18] We speculated that many people in these categories would be willing to speak with us without any participation incentive, due to the contribution their expertise could make to assisting eligible voters with different states' documentation requirements in the future.

Focus Groups with Citizens

Our highest aspiration in this study was to speak face-to-face with citizens in strict voter ID states who were previously registered or eligible to vote, but who faced barriers related to voter documentation and similar requirements. With assistance from service providers interested in partnering during the phone interviews, our plan was to select some states in which to conduct research with community members. Ideally, we had hoped to conduct focus groups as well, but if logistical issues made it difficult to recruit enough people to convene at the same time and place, we remained open to conducting individual interviews.

In the end, we largely conducted focus groups with people who were eligible to vote but did not currently have voter ID, as well as groups with participants who successfully obtained voter IDs. Some groups blended both categories. Each focus group included five to eight individuals and lasted approximately one to two hours. We designed a discussion guide for the focus group moderator(s) or interviewer(s) with questions to pose and follow up on. Focus group or interview sessions were audio recorded, transcribed, and coded for thematic clusters.

Our overall goal in this five-part research design was to provide multiple viewpoints on this public issue. We also meant for this scheme to be flexible and iterative—if we found that a particular means of data collection was not bearing results, we focused more heavily on one of the other avenues highlighted. At each step, we attempted to take an empirical look at what's happening with voter documentation requirements, with an eye toward practical solutions.

A Launching Point for Addressing Voter Documentation Challenges

Given the multifaceted nature of this issue, we were inspired to take what's called a "social marketing" approach in considering how best to assist citizens in meeting state-by-state documentation requirements to gain access to their right to vote. Social marketing uses research with priority publics to design an intervention that is tailored to the needs and desires of the people whose actions you're trying to change.[19] Social marketers identify the most salient barriers and benefits for their audience and use that information to make new interventions as appealing and as easy to perform as possible.

An article by the Center for Civic Design provides a perfect illustration of the type of thinking and results fostered through such an approach:

> When we look at election websites it's clear that there is an expected, chronological process: You register to vote, and then figure out your options for taking part, then do your homework about who the candidates are and what's on the ballot. Then you vote. But voters don't think the same way that election officials do. Instead of starting at the beginning, they start with the question, What's on the ballot? We think that what they're really asking is something like, What is important enough about this election for me to invest time and energy? What will happen in this election that will affect me and people I'm close to so much that I should do whatever it takes to vote? They're asking, Is it worth the effort[?] The way we talk about the process leaves a lot out. Voting isn't as easy as 1, 2, 3. . . . [T]here are more steps than most privileged voters think about. At each of those steps, voters weigh tradeoffs. In other words, they are weighing the benefits of taking part and the potential value of outcomes to them against the costs of time, money, attention, decision-making, and relative hassle. When information is hard to find, or there are hurdles to taking action, the cumulative effect of the barriers can outweigh the initial desire to vote. . . . Our research shows that very few people really don't care. Deep down, almost everyone does care about voting, and they feel shame for not doing it. The real problem is that voting in America is just hard. The burdens are costly and the frustration of overcoming them is cumulative. As people weigh the tradeoffs between taking part in a process that is difficult against a possible but unknowable future that they might influence by voting—it's not that they don't care. It's that they are making rational decisions that they may not even be aware of at every step about what they care about right now.[20]

Voter ID is an issue with many dimensions. Whether an individual ultimately takes action to obtain documentation and then to register to vote and vote is not just a matter of being educated about ID require-ments. Information is necessary, but often not sufficient, to bring about behavior change. Instead, potential voters need help and motivation to go through the necessary processes.[21]

We used our research to identify priority audiences; understand their current knowledge, attitudes, beliefs, and behaviors related to voting and obtaining voter ID; learn what they see as the main benefits and barriers to voting and obtaining voter ID; find out how best to reach them; and explore other opportunities and current challenges. With this back-ground, in the next chapter we turn to three broad vantage points on voter documentation requirements that provide a multifaceted picture of the challenges citizens face.

3

Different Perspectives

Citizens, Election Offices, and Nonprofits

In Wisconsin, the biggest challenge in getting people to the polls is voter registration requirements—which are documents of proof of residence. It is a very finite list that qualifies as proof of residence, [and] tends to be harder for people who are transient, students, and those who don't have driver's licenses. Then the other challenge to getting people to the polls are our photo ID laws; we have a limited set number of photo IDs that qualify for individuals to use.
—Executive director for a nonprofit focused on voting issues, Wisconsin

Every day, people working at nonprofits all over the United States help others get what they need on issues ranging from health care support to food insecurity. As part of that work, whether planned or not, they will often go the extra mile in assisting these clients with obtaining what's needed to vote. At the same time, there are staff in elections offices courting calls from eligible voters who have questions about where they should register to vote, what forms should be used, and all manner of other details. Then there's the rest of us, either registered to vote or eligible voters, who may be trying to navigate legal changes and new requirements within various states that form the subtext of our voting system. As happened in Pennsylvania, perhaps a voter ID law was just struck down in the courts, but in the weeks following we're receiving misleading mailings or television ads saying a specific form of photo ID is still required.[1] Or maybe there's been no funding put toward public service announcements for updates to a state election structure, so we're simply left to our own devices to figure it all out, even if there's little time to do so.

In this chapter, we turn to these three unique perspectives on voter documentation challenges by casting a wide net on the surprising problems that citizens face: examining the responses of engaged nonprofits, through a national audit of elections offices, and by surveying people in the strictest voter ID states. The story we tell is grounded in both a broad look at voter ID and our main concern for tracking citizen experiences.[2] Ultimately, before we dig even deeper in ensuing chapters, each of these vantage points revealed striking insights into the trials and prospects for obtaining voter ID.

The Perspective of Engaged Nonprofits

Nonprofit VOTE, the national voting engagement organization that we collaborated with for part of our project (see details in chapter 2), distributed surveys to state organizers and nonprofit staff affiliates in the ten strict voter ID states chosen for this study. We received responses from 44 participants across eight of these states, including Ohio (16), Wisconsin (9), Georgia (8), Tennessee (3), Virginia (2), Arizona (2), Kansas (2), and Indiana (2).[3] Some staff mentioned that their organizations operate nationally with branches across the United States, or with a presence in many counties.

Half of the nonprofits focused on civic and community engagement, but many positioned themselves with other areas, including advocacy, nonpartisan voter research or assistance, education, health support, libraries, family and social services, a social justice organization and community development corporation, and public and permanent housing. Clients served included seniors, youth, LGBTI, persons with disabilities, specific racial/ethnic groups, low-income populations, immigrants and refugees, college students, technical school students, those who wish to vote by mail (absentee), mental health and substance use disorder clients, politicians, veterans, and released prisoners eligible to vote or those needing their voting rights restored.

Voter Assistance Activities

We asked survey respondents if they were "involved in any kind of voter registration and/or voter engagement efforts." Fully 86.4 percent

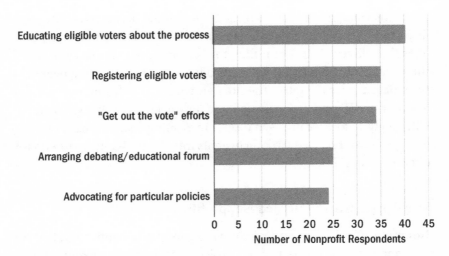

Figure 3.1. Voter assistance activities

answered "yes" to the question, while 11.4 percent answered "no, but we plan to become involved," and only 2.3 percent said "no, and we do not plan to become involved." To the question "If yes, what aspects of voter registration and/or engagement do you address? (check all that apply)," the respondents reported as shown in figure 3.1.

The survey asked, "Given your state's requirements for documentation to register to vote (e.g., Voter ID law that requires forms of documentation such as birth certificates, etc.), how often would you say voter documentation problems arise for the people your organization serves?" Voter documentation requirements presented a common problem, with more than three-quarters (77.2 percent) of organizations reporting that they occur often or occasionally. The responses broke down as shown in figure 3.2.

Given these nonprofits' connections with organizations such as Nonprofit VOTE, we expected a high level of involvement with addressing voting issues in general, and this expectation bore out in most of the responses. For those answering "often," "occasionally," or "rarely" to the last question, we also asked participants to "briefly describe any ways that your organization handles voter ID issues, if applicable. For example, what do you do to assist eligible voters with documentation requirements?" We speculated that a benefit of working with this sample might include learning about both the nature of the problem and solutions. Answers to this question demonstrated varying levels of intervention and commitment to helping citizens with these obstacles that we detail in the following sections.

Staying on Top of Changing Requirements

The majority of responses highlighted serious concerns with their constituents' knowledge about and abilities to overcome barriers to voting, given the array of voter documentation challenges and shifting rules and nuances encountered. As one example of the types of changing requirements citizens face—even within the same election cycle—one staff member shared how "day-of voting requires a photo id or proof of residency, but early voting requires only the last 4 digits of SSN. We promote early voting for that reason."[4] That it took the help of this organization to keep track of these dates and expectations provided a glimpse of the midstream organizational strategies (in serving the nonprofit's downstream clients) already at play in tackling voter documentation requirements.

Another respondent shared how the documentary proof-of-citizenship requirement had been ruled unconstitutional by a district

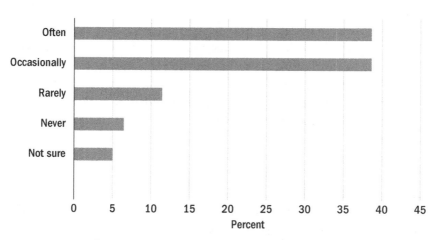

Figure 3.2. How often voter documentation problems arise for nonprofit service recipients

court in their state in 2018. Yet "it is still confusing to potential voters and our job is largely one of educating people about the laws and directing them to the proper resources, if necessary. Voter ID is still required at the polling place, however, so that is now one of our new challenges. Some people think the court ruling did away with all Voter ID rules, but that is not the case." In other words, it's vital for local organizations to do the work of wading through both the perceptions and the actual legal regulations in effect within their communities. One person shared how "community members don't have a thorough understanding of voter ID laws/policies in our community," calling for more assistance, while another described their work in terms of "grassroots volunteer efforts to educate voters to learn, know and accomplish any and all cu[rr]ent and future voter requirements." In these examples, the nonprofits served as intermediaries between citizens and shifting and confusing voter ID policies.

Working in Coalitions to Meet Multiple Needs

The most engaged nonprofits work in coalitions, or networks of other people and organizations with common goals, and follow through with all aspects of the voting process up to the limits of their capabilities. One participant noted the many audiences served and efforts undertaken by their organization:

> We conduct voter registration, education, and Get Out the Vote across the state. We find the biggest challenges when serving veterans, students, low-income and/or homeless voters, and people of color. We work to arm voters themselves as well [as] our diverse network of partners, members, and activists with the information regarding voter ID requirements. We create materials for broad distribution in print and online forums, host educational events, etc.

Despite the difficulties voter ID and similar laws present, it became clear that there's an equal and opposite energy provided by some nonprofits to get people what they need to vote. Another respondent explained, "We work with individuals and a cohort of nonprofit organizations to identify and assist eligible voters in obtaining proper Photo ID (not just

Voter ID . . . obviously there is a difference). We primarily work with the Latinx community in my organization . . . to first work with unregistered eligible potential voters to turn them into voters then get them the proper ID." These comments underscore the need for those who serve citizens at the local level to not go it alone in taking on new ID laws.

Many responses showed staff committed to doing whatever it might take to help their clients. One participant shared that their nonprofit would even "Make calls to assist Clients in ordering a Birth C[ertificate] or Social Se[c]urity Card. Take Clients to the Social Security Office to obtain [a] Card. Take Clients to the Department of Motor Vehicles to obtain a state ID," and further "Take Clients to the Post Office to get a money order to pay for [a] Birth Certificate." One person highlighted issues of translation and making the process easier for some: "We translate requirements in Spanish, do voter education campaigns, walk individuals through the process providing step by step recommendations." Another explained, "We use [an] APIA Vote in-language hotline; we also provide in-language resources; and lastly we have immigration/civil rights attorneys employed by our organization to assist clients in need." Far from putting in a bare minimum effort, these nonprofits improvise and adapt in real time to ensure their clients' ability to vote.

One of the most engaged strategies, help with transportation issues, came up repeatedly. One person noted how they played a role in a voter ID coalition that arranged cab rides to the Division of Motor Vehicles in Wisconsin "for people who need ID for voting ([our] grant [to provide transportation] is from [the] Dane County Clerk)." The organization would also reach out to City of Madison voters, who were unable to cast their votes because they lacked ID and therefore voted provisionally, "immediately after each election to provide information on how the voter can provide an ID to make their [provisional] vote count, and to offer assistance if needed," with subsequent printings of "bookmarks with information about Voter ID and voter registration and hand[ing] out hundreds of them at various locations including food pantries, libraries, and other venues." Some connections between the nonprofit, voter lists, and government offices were instrumental to these strategies, a theme that we'll return to in subsequent chapters.

Other organizations worked at the local level with people having difficulty obtaining a photo ID for voting, while reaching upward to state offices to support their work with additional resources, demonstrating a need for help from other entities. In fact, staff sometimes even brought their clients' voter ID issues to the center of the political process:

> We work with our clients to obtain the necessary paperwork—including assisting them to identify and contact the appropriate agency to obtain a birth certificate (particularly out of state), assisting them to obtain necessary fees if this is a barrier to obtaining the document, and providing advocacy and support to understand and negotiate the steps to obtain documents. On rare occasions, we have been in the difficult bind of the client not having either a valid ID or social security card. In Ohio, you can't get one without the other. This situation has required, in the past, the involvement of our local congressperson.

This situation brought sharply into focus a need both to work across state boundaries and to deal with situations in which no relevant IDs existed. The necessity of working with governmental and other agencies was also evident from other comments such as "We have joined our local election organizations to find ways to assist people & we let our community know that we are available to assist and help them solve their voter id issues" and remarks relating how one person would "discuss with [the] citizen, and refer to [the] proper agency or protocol," linking people with appropriate institutions each step of the way.

Others saw voting help as an extension of the many other services that their organizations carried out. But they also faced barriers that prevented them from following through without partnerships:

> Our work includes but is not limited to, enrolling rural community members and those in need in federal marketplace insurance, medicaid, food stamps (SNAP), cash assistance, assisted living programs, etc. Registering to vote is a final option when completing the necessary paperwork and we always encourage our clients to do so. Identification is required however, and often our clients are homeless and their IDs have gone missing. We work with partner agencies that assist our community members with obtaining proper identification so that we can provide the assistance needed.

Some participants shared that partnerships with local and national organizations such as Spread the Vote and VoteRiders remained integral to helping new voters get what they need (or, as mentioned in one comment, simply pointing voters toward these organizations), including: "When we host tabling events we have made sure an ID offering was part of the tabling." Another participant noted, "We conduct Community forums and tabling events with agencies/organizations (e.g., churches, libraries, etc.)," while another wrote, "Once our clients become citizens we register them to vote." Overall, while certainly taking up many tasks related to voter ID, these nonprofits viewed their work within networks of organizations and public assistance as critical.

Building Awareness

Other nonprofits focused on some combination of raising awareness and providing additional help for citizens in preparation for Election Day. One person emphasized, "Our primary focus is education to ensure that everyone knows what is needed prior to voting. We also have election protection teams at polling places on election day to answer questions and help with getting proper ID if that's the issue." Another respondent mentioned, "We inform [eligible voters] of required documentation . . . on our Web Page, in our Voters Guide, we host a hotline for elections answering questions, [and] pass ou[t] information at monthly Naturalization ceremonies." Another shared that they "work w[ith] schools for student ID questions, [and] assist adults with state ID requirements." These comments indicate that obtaining an ID to vote isn't as straightforward as it may seem; it too often exceeds citizens' bandwidth, requiring intermediaries and interventions.

If needed, sometimes help with transportation and funding documentation requirements enter the picture. One person said, "We educate and advocate for people who are trying to get a voter ID, including arranging transportation to the local Department of Motor Vehicles. Currently, many people can receive a free ID without having to pay for certified copies of documents, but we will try to assist with funding should that situation reverse itself." Inherent in these comments was a belief that the laws can change quickly, making previously easy tasks with voting more difficult.

Assistance with applications was offered, and citizens can be nudged toward the necessary actions: "We assist with completing any forms needed to obtain the required documents. We also provide reminders of what to take to the polls." Others noted a minor use of nonprofit resources to help where possible, for example, "If [a] copier is available, we try to make a copy of the document to be included with their voter registration." Given how challenging the expense of traveling to and making copies at a place like Staples or OfficeMax may be, the nonprofit could effectively substitute as a resource center.

Some of the nonprofits focused only on education about voter documentation challenges. A participant commented on how they do their best to "provide information ahead of time to make sure voters understand what is needed," while another focused on "education, through resources such as student voter guides, creating campus action plans and outre[ach]." Some helped clients with "education on the needed documentation and provide linkage[s] to resources." Going further, another wrote, "We actively educate the community through our Nashville Voter Guide, social media platforms, community forums and speaking engagements." The nonprofits in these cases often not only developed their own materials but served as a vital conduit to obtain local information on voting-related matters.

On the minimalist end of engagement with voter documentation requirements, some participants simply cited an awareness of the problem. As a connecting point with other community institutions that could help, others noted when and where citizens could obtain what they needed: "We provide them with the names and locations of the agencies at which they can obtain their necessary documentation." Some remarked more broadly about their services, implying that supporting voting could fit with their larger services: "We have transition-age adult focused groups/services as well as parent advocates, to help individuals meet a variety of adult needs and barriers." One isolated commenter remained resigned about the organization's clients, which may reflect fatalistic attitudes about voter documentation requirements and all other steps needed to vote more generally: "They don't vote—period."

Connecting with Online Assistance

Some assistance takes the form of linking citizens with websites. A respondent wrote that they would direct clients "to log on to myvote. gov if they are internet capable." If the person was unable to do that for any reason, the nonprofit would hand out leaflets showing "types of I[D] [a]ccepted along with tips for ways to produce documentation using other sources such as establishing residency proof by sending the 'incomplete' application to the city clerk and using their return letter requesting residency proof as the requested proof." These efforts sometimes took multiple steps and follow-up. Another participant reinforced this strategy by referring clients to "myvote.org" to start the registration process online and to see what documents would be required.[5]

Participants usually preferred one site over others as a reference or resource. As one person mentioned, "We try to stick with using Turbo-Vote because we know there is built-in follow-up for students who are attempting to register to vote." The organization didn't rely solely on its own resources and found itself adapting to local requirements and varying levels of experience with online and off-line platforms. In essence, these nonprofits often devised diverse strategies to meet the needs of different audiences.

Next Steps

Overall, we were surprised at the commitment and interventions of most of these nonprofits to address voter documentation challenges, and even more amazed at the sheer variety of methods used to help clients overcome barriers. We can't make representative claims with these data, given that we worked with a small convenience sample of nonprofits that (through their connections with conveners and Nonprofit VOTE) already skewed in the direction of involvement with voter support. Yet these responses offered insight into what might inform future efforts at helping people through nonprofits or other community organizations get what they need to vote.

To further explore these responses, our survey concluded with the following item: "We're looking to build a research network of nonprofits interested in helping eligible citizens with voter documentation requirements. Would you (or the appropriate person at your organization) be willing to participate in a phone interview to help us learn more about how your organization and the people you serve have been or could be involved in assisting eligible citizens with voter documentation requirements?" Among our respondents, 61.4 percent (27) answered "yes," and 36.4 percent (16) answered "maybe—I need more information" to this question. Only 2.3 percent (1) answered "no." We contacted all of those who answered "yes" or "maybe" to see if they would be willing to participate in the further interview with us, while also exploring the potential for a site visit to each respective nonprofit's state to speak with community members.

The Perspective of Election Offices

We called 150 election offices across the ten strict voter ID states. As discussed in chapter 2, according to our plan and to keep the scope of inquiry manageable, we called 15 in each state to provide a sampling scheme parallel to the state with the smallest number of counties. We contacted the five most populous, five least populous, and five others that fell within that spectrum during their business hours to see what the experience of seeking to understand and receive help with voter documentation requirements might be like for citizens trying to work with this part of the electoral system.[6] The experience was eye-opening.

Knowledge about Documentation Requirements

To our initial question, "Hi, I'm calling to find out what is needed to vote in the next election," eighty election offices mentioned voter ID unprompted, while fifty-eight failed to mention voter ID, and we received no information at all from twelve due to calls going to voice mail or for other reasons (we'll return to this issue). In other words, for those answering our calls, 53 percent spoke about voter ID spontaneously, while 39 percent failed to mention anything about this issue. A qualification is in order: in the process of conducting research with this question, given the number of initial responses generally along the lines of "You need to register to vote," we believe this question could also have more clearly asked about specific documentation requirements, and may have been confusing for respondents. Then again, people calling who are not aware of documentation requirements would not necessarily know to ask about this. That's why we asked more generally first—to see how the office responded unprompted—before turning to a relevant follow-up question for clarification.

Our follow-up question for those not mentioning ID—"What about ID?"—certainly clarified the nature of our inquiry. On a more hopeful note, fifty-six out of the fifty-eight who failed to mention voter ID talked about it when prompted. But these calls got interesting when we inquired into the details of what exactly was needed. If the respondents described the types of ID accepted in their respective jurisdictions unprompted, we made a note of that. If they didn't describe any, we asked the follow-up question, "What kinds of ID do you accept?" In either case, if only a general description (e.g., "You need a photo ID") or no description of specific forms of documentation was provided (e.g., no mention of a driver's license, US passport, or other specific ID), we marked "No" on our sheet (see appendix C). If specific forms of documentation were described unprompted, we marked "Yes." Eighty-three of the election offices specified the forms of necessary documentation unprompted, while fifty-three did not, and the remaining fourteen gave us neither answer, for reasons such as receiving an automated voice mail or being transferred to another agency or office with this question.

After this, we asked the question, "What if someone doesn't have any of those IDs? How can they vote?" Thirty-three out of the 150 offices mentioned provisional ballots, while 105 did not (although provisional ballots are not standard practice in every jurisdiction). We also took note of whether, in response to this question, the respondent made any other effort to describe how to obtain a valid ID; forty-six provided a further answer, while ninety-two did not (but a "No" here could indicate that the respondent felt they had provided all the necessary information to the questions and needed to go no further).

The "Citizen Service" Experience

We also took notes on almost all the calls to understand the qualitative experience of phoning election offices to find out about voter documentation requirements. Since finding contact information for all these offices required internet searches, we noted the stark contrasts between different jurisdictions' websites that alone could be of help or an obstacle to learning about voter documentation or ID. Some websites were incredibly elegant and user-friendly, while others had confusing content and architectures. Some had features like "precinct locators" that helped voters check their registration status, or clear lists of requirements for voter documentation or ID, while others lacked such features.

In general, counties with larger populations tended to have more robust and well-developed websites. On some county websites we couldn't find any information on voter registration. For one Virginia county, the voter registration portion of the website was "under construction," and we received no response from the office, despite phone calls. We made four attempts to call the election office in another Virginia county but received no response.

Election office staff sometimes postponed answers to our questions by sending us elsewhere. Many staff, sometimes uncomfortable about the specifics of our questions, were quick to send us to their websites for steps and instructions. This raises the question of what the experiences of looking for information would be like for those who have any kind of difficulty with internet access or who lack good connection speeds. In general, staff just assumed that the internet site would be easy to find and navigate. We would sometimes hear that a "passport" or a "student ID" would work in the state (for the first time after many calls to offices within the same state), suggesting that those unlikely to go to a website or who might have difficulty with it could receive different information since the responses to the calls alone might have been understood to be comprehensive.

Sometimes our calls were transferred to another person or agency. If we merely asked what specific forms of documentation would count, we were immediately transferred to someone else. If election office staff cannot answer these basic questions, it speaks volumes about how confusing this process can be and underscores the need for local government to prioritize staff training to help citizens to vote.

Frequently, only one form of ID would be mentioned in a telephone call (such as a driver's license), and more than once we found that an election office's automated phone system didn't have voter registration as an option to get information over the telephone. One automated system in a Wisconsin elections office only offered the option of dialing some-one by name; when we entered the name of the clerk, we heard only a person's first name (no last name). The agency's website had the same information as its telephone message, but we finally found the extension. Many citizens would likely give up after the frustration of telephone calls like these. The extension number had to be called three times, so we fi-nally just left a message. In some cases, the county office made clear that it was not in charge of voting, and subsequently transferred us to other government entities.

Often getting through the first few steps to reach someone knowl-edgeable required patience and perseverance. Some systems were fully or partially automated and required either leaving a message or being placed on hold for up to ten minutes. One call started with a circuitous automated system, inviting the caller to press "0" for assistance, but with no options for voter registration or elections. The line provided a num-ber to a local courthouse and one individual, but upon calling that num-ber, we were put through to city hall. Another phone call started with an automated system; we selected the option for voter registration, and that option only asked if we wanted to change our information online. This then required going back into the menu to find the option for the operator.

Of most concern, some staff didn't know certain details or remained unsure of the answers to our questions. As noted with the results of our initial binary questions, perhaps due to not knowing all the spe-cifics, staff pointed us quickly to their own websites or other websites (e.g., azsos.gov) for a full or better list of information. One person admitted that she was the only person in the office that day and wasn't sure if she was giving us the correct information, so asked us to call back the next day. During one call made at 9:20 a.m. (to an office open from 8:00 a.m. to 4:30 p.m.), we were told that "none of the elections people are here."

In one county in North Dakota, we spoke with someone who had no information available regarding the voting process. This person asked if we wanted to leave a message with the county auditor, who was not available at the time (this was at 9:55 a.m. in this jurisdiction on a Monday). In Wisconsin, too, we spoke to someone who was not the typ-ical person for calls like this, who let us know that the relevant person was busy working on budgets and audits. This conveyed to us that many of these offices had only one knowledgeable point person. Yet we were left pondering why the basic details of voter ID would not be within every staff member's purview. This situation also raised questions about what might happen if a staff member most familiar with voter ID should leave or be unavailable for any period—the lack of distributed knowledge leaves such matters to experts alone.

Sometimes the amount of prompting we had to engage in for answers was remarkable, especially because we (unlike many eligible voters) were familiar with the issue of voter documentation requirements and knew in advance what kinds of questions to ask. Underscoring the findings from our previously noted binary questions, in one county the staff member who answered the phone gave us little information throughout. When asked about valid forms of ID, she said a "photo ID," and when asked about what types would count, she simply told us whichever ones the state requires. When asked to further elaborate, the officer stated that she did not know that information at that moment. On a different call, when we asked about having no ID, we were told, "You can't [vote]," a message provided many times when we asked this question. Furthermore, in one Wisconsin county we were told that you had to be a resident of that county for at least ten days before being able to register to vote, while in a call to another Wisconsin county, we were told the requirement was thirty-eight days. Conflicting messages abounded.

Standardizing Election Offices

Despite these issues, we don't want to overstate the magnitude of the problems encountered in the process of making these calls. The majority of election office staff were friendly and helpful in explaining, for example, that only a birth certificate or Social Security card would be needed (depending on the state); that ID would only be needed if we were voting at the polls on Election Day; that one would only be able to participate in federal elections without specific forms of documentation; or in general providing information about voting centers, precincts, and polling locations related to voter ID challenges.

We also learned about information unique to each jurisdiction. In Arizona, for example, we learned from one office that if you don't have an ID in the voting booth, the state will give you time to get an ID. In Georgia, we received information about similar provisional efforts such as temporary voter IDs being available if certain requirements were met. In North Dakota, we learned that if one does not have an ID, the ballot can be put aside for seven days during which the voter can prove residency, if that includes presenting a document that has a current address. In Tennessee, we were told that one can vote provisionally without an ID, but would need to present a photo ID within forty-eight hours for the vote to be counted (and the only two reasons to not have an ID, according to Tennessee law, are for religious purposes or being a member of an indigent community).

These mixed experiences with election offices again pose a crucial question. Overall, if "one person, one vote" remains a democratic ideal, we must ask why the United States has a system of electioneering that results in such vastly different online and off-line experiences for citizens. The information we received from those working in election offices was much more about the fortuity of which individual agency employee responded to the call than not. For those who find the process even harder to navigate (e.g., immigrants, citizens for whom English is a second language), a goal emerges even more clearly: standardize voting practices so that all have an equal opportunity to understand and to take uniform, easy steps to have their votes counted.

The Perspective of People in Strict Voter ID States

We used Amazon's MTurk platform to prequalify survey participants from the ten strict voter ID states chosen in this study (see table 3.1 for the percentages from each state).[7] After conducting an initial test to make sure we would obtain a sufficient number of responses, and consistent with the literature finding that those most likely affected by voter documentation issues include the elderly, youth, and people with low incomes, we also used MTurk's prequalification categories to limit respondents in the strict voter ID states to eighteen-to-thirty-year-olds, those fifty-five and older, and the personal income category of less than $50,000.

TABLE 3.1. Percentage/Number of Prequalified Survey Participants from the 10 Strictest Voter ID States

US State	Percentage of Prequalified Survey Participants	Count
Arizona	10.6	23
Georgia	17.4	38
Indiana	9.2	20
Kansas	2.8	6
Mississippi	2.8	6
North Dakota	0.0	0
Ohio	18.8	41
Tennessee	11.0	24
Virginia	17.0	37
Wisconsin	7.3	16
None of the above	3.2	7
Total	100.0	218

Visualizing ID Issues

After providing their informed consent, 223 participants filled out our survey in whole or part via a link to our Qualtrics research site. All these participants responded positively to the first survey question ("I will provide my best answer"). Their responses are presented in table 3.1.

Our youngest participant was twenty and the oldest was seventy-seven, with an average age of thirty-four. Some 81 (37.3 percent) of the participants listed said that they were male and 136 were female (62.7 percent). Three participants (1.3 percent) checked off that they were Asian/Pacific Islander; 42 (18.3 percent) were Black/African American/Caribbean; 11 (4.8 percent) were Hispanic/Latino; 172 (75.1 percent) were White/Caucasian; and 1 (0.4 percent) was Other. In terms of household income (i.e., the participant's personal income could have been combined with that of a partner or another person), 81 (37.33 percent) said they made less than $25,000; 105 (48.39 percent) listed $25,000 to $49,999; 24 (11.1 percent) listed $50,000 to $99,999; 4 (1.8 percent) listed $100,000 or more; and 3 (1.4 percent) declined to state their income. In terms of education, 25 (11.5 percent) completed high school (with 1 [0.5 percent] indicating that they did not complete high school); 95

(43.8 percent) had completed some college; 78 (35.9 percent) had completed college; and 18 (8.3 percent) had taken part in postcollege studies or graduate or professional degree programs.

We asked, "Politically, which party do you identify with the most?" As illustrated in figure 3.3, about half the sample were Democrats (98 total; 48.2 percent), and the other half were a mix of Republicans (49 total; 22.6 percent) and Independents (60 total; 27.7 percent), with None (5 total; 2.3 percent) and Other (5 total; 2.3 percent) in the minority.[8] Overall, 92.79 percent listed that they were registered voters, 6.31 percent were not registered voters, and 0.90 percent were not sure.

Two conditions are worth noting. One is that, because we used a convenience sample, we can't make representative claims from these data. The other is that, compared with the 64.2 percent of reported registrations to vote in the US population in the 2016 US presidential election,[9] for instance, the MTurk sample overrepresented registered voters. Responding to the question, "Did you vote in the most recent presidential election (2016) or any other state or local elections in the past two years?," 90.4 percent answered "yes," and 9.6 percent said "no," which also deviates from averages for the US population. According to the United States Election Project, 60.2 percent of eligible voters cast their ballot in the 2016 US presidential election.[10]

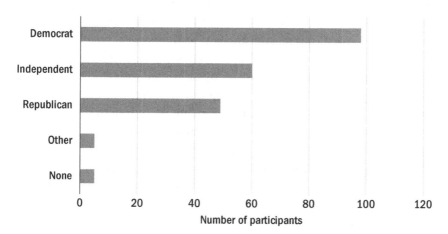

Figure 3.3. Political party identification

On the other hand, the data obtained from this sample spoke to many of our research questions of interest. To the question, "Does your state have specific requirements regarding showing a form of identification in order to be allowed to vote?," 72.52 percent said "yes," 4.5 percent said "no," and 22.97 percent said "not sure." These results are from a sample of respondents all of whom live in strict ID jurisdictions, running parallel to some literature showing that people are generally aware of their states' having voter ID requirements. Yet, that sixty-one participants—more than a quarter of our sample—either got the wrong answer or didn't know illustrates significant confusion about their states' requirements to vote. When we asked, "Do you have identification documents that you could use to prove your identity if required for voting purposes, such as a driver's license, state-issued ID card, US passport, or other official photo ID card?," 99.1 percent said "yes," and only 0.9 percent said "not sure." This still leaves open the question of whether the specified identification matched what was required by each state. But at least for this sample, citizens were quite confident that they possessed the needed documentation. That so many of the participants had ID makes some sense, given that Amazon verifies its worker identities through Social Security numbers and, in some cases, minimal additional documentation.

The most useful findings involved participants' responses to questions about help with voter documentation and other people they knew who struggled with requirements. Figure 3.4 shows respondents' answers to the question, "Have you ever sought help or received help in obtaining identification documents from any of the following?" (they could click on multiple categories as appropriate, so the percentages in figure 3.4 reflect that participants could be included in more than one row):

Although less than half of the total participants at 40.07 percent (not included in figure 3.4), in descending order, government agencies constituted 23.69 percent; families, 18.82 percent; friends, 6.62 percent; voter registration workers, 5.23 percent; religious organizations, 2.09 percent; nonprofit organizations, 1.74 percent; other, 1.39 percent; and political parties, 0.35 percent. For other, our participants clarified, "Birth certificates, etc. were obtained thr[ough] family, court house, and school at one point," "Obtained photo for passport at a store," "DMV," and "I tried asking my blended case manager but it hasn't led to anything." At least for this sample, we learned that while government agencies still

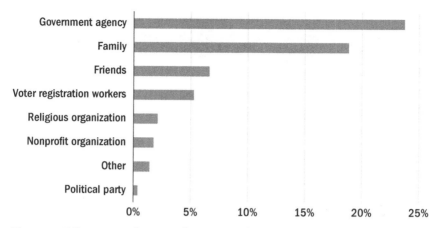

Figure 3.4. Where respondents sought or received help in obtaining identification documents

do most of the work with identification documents, working through one's immediate circles of family and friends is more influential in obtaining documentation than assistance from organizations (e.g., voter registration workers, religious organizations, nonprofits), which we had assumed would play more of a role. The more we thought about it, the more it made sense that documents such as birth certificates would likely come from parents, in particular.

To the question, "Would you be interested in receiving free help from a nonprofit organization or other type of organization to obtain official identification documents?," 18.26 percent answered "yes," 20.09 percent said "not sure," and 61.64 percent said "no" (figure 3.5). That approximately 40 percent of respondents answered "yes" or "not sure" to this question illustrates that, despite the low number who had ever received help from a nonprofit, there was still substantial interest in this possibility.

Following these inquiries, we posed the question, "Do you know of other people (not including yourself) who have not been able to vote because they did not meet voter identification requirements?" In response, 61.6 percent of participants said "no," and 10 percent said "not sure." "Yes, 1 to 2 people" received 24.7 percent of responses, and "Yes, 3 or more people," received 3.7 percent (figure 3.6). The responses indicate that these

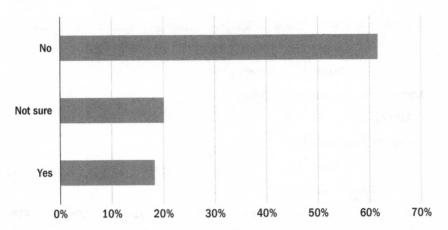

Figure 3.5. Respondents' interest in receiving free help from nonprofits in obtaining official identification documents

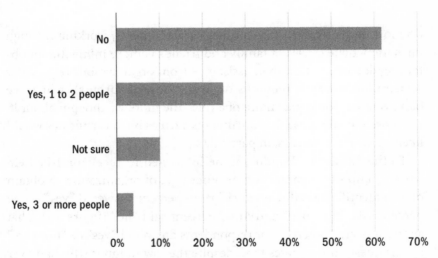

Figure 3.6. Knowledge of other people who have not been able to vote because they did not meet voter identification requirements

problems and those affected by them are known, and that it's worth taking a deeper dive into how such challenges impact people in these states at the level of everyday life—a task we undertake in subsequent chapters.

Additionally, we sought participants' views on a variety of voter-related questions to examine what individuals in this sample thought about issues from the importance of voting to voter fraud. The results in table 3.2 show that on a 5-point scale (with 1 meaning "strongly disagree" and 5 meaning "strongly agree"), our respondents largely thought that those who are eligible should be able to vote in public elections (mean = 4.32), while valuing the right to vote (mean = 4.51) and taking pride in the possibility of voting in the next election (mean = 4.21). The most noteworthy finding was that respondents believed that *requirements to show ID before voting are critical to preventing voter fraud* (mean = 4.01), revealing that—no matter what extant research highlights about the lack of evidence for voter fraud—this sample of citizens across party lines still believe that fraud is a danger and that voter ID is needed to combat it.[11] This shows how deeply a narrative

TABLE 3.2. Voter-Related Issues

Statement		Minimum	Maximum	Mean	Standard Deviation	Variance	Count
a.	Everyone who is eligible should vote in public elections.	1	5	4.32	0.83	0.68	218
b.	The requirement to show identification before voting is important to prevent voter fraud.	1	5	4.01	1.15	1.33	218
c.	Voting is not worth the effort.	1	5	1.83	1	1.01	218
d.	I value my right to vote if I choose to do so.	2	5	4.51	0.63	0.4	218
e.	It's easy to obtain photo identification that can be used as proof of eligibility to vote.	1	5	3.72	1.04	1.08	218
f.	I would be proud to vote in the next election.	1	5	4.21	0.93	0.86	218
g.	I don't care very much about politics.	1	5	2.17	1.19	1.42	218
h.	Voting is for other people, not me.	1	5	1.74	0.99	0.98	218

Note: The participants' views are ranked on a 5-point scale, with 1 meaning "strongly disagree" and 5 meaning "strongly agree."

of voter fraud rather than suppression appears to have sunk in to many citizens' thinking. An above-average number thought it would be easy to obtain photo ID to vote in the next election (mean = 3.72), while our reverse-coded questions received minimal support, including voting not being worth the effort (mean = 1.83), not caring much about politics (mean = 2.17), and voting being for other people, not oneself (mean = 1.74), meaning that for this sample, at least, an expectation for civic engagement was a norm.

To place their experiences in context, at the end of the online survey we also asked participants if they had any comments to make after having completed all these responses. Most comments indicated that they enjoyed the survey and found it easy to complete and clear. One person appreciated that it was "well worded while still maintaining neutrality." Another wrote that doing the survey itself "has made me more aware that I need to get registered to vote"—*showing the unexpected potential for research itself to open spaces for voter engagement.* Similarly, another participant felt motivated to proclaim, "All legally eligible people who want/try to vote should be able to do so!" Other calls to action included: "I hope the survey results will be used to get out the vote!" and "I hope you do help those who have trouble getting I.D.s Thank you." Consistent with the generally positive beliefs about voting in the survey, our participants took pride in their identity as voters (or eligible voters), with a near-evangelical belief in the need for others to have access to that identity as well.

Some related the successes they or others had (or should have) on this topic. One citizen wrote, "It should be easy for anyone to go to the DMV or elsewhere to get an ID for voting if they don't have a driver[']s license." Another documented some initial challenges that had been overcome: "I did have one problem in Ohio getting my name changed on my voter registration. I contacted the office and still couldn't get anything done. Finally the lady at the voting place was able to change it for me. Cards are no longer required here so we use [a] driver[']s license." One person explained, "When I went to vote, they asked for my driver's license. My little brother didn't have a driver[']s license yet, but was able to easily get a photo ID from the DMV, and was able to vote afterward."

These assertions did not translate into a belief that voting was equally within the reach of all, though. Some participants expressed empathy for what others may face, confirming that their positions in life might be quite different. One respondent wrote, "I am lucky, in that it was easy for me to obtain photo identification because I am a [W]hite middle class male. However, for some people, it is NOT easy to get a photo ID, such as those who live in the city and cannot afford to travel to the necessary places to get an ID." Such comments present a keen awareness of how ID issues might play out beyond one's own situation. Another participant wrote, "I have never had a problem voting in my state. But then, I am a senior [W]hite man."

How voting worked in one's own and others' cases exposed some confusion, with one person telling us: "I completed the mail in ballot, so I was unsure about voter identification (how they check when you go in person to vote). Also, I answered that I knew some people who did not meet the requirements, but am unsure if they did not obtain proper identification or simply did not register in time." One respondent expressed skepticism about the effects of voting: "I think everyone should vote, but as things stand it isn't worth voting as a single person." Overall, across a broad convenience sample of people in strict voter ID states, opinions mainly supported the view that voting is important, that it should be easy and accessible for all, and that election integrity must be maintained.

These larger statistical data with qualitative responses from engaged nonprofits, the experience of contacting election offices, and people across these states provide a backdrop for what does and could happen on the ground with voter documentation requirements. In that spirit, we next turn to experts and others well connected to this issue, who offer more granular views about the havoc voter ID wreaks around the nation, including what should be done moving forward.

4

Breaking Down the System

Problems, Challenges, and Opportunities

With voter ID, the devil truly is in the details. While it's common in places like the United States to think that most problems derive from individual choices, people's actions never take place in a vacuum. Just as asking low-income families to eat lots of fruits and vegetables in an area where there are no supermarkets with fresh produce is unlikely to create real change,[1] a person may want to take care of voter documentation requirements to vote, but the systems around them may make it difficult, and sometimes impossible, to do so. Part of understanding and addressing the citizen experience with voter ID, then, must involve insights into individuals' capacities within the demands of communities, networks, and institutions.

The themes in this chapter derive from interviews with experts of various kinds on US voter documentation requirements. In total, we conducted thirty-eight interviews with nonprofit staff, government employees, executive directors, data and policy directors, program and outreach managers, community relations staff, founders, deans, ethics officers, CEOs, copresidents and vice presidents of various voting-related organizations, and county clerks and elections officials. To understand how this issue has been playing out nationally, we also interviewed health consultants, office administrators, lawyers, academics, and community service providers across almost all the strict voter ID states.

These participants worked in organizations such as election research centers; nonprofits dedicated to racial, gender, and immigration justice; foundations; advocacy networks; civic engagement nonprofits; county recorders' offices; and veterans' rights organizations. Some worked in political parties; law schools; coalitions; community organizations working on homelessness, affordable housing, and health; and even nonprofits dedicated to voting assistance.[2]

This chapter moves from a focus on the barriers that people experience with voter documentation requirements to the suggested solutions that those with a deep understanding of these challenges consider feasible and creative. Let's start with the breakdowns or current gaps that need to be closed between the United States' citizens and systems when it comes to voter ID and related issues.

The Breakdowns

Time, Money, and Transportation

Consistent with background research, the most basic challenges of time, money, and transportation came up across our interviews, but with many more complexities than we had expected. To start with, those who gave us a comprehensive overview of what they've experienced provided helpful perspectives on voter documentation requirements and their effects. Many attorneys had an acute sense for both on-the-ground and systemic problems. A senior legal director articulated the voluminous challenges connected to voter documentation requirements: "When folks have such limited resources, limited time and a lot of strain on their resources . . . and have lots on their mind, the likelihood that they are able to devote time and resources and [that] kind of space in their mind to think about voting and what they need to do in order to prepare to vote [is curtailed]." People in the United States also tend to move a lot from state to state. That many states have different voter registration deadlines makes it even more challenging to navigate the maze of varying expectations that citizens face.

Expanding on details that we heard from engaged nonprofits, we discovered that what may seem like simple actions for many citizens, such as printing up a voter registration form at one's office or home, can be incredibly difficult for some people. For example, "If you don't have a home office then you are talking about either having to go down to the voter registration office, which is one trip, going to the polls and vote, which is two trips now, or you have to go to a Kinko's or something to print out the forms." On top of this problem, issues of illiteracy and the challenges that homeless people face in having to include a residence as a prerequisite to voter registration compound these issues. In the United

States, peoples' literacy rates with government documents and similar technical forms aren't always on a par either.

Documentation requirements frequently make it impossible to run voter registration activities that were typical and accessible before ID laws were passed. Voter registration drives have become hard to run in the strict ID states because previously registered or eligible citizens don't carry documents such as birth certificates with them as they make their way through the average day. Few people make a trip to the supermarket with their passports, for instance, so a voter registration drive out front would be able to do very little for such a person. Basically, as the legal director told us, many people, and especially students, don't have these documents on them in person, and

> do not have it at home. Their parents have it or they do not have easy access to proof of citizenship. One thing we run into in voter ID [and] is similarly an issue here is for elderly people, the likelihood that these documents, especially [for] elderly poor people, have been lost; people experience fires, a lot of people move a lot, and documents get lost. They may not have the easy and well-established personal record as some of us might have. A huge number of people that I have encountered while doing research on these issues and cases, a lot of people tell you that at some point they have lost all their records. At some point, I got kicked outside of a house, I got evicted, I had to move suddenly, I have experienced domestic violence, I mean you name it. Someone has a reason that at some point they lost a lot of their documents. . . . I really do think that the biggest burden is that some people do not have the documentation on them . . . if people, for example, if they just go to the disability office and the office is complying with the National Voter Registration Act and it offers them voter registration options, they can't really use them without an additional trip because they do not have their birth certificate on them. The National Voter Registration Act, it is really created to help meet people where they are and get them registered to vote, and this makes that impossible.

Overall, if organizations are to have any impact by helping people deal with documentation requirements, they must realistically deal with these documentation challenges across institutions and states.

The director of a nonprofit that helps people get voter IDs told us that money is one of the most basic challenges for many people. She mentioned that in her state (Tennessee, but the group also works in other states), the average ID cost is 40 dollars, but about 57 percent of the people they work with don't have birth certificates.[3] The average birth certificate costs somewhere between fifty and eighty dollars, and then there's the issue of needing an ID for a birth certificate (a challenge we'll expand on in the next section), showing how this process can turn into a significant undertaking. When you add transportation costs in time, money, and availability to this mix, "a huge part of it is just the bureaucracy and the confusion." Amplifying the confusion at the core of this book's argument, the director underscored:

> These laws are massively confusing and post 9/11 it's become almost impossible to get an ID and so people just don't even know where to start. And these are parts of the population that [are] the most forgotten. You know, that [have] suffered the most in this country. And so everything is harder, everything is harder. And being able to go on a website and go to the DMV and figure out what you need to get, all of these documents and find the money like that is, it's impossible. And we, we help people who haven't had an ID in twenty years sometimes, right. Or someone whose ID was lost or stolen five years ago and they're devastated without it. Right, it's, this is not a group of people who have the resources . . . or tools in order to be able to get to find things. So the money and the transportation and the bureaucracy are definitely the, the three biggest things that we run into and are . . . the three biggest reasons that people don't have their ID.

Note the director's judgment that coming up against these systemic constraints can make getting voter documentation "impossible." Compared with the views expressed by people across strict voter ID states in the last chapter (from those who had ID and were already registered to vote, by and large), who thought that getting an ID should be a relatively easy undertaking, here we find that for many "forgotten" populations, bureaucratic dealings related to time, money, and transportation become insurmountable obstacles. Although there are common challenges that citizens encounter with voter identification, it's often the unique combinations of these requirements that really bring home the havoc these laws are wreaking.

We learned from the staff member of another nonprofit how "voter ID has been difficult and confusing in Indiana. It is a little bit better now with some of the changes in utilizing student ID and those IDs being accepted as government IDs," but access to voter registration and voting still raises transportation and time issues that are especially hard for those with disabilities. Getting a birth certificate in Indiana can require going to another state or county or trying to get a duplicate birth certificate that requires money: "That is a complicated step for many people. It is also expensive."

Circular Traps

The idea of a "circular trap" sums up one of the main trials that citizens face with voter identification requirements. What seems like a simple problem to solve on the surface often rests on an iceberg of problems beneath. We spoke with one lawyer who provides legal services for low-income clients and those with disabilities, who said that "about 40 percent of my cases . . . involved helping people obtain legal ID" and had "testified as an expert witness on the difficulties that low-income folks face in obtaining legal ID." Like many of the stories we heard, the following explanation of circular traps is worth quoting at length to understand the dilemma of a series of unresolvable, interdependent conditions. Concerning the main issues voters in Pennsylvania had to tackle (a state in which the voter ID law was eventually struck down), the attorney offered the following description:

> It was very difficult due to the expense of obtaining birth certificates [BCs]. Vital Records [VR] units require applicants to submit state-issued photo ID to obtain BCs, so when someone needed an ID to get the BC to get an ID it was a circular trap. The expense of paying for BCs was also a hardship, or for folks born out of state, knowing how to order one. Some states require notarization of the applications if the person orders by mail. That posed a problem of expense and also not having ID to show to a notary. And for many older people who were born down south, there was often the absence of BCs. I had clients who were born in hospitals but

the VR unit had never recorded the birth. More common were the situations where people were born at home and the birth was never recorded. In those cases "Delayed Birth Records" had to be created, which was a costly and time-consuming process. Most VR units require three separate documents that are fifteen years or older, which have "birth facts" such as name, parents' names, date of birth, state, and city of birth. If there are any typos or conflicting information in a document, it is not accepted. In that situation we were required to petition the family court in Philadelphia to issue an order requiring the VR unit of the state where the person was born to create a delayed birth record. The legal department of the VR unit of the state of birth then parsed through the petition, and could oppose it, and then if the order was issued the legal department would scrutinize the order and might object to some of the birth facts the Philadelphia judge put in the order. The whole process would take years from start to finish and would be tremendously expensive for the individual if legal services was unwilling to do this pro bono.

In cases like these, citizens face colossal challenges. The cascading list of problems highlights how much help someone facing these hurdles may need, even to the point of enlisting an attorney's services, which can cause the costs of voter documentation to skyrocket well beyond one's means.

Government agencies and related organizations amplify circular traps when the forms of documentation people need pile on top of one another. We heard from one respondent that in states like Wisconsin, *the challenges of residency proof have become more of a barrier to voting than ID.* She mentioned that her agency's clerk had measured the effect of proof of residence to register to vote, "and it's actually keeping more people from voting than the ID," since Wisconsin has a strict law for demonstrating one's residence. North Dakota and other states have been in the news for proof-of-residence requirements that have the potential to exclude whole communities (e.g., Native Americans) from the ballot box.[4] Citizens may think they're prepared to vote, only to find out that they need an ID showing proof of residence, at the same time as proof of residence is needed to get an ID. Although these laws may have started with the best of intentions to preserve election integrity, in effect they end up perpetuating pernicious and politicized circular traps that can put voting out of reach.

Variations in State and County Requirements

Although the requirements for voter documentation vary across states, there are federal expectations that carry across the United States. An associate dean at a law school reminded us that the federal Help America Vote Act requires states to have a floor for voter ID. That is, "any voter who registers by mail has to have either the driver's license number or SSN [Social Security number] on their registration form matched up to DMV or Social Security databases, or show one of a fairly broad series of documents (including utility bill, paycheck, any government document with name and address, etc.) before voting for the first time." Yet, in practice, these attempts at standardized principles and practices frequently pit federal expectations against an onslaught of niche state and county requirements that create uneven experiences for people.

Many institutions charged with regulating or implementing voting requirements are hence shifting their strategies to stay on top of the confusing array of documentation requirements. A senior legal director for an organization working on voting underscored how, "With respect to voter documentation at registration, this is a relatively new kind of issue. Registration as a general matter, just the requirement that you need to register is very old and is the biggest barrier to voting that there is in the United States." Some states don't have voter registration or have same-day registration, making our election system necessarily unequal at the earliest stage of the voting process, creating both dissimilar expectations and different obstacles on the way to voting.

We heard the same idea repeatedly: the variation in documentation requirements and approaches between states, and even counties, constitutes a far greater challenge for citizens than federal rules about voting. Although a federal court ruling in Kansas in 2018 made it easier to register to vote by getting rid of the state's proof-of-citizenship voter law[5]—or, as the president of a voting group told us, "Now it's a matter of throwing out a form and a sermon that one is a citizen"—it's instructive to see how all this variation plays out, since so many states continue to update and apply their own rules for voter registration. It can be hard keeping up with all of this, especially in the environment that has followed the 2020 US general election. The president of the voting group told us that, unbelievably, there is a difference across the 105 counties in Kansas. What our county was doing was sending out postcard reminders, two of them, to individuals that had not fulfilled the documentation requirements for proof of citizenship. Then if they never heard back after a certain period of time, the county under the direction of our secretary of state, took those people off the roll. As far as the person was concerned, if they paid no attention to those postcards or waited too long, there was a ninety-days waiting period supposedly after the last postcard, then they were taken off. It really varies in our state in what was really happening. It varied by county. Now with the new federal ruling, as of a week ago, the election office here accepts both the Kansas form, which [was] used to require proof of citizenship, . . . or the federal form.

Without fully solving the problems of variation, that it took a federal ruling to create some needed uniformity is telling. Yet the effect of laws being overturned can create new confusion too. An office administrator for a voting organization in Kansas mentioned, "It was a crazy mess of how do we advise people in the most prudent way to register to vote so that once this court case [is] settled, they still have the right to vote. So it was very tricky." Moving to a state such as Arizona can be even more complicated. We learned from one interviewee that proof of citizenship is required for state and local elections, but due to an electronic system currently in place, people can still vote without documentation in federal elections.

The difficulties of traversing state lines and the ironies of "free voter IDs" don't help either. In Wisconsin, a participant described how the problem with the state's photo ID law is that only a limited number of IDs are acceptable. State university IDs are not viable (i.e., presumably not accepted by the Board of Elections) forms of ID for voter registration, "so for students who come from out of state but live in state during the school year, which would be during elections, they often have a hard time securing ID that would work for them to vote." This participant's organization therefore conducts a large public education campaign around these issues for students, the elderly, and people who move a lot. In this work, "The state does provide a free ID; however, it's been documented by several individuals who have helped secure free ID that there is often a cost involved, which means maybe obtaining a birth certificate. There is a fee involved and then all the time invested in securing the components that are needed to get a state free ID. Those kinds of things are quite challenging." In this regard, "free" voter IDs simply perpetuate the major problems associated with documentation requirements—and are anything but free. They present many eligible citizens with the illusion of an easy-to-obtain product but add another step to the already cumbersome process of procuring needed documentation in the first place.

Many people have housing situations that further complicate the already complicated variations among state and county requirements. Another participant from Wisconsin explained that for students to demonstrate their proof of residence, they could use the university's housing list, but for those living in private housing, "it's sometimes difficult because, for instance, the permitted proofs of residence are things like utility bills, which are only in one person's name. And so if you've got five students living in an apartment, only one of them has proof of residence." We heard from another respondent that sometimes a university or college residence will work, "but only if the voter also can provide a fee receipt within the last nine months, or the institution revised the certified housing lists to the municipal clerk." This means that certified housing lists for dorms can be obtained, but most students will not have met the housing-related fee requirement. In addition, "Seniors are also an issue. They had let their driver's license lapse. Or in the case of retirement homes, they came here to be with their children and so they don't have a valid Wisconsin driver's license." These examples highlight how only strategies that reflect the huge variety of dissimilar regulations across jurisdictions can meet the needs of diverse groups of eligible voters. Another nonprofit director in Wisconsin similarly explained, "Our elections are all decentralized. We run 1800 different elections and our, you know, [the] state election commission doesn't really have any authority for the most part." Working out the different requirements for elections across fifty states is difficult enough, but add to that potential variations across the 3,141 counties in the United States, and disconnections between citizens and election systems abound. From another participant we heard the following: "In Wisconsin, if you are older or just disabled, you can get a permanent absentee ballot. You can get on the list to get one and then you don't have to show an ID. . . . of course you have to ask for that before the election." The requirements for elections vary not only by county and state but also for particular populations who can easily fall through the cracks because they don't know what requirements apply to their individual circumstances.

At the same time, life changes frequently affect what's needed in crossing state borders. The past president of a voting rights organization in Wisconsin told us that many elderly people move to cities such as Madison to be near family, and when they move to independent or assisted living facilities they no longer need to drive. Ultimately, "They don't think about the fact that they're going to have to present an ID at the polls . . . this is a fairly common thing. And I don't think our legislature really intended this either. I don't think they were trying to prevent older people from voting. But there are a number of older people who moved from another state and they're not going to get a driver's license ever because they're not really planning to drive." We'd infer that for these types of voters, the idea of not having a car (with all its ensuing expenses) may be a welcome relief, yet with the unintended consequence of blocking access to one of the most valued forms of voter ID. When one moves from one state to another, there's also the issue of getting off the rolls in one state to get on the rolls in another. The Electronic Registration Information Center (ERIC), which we discuss further later, has been the most sweeping tool for helping with this issue. To date it has "helped a bipartisan group of nearly two dozen states correct almost 4 million out-of-date voter records, and led to these states registering almost a million new eligible voters."[6]

Online Difficulties

Contrary to a common understanding that the internet should make life easier, sometimes challenges with voter ID lie in understanding online procedures that are anything but intuitive for voters. One woman who cochaired a voter ID coalition of about thirty organizations in Wisconsin and who works with people who must move frequently said, "It turns out that registering online is not all that simple," prompting the coalition to engage the issue. First, to provide assistance online, volunteers or workers themselves need to acquire new, current software electronics and technologies, as well as hardware, like different phones and tablets that have their own learning curves.

Second, where the different norms and expectations across states present one source of frustration, the differences between online and off-line voting systems beget another source of the chaos that voter documentation requirements have created on many levels. A staff member for a foundation that conducts a lot of overseas outreaches dedicated to helping people vote (including work with data and systems built around this work) expressed alarm at the lack of standardization between online and off-line systems' due dates, especially for

> domestic voters, the deadlines are different for every state. There's nothing uniform. . . . For example, you may have a deadline for registering to vote that is October 9. But if you registered to vote online, your deadline might be October 16. If you do it in person you might get a totally different date, you can have, there's no longer one deadline. There might be federal deadlines depending on how you execute the action requested. But overall, the, the issue of deadlines to register and deadlines to request an absentee ballot [is] what causes a tremendous amount of fallout, [a] huge amount of fallout. The promotion is always around Election Day. . . . they [voters] can't cope with that.

After working to provide people with information online that could assist with the lack of consistency for voting regulations, the staff member told us, "After years of dealing with it, we saw that there is no standardization, no uniform way of presenting exactly what you're talking about," and due to the "decision on our government's part to not issue automatically ID to people, we have hundreds of types of IDs." The participant's organization has therefore been doing all it can to make and update lists of voting requirements and voter ID standards by state. In a day and age in which automation has become the norm we, too, ask: Why aren't IDs automatically issued to people? Why do we have election systems premised on a need to "opt in" to begin with? Why not create automatic procedures where to "opt out" would require the substantial work that many citizens face just to get on the books and vote? Other modern democracies have systems that provide for this—European

Union countries ensure that newborns are registered at birth, for example.[7] We'll return to these critical questions again.

Third, putting together lists of acceptable documents whether online or off-line presents its own problems. To achieve anything like an updated, iterative list that's flexible enough to keep track of policy changes in different jurisdictions means creating an intimidating document. As our participant pointed out, "It's mind-numbingly long. It's supposed to be an option, but options are scary. 'Oh, what's all this, do I have to bring it all?' Who knows what they read or don't read?" In other words, simply providing the information doesn't necessarily speak to the barriers that people have upon seeing lists of IDs. The experience can be overwhelming both for the originators of these documents and for those on the receiving end. From the respondent's viewpoint, the presentations available now and the ease of using the information provided could clearly be improved to be more audience-friendly both online and off-line, supplementing the back-end work that election officials and others are doing to get correct, updated information.

We came to this project understanding that state variation played a large role in voter documentation challenges and in suppressing votes. Our findings from the election office audit certainly support such a claim. But we were genuinely astonished that county-level differences would also figure so prominently in this story, especially with respect to the disjuncts between online and off-line capabilities and the ability to vote within the same election cycle.

Delays in Receiving Documentation

The length of time that people need to wait to obtain documentation must be reasonable to guarantee wide access to voting. One nonprofit staff member in North Carolina told us that children whose parents are immigrants can become US citizens by virtue of their birth in this country, but they experience a time lag for a certificate of citizenship or naturalization. During the Trump administration (among other reasons), those papers took a lot longer for the US federal government to process. The time for processing used to be about four to six months, but it could now take from sixteen to twenty-two months to process a

certificate for children when they turn eighteen. Overall, as our participant mentioned, "That is affecting the elections in November. . . . we are
having difficulty in registering those young adults for voting." Under
these circumstances, the varying voter registration deadlines that states
provide become moot, since the federal delays can set first-time voters
back, effectively shifting their real voting age to nineteen or twenty, or
the age at which they could vote in their first presidential election to
twenty-two or beyond.

People can also be turned away from polls for having expired driver's
licenses. Someone may go to the polls not realizing that their license has
lapsed by even a few days or a month and be turned away for not keeping their ID current. A past president of a voting rights organization in
Wisconsin described the story of one voter she had worked with:

> I talked to an older woman who had been in Florida for the election, the
> week before the election and somehow, in giving her driver's license to
> the TSA or something, or who knows, she had lost her driver's license
> at the Florida airport, so she went to the DMV to get a new license. But
> somehow—I don't really fully understand this—but somehow you can't
> get a replacement license the same day you go there or something. And
> then they were mailing the license from Florida, you know, they found it
> at the airport. But of course it didn't come in time. I mean, it was a mess.
> She, she'd said she'd voted [in] every election. She was my age, you know,
> in her late sixties and she couldn't.

While cases where people can't get what they need to vote across long
periods of time are certainly concerning, sometimes having a delay of a
single day can affect a person's ability to register to vote or vote.

Fear, Distrust, and Language Choices

Unfortunately, whether grounded in perception or reality, fear and distrust of public institutions and of those in public service exact a toll
on people's motivations to pursue IDs for voting and other purposes. A
staff member at a legal nonprofit in North Carolina told us that people
in their community tend to have a lack of trust about who is going to
register their vote and what will happen to their information. In a time

when there's already so much data surveillance, it's not unreasonable for vulnerable populations to assume that powerful actors and institutions could use their information against them.

Particularly in the case of immigrant communities, if someone comes from a library or the DMV and says, "Hey, fill out this application," they may be viewed with suspicion. So "having an organization, a nonprofit that they are familiar with, that's run by immigrants themselves is a plus." Trust is everything. Many immigrants "are also fearful because there's just a lot of misconceptions or a lot of news out there in the media that the federal government is revoking citizenship, revoking documentation." Even terms like "documentation" may be intended as neutral but come loaded with negative associations for certain groups. This is often the problem with some forms of language used by government entities that, in seeking to signal a nonpartisan and neutral tone, don't take account of the deep emotional discomfort different audiences bring to formal legalese or to particular words or phrases.

In general, many people are fearful about bringing documentation to or registering with the government in any way. As one participant remarked, "That's one thing I think is essential and should be pointed out. Fear has increased."[8] In this light, seemingly innocuous questions about documentation may foster dread and anxiety. To an immigrant, a question about a birth certificate or any number of other documents could be responded to with: "Huh, why are you asking me for my papers? Are you immigration? Are you the government?" So those working on voter documentation requirements need to be especially mindful of the nature of their language and the questions asked and to think about possible negative responses. We learned from our interviewees that, within some communities, online apps like Whatsapp have been used to share information among people with green cards, or people with citizenship being deported or whose identification has been revoked. Despite the fear and distrust, this shows that people who are wary of government communication are willing to turn to local, trusted others, even online, to find reliable information.

Fear, distrust, and language choice issues highlight an intriguing contradiction about how to present voter documentation requirements. The most accessible pathways to voting in the future would arguably come from federal and national policy changes on voter ID, but the government itself is the entity most feared and distrusted by many immigrant communities. Whether or not federal or even state government policy changes take place, fear and distrust are best addressed by community-level, trusted others, begging local assistance from nonprofits and community organizations. In an era when many citizens are distrustful of government for a host of reasons having nothing to do with being an immigrant or a member of a marginalized community (including libertarians and many citizens on the political left and right), the stakes for local mediators are also raised.

The Voting Rights Act requires that voting information and resources be available in foreign languages.[9] This issue flared up in New York City during the COVID-19 pandemic, with journalists covering how the Board of Elections hotline "eventually routes English and Spanish speakers to other channels, such as county Board of Elections offices. But it does not offer an option for interpretation for New Yorkers who don't speak these languages, nor does it provide information in the three other languages—Korean, Bengali, Chinese—that the registration form is printed in. Then there's the DMV's online submission form: It's only available in English and only accepts New York state issued IDs."[10] If as progressive a city as New York has still not caught up to the Voting Rights Act's requirements for linguistic access to voting, this issue is likely amplified in other cities and states.

We learned from an executive director in Arizona that Latino communities and voters also don't want to make the wrong choices in their voting. People within these communities would often rather not vote than vote for someone who could harm them and their families. Like many Latinos, those in Central Asian immigrant communities may sometimes veer toward avoiding the voting process when they consider what they hear in their surrounding vicinity. They can question why they would show up and vote for most politicians who appear to "just turn around and demonize me and my family and my community anyway," making civic participation, or at least having confidence about voting, unlikely. With so many elected officials targeting the legality—and humanity—of vulnerable populations in the news, voter documentation requirements cannot simply be addressed as a stand-alone issue without addressing other matters related to voting, the lived circumstances of different communities, and, overall, the barriers of fear and distrust in many people's lives.

Although trepidation over accidentally casting a vote for a person who could cause harm to community interests looms large in the decision to try to vote, creating any level of confusion at all about voting dates, locations, and other variables has its own afterlife. Making voting complicated and confusing plays into fears that one won't get the process right, or that something could go wrong at any stage. At the same time, information about the candidates and issues can be hard to come by, and instructions for how to vote sometimes present an additional difficulty, as one interviewee shared: "As we're constantly changing our election processes, in some ways for the good, you know, with more, more, and more people voting early, and, and more and more options to vote, that can also still be very confusing about, OK, so on this day I can go anywhere in the county, but on this day I have to go to my specific polling place or my ballot won't count?"

Again, working through local networks is at least one way to combat confusion and alleviate eligible voters' concerns. A nonprofit director who works across many states told us, "There's a lot of fear, especially right now, right about what's happening." If you're an authority figure of any kind, various populations can easily interpret your presence as Immigration and Customs Enforcement (ICE). So she always partners with and has an intermediary who knows the people within the community. She points out that "if you go in and say 'do you have an ID,'" then "people will literally run from us. So you have to go through a shelter or food bank or a school or church, someone they trust who will say no, they're OK, we've vetted them, they're going to work with you." This led her to conclude that, for providing realistic, successful local assistance with voter documentation requirements, "our whole lifeblood is local partnership."

Limited Resources and Bandwidth

A serious impediment to citizen engagement is the generally limited resources and bandwidth that local organizations themselves have for addressing voter documentation requirements. An office administrator for a voting organization in Kansas told us that there are "limitations on what, how much can we actually do, given that we're all volunteers . . . [and] a lot of historic organizations, we're having . . . challenges getting younger members to join." One implication is that if nonprofits rely solely on volunteers, engaging in voter assistance may become too much of an ad hoc operation to adequately address community members' numerous needs.

On top of that, as much as local governments help connect nonprofits and other community organizations with critical resources and assistance, they are often strapped in terms of their available capacity to act given time, personnel, and other nonmonetary constraints. We heard from a nonprofit staff member in Arizona that the lack of information potential voters receive often has to do with elections officials' dearth of resources too, highlighted by how nonprofit groups largely run the biggest registration drives in the state. So,

> if registration is a government-imposed process, then it stands to reason to me that there should be some significant government resources put into helping people get through the process. . . . and a lot of our counties are really understaffed, just in, I mean, especially this time of year, they are just swamped with processing registration forms and they're also reviewing petition signatures for candidates or ballot measures, and they don't have the time to be going out into the community, to register people or to tell people about when and where to register and when and where to vote. So lack of information really is a big issue and that's, that's related in part to [a] lack of resources and lack of seed investment in our election infrastructure.

Citizens need a concerted, systematic effort to fill in the knowledge gaps that government institutions leave in their communication. As aptly pointed out by the staff member quoted earlier in this book, it's unreasonable that the system demands that people know about voting processes and obtaining an ID without providing what's needed to carry through on these expectations.

We heard similar sentiments from county offices. One staff member at a county recorder's office in Arizona told us about how disjointed the two-tier federal and state systems regarding requirements for proof of citizenship have become. If a completed state form arrived at the county office and did not have proof of citizenship anywhere on it (or attached to it), they would often send out a letter to the person who sent it; however, the forms were put in boxes, and "we had no proof that the letters were sent [back to the filer] because the staff was not keeping track of that." In one respect, this is partly the fault of the county and not of a two-tier system. What was described by the staff member was a result of limited resources at the county office to follow routine office procedure. Some of the problems of tracking outreach (or, to go even further, evaluation) show that, despite many individuals' best efforts, some potential voters fall through the cracks simply because of government offices' available resources and bandwidth.

The limitations on what state and local governments can manage create a gap that other organizations must fill, particularly nonprofits that already lack sustained funding and are primarily engaged in other forms of service delivery. We heard about the resource problems that one county elections office faced in this regard: "We don't actively go and seek that voter documentation. We do it by promoting what they need to do in order to provide that documentation. We will proactively go and remind those voters that they need to show that documentation if we were the ones to register them to vote. But that is about all we can do in our capacity, we are a few people for a county of 2.5 million, so there is only so much we can do." Whether strapped for cash or other resources, ironically, governments themselves are often ill-equipped to tackle the documentation challenges that their own policymakers have put into law. When the rhetoric of politicians fails to meet the realities of implementation, voter ID unintentionally or intentionally functions to exclude citizens from access to the ballot box.[11] At the same time, a failure to fund state and local elections offices reflects at best a woeful failure of government to take voters' rights seriously.

A running theme throughout our research was that the vagaries of human judgment, error, and other limitations (e.g., government workers just giving up) play a prominent a role in administering the confusing array of policies around voter documentation. We found out that elections offices sometimes throw in the towel on policies and procedures because of the hassle they cause. One participant told us that she was speaking to someone at a voting convention in Wisconsin about the problems in their district, and this person complained that "their polling place just won't give out provisional ballots [be]cause it's such a nuisance. They don't tell people that it's available. So that's another barrier." Understandably, the additional steps such processes require are a hurdle not only for citizens but also for those who must administer a function that carries with it so many layers of complexity. And who would know to ask for a provisional ballot under such circumstances, or that they had the right to do so? The potential for misinformation or burnout that might lead staff to deal only with the voting problems that seem more urgent can leave voters confused, enervated, and, ultimately in too many cases, deprived of their votes.

Our participants even critiqued the lack of effort they observed their local and state governments making from state to state. A program director in Wisconsin remarked: "Our ID laws are very restricted. What we have found was that the state did not dedicate enough resources or enough training to basically adequately ensure that folks were able to get IDs without cost if they needed them, and were able to get them in a way that allowed them to vote." In the face of these obstacles, the organization "supported a number of groups that are working to get people IDs. Yet there are also a number of pretty significant barriers," making "voting very difficult for certain populations in the state of Wisconsin." When systemic difficulties are added to this mix (as we heard from, among others, a participant in Indiana)—such as closed primaries that require people to name their political party to have a vote in election primaries and that exclude independent voters, for instance, the discouraging roadblocks escalate.

Multiplying Obstacles

Expanding on a detail we heard about earlier, people face multiple rounds of obstacles, often unique to each state, when trying to vote. The executive director of an advocacy network conducting voter education, policy work, and lobbying in Arizona told us: "What's often overlooked about Arizona or little understood about our, our voter ID law is it, it really has two components of both ID at the polls and proof of citizenship to register to vote," which is a significant challenge for people on Election Day.

He continued to explain that for many people who are trying to register to vote (and especially young people, university students, and people of color who are more likely to have voter ID problems), the goal must be to get them onto a permanent early voter list so that having a material ID at the polls can be avoided. Overall, "The more the system gets complicated, people are just confused about how and when they can actually participate as well." Confusion begets more confusion.

Elderly people are considerably impacted by the multiplying obstacles ID laws present. The executive director told us about one elderly woman:

> She's 104, from Brooklyn, who I know because a friend of mine is representing her sort of pro bono, trying to help her get registered to vote here. And, you know, she has never had an Arizona driver's license. I'm not sure when she came out here, but my assumption is like many people, she retired to Arizona and so has just never had an Arizona driver's license and is having a really hard time tracking down a copy, an original copy of her birth certificate. I'm from New York state and it's, you know, it's just taking a while to get that and she was really hoping to have it in time to register for our primary election and the deadline is July 30, so coming up. And basically because of the purpose of the proof of citizenship law, she's just stuck waiting for New York to get back to her. . . . in many ways, proof of citizenship actually poses a bigger burden here than even voter ID does.

The director in Arizona summed up the disorienting, confusing experience that takes place for many citizens both in considering candidates and initiatives on the ballot and attempting to fill out ballots. Voters recurrently feel that they don't have the requisite information to vote. Even when Arizonans get past the obstacles to vote and are facing the ballot, they are confronted with long ballots where "we vote for things like your constable and a whole bunch of county offices, but nobody can tell you what they do." There's also what's called a Missouri plan for judges, who are up for retention elections, "So the back of your ballot can be the names of sixty judges and a yes or no. And that's on top of all these ballot measures and . . . so that's just one area in which people often feel, just feel, ill-equipped to vote." The experience of having more than sixty people on a ballot is not a consistent standard across jurisdictions. In many states and counties there will be far fewer, and in many, we would speculate, perhaps more.[12]

Once again, no two people from different areas of the United States will have the same standards or experience en route to voting, and no two will have the same standards for what is on the ballot and how they will find out about who and what they are voting for. We don't want to understate how many people are genuinely helped by the system and get what they need to vote, despite these kinds of requirements (consistent with research showing that approximately 11 percent of people in the United States, more then twenty-five million in total, are negatively affected by voter documentation requirements). But the on-the-ground experiences of many of our interviewees highlighted how there are many more layers to what will seem like the "job" or value of voting to some. Those factors compound beyond the already cumbersome experiences of getting qualified to vote, getting the documentation to vote, and having the opportunity to cast a vote.

In Arizona a staff member at a county recorder's office mentioned the following:

> For the homeless people to vote, that's a big barrier. In fact, I was just dealing with a gentleman who's homeless. He was Japanese, so it was hard to understand him, but it was just today and I was trying to help him, but he, he did get registered to vote. He has registered using a homeless shelter address. Fortunately for him, he gets his mail there. But some individuals still register using, most of them use that same address that he used, and they're so transient that you can't, it's hard for them to get any type of mail or any type of election materials because they don't have the resources to do that. They don't have computers, they don't have smartphones, they don't have televisions in the shelters, they don't have this, they don't have that. So it's hard for them to get educated on how to, how to register, how to vote.

At each step, what's seemingly simple for one citizen becomes a labyrinth to overcome for others. More concerning is the way that, over time, laws and regulations that were once more inclusive have begun to resemble, de facto, discriminatory standards that it took years to abolish from the

US Constitution's original framing. At that time only property-owning (and, in the original vision, White male) citizens could vote, and these individuals made up only 6 percent of the population.[13] Yet the more documentation to register to vote is tied to having an address in the present, the greater the return to this exclusionary standard for voting.

For many people, both knowledge of what's happening in their political context and the timing of certain voting events become difficult to ascertain. An executive director of a nonprofit foundation in Ohio offered, "What we do have in the state of Ohio is that laws are often changed and the community isn't always aware of [how] those laws changing . . . can affect them. . . . I know the impact on voter documentation is important." Between this problem and needing to get student populations the correct state IDs in time for voting, this nonprofit usually starts its process to help people get IDs, register to vote, and ultimately vote in August (three months before Election Day!), showcasing how much planning and foresight are necessary to jump through all the hoops.

An additional barrier, in the opinion of one county clerk, is that eighteen-to-twenty-four-year-olds do not turn out to vote because they often think the system is "rigged," especially since the 2000 US general election. And many people who are lower on the socioeconomic ladder feel too busy. Overall, people may be making perfectly rational decisions that they have neither a big enough stake (e.g., because they've never seen what their vote gets them) nor the free time to deal with voting when they are more concerned with getting the next paycheck to pay the rent, feeding and taking care of children, and more.

The clerk observed one bright spot: an uptick in citizens using provisional ballots when they were encouraged to get out and vote, even if they did not have an ID. Senior citizens face additional obstacles, however. One participant said, "We deal with a lot of seniors. They don't keep their IDs and things up to date. They are not able to just run out and get to the DMV. There isn't one that is relatively close to the area that we serve. They would literally have to leave the city and probably go through two cities to get to an ID facility." Adaptation to the unique needs of certain groups and individuals thus remains paramount to adequately addressing requirements.

Identifying People Who Lack Voter ID

People who lack voter ID can be hard to identify. We heard a lot about how 11 percent or so of people in the United States fall within this category; one nonprofit director told us that there are "markers of the people who are affected by voter ID laws," including elderly people of color, the homeless, returning citizens (people returning from out of state and people who have served sentences), and students who are about to graduate from high school (who are already eighteen). But there are also a lot of demographic and other indicators that apply within those categories, such as people who have a history of substance abuse, women fleeing abusive domestic situations, and the largest percentage of people their organization works with: people who desperately need an ID for a job or home or medical care. These are typically disadvantaged populations who have not thought about voting, "because you can't think about voting when you're not a full person."

Working with networks or organizations that help specific groups offers some help. One participant told us that their organization's strategy is to work with, for instance, groups dealing with accessibility issues, "like the National Federation of the Blind" and others that are usually happy to assist and provide feedback on voter engagement efforts. Nonprofits and other community organizations are doing their best to identify individuals who fit into specific groups, but it is a heavy lift for the institutions and volunteers involved. In a webinar, David Griggs, the executive director of VoteRiders, described how his organization is working on identifying people who lack documentation. Griggs and his team are developing software to identify the broader universe of those challenged by voter ID requirements. They're also developing parallel "chatbot" programs that use mobile phones to lead people through the steps needed to get what they need to vote in certain areas.[14]

A final distinction must be made about finding those who lack ID: the difference between needing a non–photo ID and a photo ID can be substantial, since many states now require the latter. A staff member from a nonprofit in Virginia told us: "The picture ID is one of the barriers. I personally work at the polls and that is the one issue that happens to come up more than anything else. I have sent people down to the registrar's office, if they had come in early enough to get a picture made."

To identify people who will need an ID, this distinction must be made in states with strict photo ID requirements compared with those with less onerous standards.

Improvements with a Price

Anytime we thought about a one-size-fits-all strategy to address voter documentation and registration challenges, our respondents provided exceptions that demonstrated a need for personalized and culturally sensitive approaches. The executive director of an advocacy network told us that in many urban and rural tribal communities in Arizona, people have issues with the mail ballots that now increasingly make up a large percentage of the voting system. We heard that about 75 to 80 percent of ballots in the state are now cast by mail, so that people on the Navajo reservation, for example, who don't have reliable, accessible addresses, or who don't live close to cities or towns, fall victim to these trends' consequences.

Like the often-stated intentions behind voter documentation requirements (e.g., preservation of election integrity), sometimes the advances in one aspect of voting create negative trade-offs for particular communities, in this case between the ease and access of voting by mail, and the problems that mail-in ballots create for communities where not having a physical address becomes a barrier to voting. In general, policymakers and voting rights advocates in the United States would do well to think through how each voting advance may create harmful obstacles.

Even states with less strict documentation requirements continue to confront haphazard trade-offs. The leader of a coalition of progressive nonprofit organizations dedicated to issues of civic engagement and voting in Virginia (whose "partner organizations focus on the New American Majority, so those voters that show up in presidential years and don't typically vote in off years and those are primarily made up of people of color, low-income folks, and young people") mentioned, "We have one of the least restrictive photo ID laws in the country, so from that perspective we're better off than a lot of states, but it has still been a struggle for some folks, yes." In Virginia, there's no-excuse absentee voting and no automatic voter registration,[15] which the leader saw as barriers to participation (i.e., although states such as Virginia don't require a formal excuse to receive a ballot, improving participation, the price is that citizens still need to make a request for a ballot and, like almost everyone else in the United States, they aren't automatically registered to vote). On top of this, limited hours for polling places and a curtailed number of polling places can exact costs for people who have travel burdens and often end up—and expect to end up—waiting in long lines to vote.

Knowledge Deficits, Misconceptions, and Misinformation

Getting citizens to act is its own hill to climb. Attacking knowledge deficits is another, and responding to misinformation yet another. A lack of information creates confusion about voter documentation requirements and voting, feeding into attempts at voter suppression. A programs and outreach director for a national voting organization said that the basic issue that comes up most often for them is voters' lack of information about polling place locations.[16]

On top of this, dealing with both the amount of information available about voting, which can be overwhelming, and the need for help in sifting through all that information to make realistic and actionable decisions creates a paradox for eligible voters. The director told us, "We still see such a role for groups like us, even in this day and age of there being tons of information online and at your fingers," meaning "there's still just a . . . large lack of information, especially in . . . the most underrepresented communities," so the necessity for the organization's work "has just gotten bigger, not smaller, in recent years." The paradox of having too much information and too many sources to wade through, combined with information gaps, underscores the need for intermediaries to act as helpers both in selecting the information relevant to communities concerning voter identification and in providing a base level of knowledge for carrying out those tasks.

Lack of knowledge is bad enough, but even worse are the misconceptions and misinformation many people receive or surmise. One participant in Ohio elaborated: "The turnout among Cleveland's and East Cleveland's population is low compared to the rest of our county. Some of them are concerned that if they register, they are going to be called for jury duty."[17] A participant in Indiana also told us that their organization was trying to clear up a common misconception among community members that juries are selected from voting polls (they are actually selected from driver's licenses in Indiana). Similarly, "People think that given the districts and situations in Indiana, that it's not going to make any difference and that the outcome is going to be clear from the start. Some areas don't even have two candidates running." If someone starts from a position of thinking that what they do won't make a difference, the additional hassles of getting documentation, getting to the polls, and voting will seem pointless.

The deliberate misleading of voters for partisan purposes exacerbates this mix. For example, at times false information has been disseminated through social media and other sources giving the wrong dates for the election or providing bogus threats about the legal consequences of voting. A woman in Texas who was unaware that she was ineligible to vote ended up being given a cruel jail sentence.[18] Partisan responses from the right claiming voter fraud were eventually tempered by the case's details, where it became clear that she didn't know or understand how changes in voting had affected her, in a time when circulating misconceptions and misinformation are all too common.

Misinformation about documentation requirements even happens in states without strict voter ID. From a national perspective, the rhetoric of voter ID doesn't remain static. It has seeped into the consciousness of people in times and places where it doesn't even belong. One staff attorney and program manager for a nonprofit in California explained, "Some people who are eligible to vote and give their name and address have non-Anglo last names and are often asked for an ID because the poll worker does not understand the last name. This has been experienced by voters as a form of asking for ID when it is not required." Subsequently, the network of nonprofits that his organization is affiliated with has "urged that poll workers ask people whose last names are non-Anglo and therefore not always understandable to the poll worker to ask these voters to write their names down so that the spelling is clear (rather than ask them for an ID)." Misconceptions abound about what is appropriate within and across these different voting situations.

We heard about similar issues in voter ID states such as Pennsylvania. One person spoke about how, when the strict voter ID law there was in effect—especially for those on the fence about voting, and in the face of other hurdles in the state such as voting being restricted to one Tuesday with no same-day registration—one problem was that "the state put out materials that were misleading." Volunteers occasionally observed in field reports that people were told at individual polling places that individuals' voter IDs were inadequate, when that was not the case. This participant's organization would call the secretary of state to complain on these occasions.

Voter documentation requirements aren't confusing only for voting-eligible citizens. We found that sometimes many different stakeholders had to be educated about the problem. One policy director for a nonpartisan organization in Pennsylvania told us that, before the voter ID law was struck down in that state, "Board members of the organization were not aware of the impediments presented by voter ID laws, and in fact questioned what was wrong with having a requirement." Nonprofit staff had to educate the board about the disproportionate effect on lower-income voters and older citizens who didn't drive or whose licenses had lapsed. Many of these lessons centered on how "people were unaware of the requirements, did not have the necessary documentation, did not know where to get voter IDs, and could not always necessarily obtain the necessary documentation." Making matters worse, the Pennsylvania Transportation Commission remained responsible for providing voter IDs, but only some of its offices could provide them to those who had the required documentation.

Whether generated by misleading sources or assuming inaccurate beliefs, misinformation and misconceptions pose one of the largest challenges to voter registration. One nonprofit staff member underscored how "here in Ohio, . . . those who have had a felony, [and] have served their time have been dropped and have to reregister to vote. Even though that is their legal right, there is an overwhelming general belief that if you [have ever] been in jail you could never vote again. That is a hard misconception to overcome."

One participant also told us, "I run into apathy, far more often than I run into an actual barrier. . . . a common one is that I can't vote because they don't want to register to a political party. I hear that one a lot. Where they think that there is a barrier in front of them but there isn't." Some states require citizens to affiliate with one party over another to vote in primary elections, but the rules around this issue vary from state to state.

Racism at the Ballot Box and Immigrant Challenges

The thoroughly racialized and politicized nature of voter ID was at the core of experiences described by many of our interviewees. One immigrant participant was a new US citizen in Ohio and a staff member of a nonprofit that helped us organize the focus groups. She was not a participant in the focus groups, but as a community member she wanted to share her experiences with identification and voting with us, especially since she knew the law and had such deep experience navigating her state's ID requirements as an immigrant. She recounted a story of her hopes for voting that were subsequently dashed by a racially charged encounter with some poll workers:

> For Ohio we had a two ballot issues, issue one, issue two, and then we had candidates. So I was all excited to go to vote and I just, unfortunately we realized that when I got to the polling place that my ID was missing, I somehow misplaced [between] the office to the voting place, my driver's license. So I went there and I told them that . . . I just realized that I don't have my ID. Is there any way I can vote? And all of the poll workers there told me that I couldn't vote. . . . They said, do you have . . . a statement, like a utility bill or registration or something that has your name or your address on it? I said, I just realized that I don't have it on me . . . until a lady from the corner said, "Oh, you can do provisional." . . . And then she started explaining to me the procedure, and this was the most interesting part. She started explaining the procedure: "So I don't know how it works where you come from. But, and I actually don't know how it works there so, but it works differently from where you come from." That's how the explanation started. So, that was not good. . . . I just voted for the issues. I was so upset. I did not vote for the candidates. I was like, they don't want me here. I took the provisional ballot, I voted and I told her, I know about provisional, how it, how it works. I know the procedure.

For our interviewee, this experience exemplified a feeling that many newcomers to the United States can have under such circumstances: that they must get everything right to become or be regarded as a citizen during voting time. It also shows how easy it is for comments, however intended, to discourage people from voting. As the participant explained, "You're all excited and you get that 'where you come from' kind of comment, those little things, it, it matters for [a] new voter."[19] The experience made her think about how much more difficult it may be for others too, such as those with disabilities.

The same interviewee told us that even getting a driver's license may seem like a simple activity, but that for first-time citizens passing both the written test and the road test alone can prevent many people from getting access to an ID. This raises the question of why a driver's license should ever be a top requirement for voting, as the most valued form of ID in many states. That's worth repeating: *Why should a written test and road test for driving have anything to do with determining one's eligibility to vote?* If driver's licenses are prioritized for voter ID, in effect, you have a form of voter suppression equivalent to the literacy tests that intentionally served to exclude minorities and other targeted populations from voting. One can imagine hypothetically how arriving in this country from abroad, perhaps while trying to learn a new language, and perhaps on top of taking tests, makes these matters more challenging than for domestic citizens. And if you come from a city in another country with an efficient public transportation system and never had a need to drive previously, even more so.

To get a state ID some years ago, the immigrant had to collect her bank statements and a proof of address and then wait in long lines. And, as was noted, if you don't make it to certain places in time, such as a Department of Motor Vehicles office, you must come back another day. For those new to the United States, home addresses will also likely change within brief time spans, as their current addresses may not be permanent addresses. In short, even for immigrants who have already become citizens and gone through the process to do so, getting a state ID can take time and exact high costs. Even utility bills must be from within the last twelve months in some jurisdictions. This may not be unreasonable, but for people moving between apartments or going to new homes, these changes can directly conflict with such requirements.

Our interviewee shared that she also found confusing the conflicting information on the secretary of state's website in Ohio and the DMV's website information about temporary IDs. She found the DMV site said temporary IDs wouldn't work for voting, but the secretary of state's site said they would: "So there's this disconnect of information [that] I think is going to cause a lot of problems for voters and poll workers." Not all parties come to the stage with the correct information, sometimes through no fault of their own. From the perspective of an immigrant, the information gap is, in sum, a more extreme burden.

Ultimately, she urged us to consider that there aren't "enough cooks in the kitchen in this case [to help people with voter documentation] because . . . the scope is so huge and you need everyone to come together and help out. So, it's just making sure that we are all giving out . . . consistent information." In a comment we heard many times from others, she also emphasized, "I think we should get automatic voter registration on board. We should bring that in Ohio. And I think that will really eliminate a lot of those confusion problems about IDs and . . . the day [the] registration deadline is coming up, those kinds of things." Furthermore, automatic registration would save money by reducing paper registrations and processing, making opt-out rather than opt-in the defining feature of all voter registration systems.

With all these issues at play, it is easy to see why "there are so many unregistered voters in the United States that they exceed the total combined populations of the largest one hundred cities in America—from New York City to Birmingham—by nearly sixteen million people."[20] As a form of suppression, voter documentation requirements are designed to exclude, and anyone concerned with every citizen's right to vote should reject them in their current form.

The Opportunities

As much as we learned about the problems between citizens and systems in US elections, we also gained knowledge about many notable opportunities for addressing these challenges. In the second half of this chapter, we turn to potential solutions for the frustrations voter documentation requirements continue to cause locally and beyond.

Link Public Services to Elections to Motivate Citizens

Many of the experts we spoke with offered important perspectives on what it would take to solve voter documentation challenges. Linking existing public services to elections was chief among them. An elections director in Arizona described how "our constituents may not have current or any form of state-issued ID. This hinders their ability to vote and be a part of the process." To address the issue, it would be critical "if they saw a connection between the type of service they are getting and the elected that lead." This is what candidates routinely offer when they run for office. But in the case of election procedures, the encouragement would be in the nonpartisan context of getting citizens to think about getting documentation—a much earlier part of the process than hearing candidates campaign—in time to influence elections regardless of ideology. For example, connecting election outcomes to educational opportunities would help inspire citizens to try to get what they need to vote, since "education continues to be the number one issue in Arizona. More people are aware that Arizona is near the bottom in nearly every education metric. They want better schools and they have the chance to change education policy in November." By implication, nonprofits, elections offices, and community organizations could motivate citizens to get the documentation they need to vote with messaging that's connected to the importance of valued public services or local issues.

This way of communicating with potential voters fit with what we heard about audience passivity regarding voting in general. Another interviewee from Wisconsin affirmed: "I think voter fatigue or issues fatigue, motivation is always one that we work on. Making sure that the issues connect with the people, so that they are prepared for when they go to vote." It's not enough to talk about getting voter ID as an imperative that should be self-evident. And none of this requires taking a partisan position or advocating for any cause beyond selecting a general issue of relevance to people particular to their locality.

Whether barriers are imagined or real, addressing voter documentation requirements can't be separated from the task of motivating audiences to want to register to vote in the first place. Some people may find that forms of documentation are more applicable to their interests than others. A lawyer pointed out that her office held a "free monthly birth certificate clinic to help people get the cornerstone of obtaining state-issued ID. We did this before the voter ID [law] and continued after the law was defeated." Offering help for ID that may not be directly related to voting can act as a stimulus, since those IDs are important to people for other, more pressing matters in their lives, such as receiving Medicaid, school enrollment, or even procuring a marriage license. As a nonprofit staff member in Indiana put it: "I think people generally will vote [and by implication get the ID they need] if they believe that the result will affect them personally, especially if the effect will be positive for them."

General messages about elections themselves can support a point to get voter ID indirectly. This communication is not necessarily about making voter documentation challenges personally relevant, but about the impact individuals' votes can have. One government representative told us that their "state tries to emphasize close votes in some elections to persuade people to vote." Furthermore, using media effectively must be given attention. To influence people, one elections director noted, "We are doing more digital outreach this cycle. Reaching people via social media or text is more effective for younger voters than mail, door knocks, or phone." With or without face-to-face efforts, online strategies can play a key role with such groups.

One way to strengthen these motivating connections between voter ID and receiving public services is to add social opportunities to the mix. One participant said her organization "informed/educated voters about the voter ID requirements wherever they were able to do it: community groups; churches; lots of libraries—wherever they could get a forum." And her strategies to get messages out were developed to be practical and cost-effective. Her organization also "trained others to train people on voter ID laws."

The influence of social norms must be absorbed into a messaging campaign. A big part of creating change involves "seeing momentum in the community that voting is considered important and that other people are voting." Social proof, or the belief that when other people are doing something it is worth doing ourselves,[21] has long been one of the top communication strategies for generating change. The first step here would be to connect voter documentation requirements to social associations and events important in people's lives, and then to do everything possible to build on that initial motivation.

Hyperlocal, Personalized Strategies

A nonprofit director provided one of the most remarkable examples of helping citizens get IDs that we came across. Because she found little being done to assist people with identification after the 2016 presidential election, she started an organization dedicated to helping people to get ID. In effect, she explained, "the way that we operate is we train hyperlocal community chapters" through the use of volunteers who work in a one-to-one capacity with people who need photo ID, "but also to get jobs, housing, medical care" and more. The organization pays all the fees required for getting IDs and partners with local organizations such as county jails, homeless shelters, food banks, high schools, and community colleges. Since about 11 percent of the population lacks IDs, the organization's volunteers walk each person served through the entire process, whether that means physically taking them to the DMV or making sure they get registered to vote online or off-line. The organization also does follow-up work to make sure each person is educated on the issues and can get to the polls on Election Day.

In addition to being a solid, developed strategy for helping people get what they need to vote, personalization provides more than a transactional encounter. It can encourage the civic bonding that so many theories of democracy promote. Amid all the complexities and challenges of voter documentation, we heard from a founder and executive director of a nonprofit foundation in Ohio that links with civic engagement outcomes should be made explicit in all efforts to assist people with voter ID. The director said: "It's not unlikely for you to walk into one of our community conversations or one of our civic education classes and have a seventeen-year-old . . . dialoguing and discussing with a seventy-five-year-old. . . . we're very multigenerational. We bring generations together to find common ground and to come up with acts and plans to move agendas forward." Pairing volunteers or others with those needing assistance can be carried out strategically, having diverse individuals come to know one another, and forging civic friendships and potentially longer-term relationships between people in communities.

These findings were quite unexpected. We started this project thinking about addressing voter ID and related challenges as the minimum that could be done to nudge people toward a most basic public act. But over time, we learned from others that voter ID could also stand at the crossroads for other forms of civic engagement.

Everyday Locations and Piggybacking

Reaching people in their everyday locations is more effective than inviting people to come to an institution or event. This strategy seems simple in principle but is often bypassed in practice. Our participants mentioned the theme consistently: go to where people are to help them out. In one state, we learned that some of the greatest barriers to voter registration occur with people in assisted care facilities who are eligible for state assistance but have no state ID because they no longer drive. In these circumstances, some "state employees went into these facilities to help give them IDs." As a variation on the last theme, more could be done to travel to places and spaces where people can be found who likely face voter ID challenges.

An associate dean at a law school told us that "the people who don't have the kind of ID you need for voting are often people who don't have the kind of ID that helps with all kinds of tasks most of us take for granted," including those who are poor and elderly in urban and rural areas. What matters is that "for the folks lower on the socioeconomic rung, there are a number of organizations and entities that help them with daily life, and also in that process help with ID: community economic organizations and legal aid and the like. They're not focused particularly on ID for voting as much as they are on ID for 101 other reasons." Previously, we discussed people's other needs for ID to support an interest in voter ID. Similarly, going to where potential voters are, in the places they inhabit socially and through links with service organizations, and attending to their interests in specific issues can be a powerful way to reach unengaged populations. Hence, a type of piggybacking strategy with organizations that work on related projects may prove useful, especially since nonprofits and other social service institutions are well suited to address common problems with IDs. Given the limited budgets and time available to so many nonprofits that work on community challenges, targeting the everyday locations and places where citizens probably lack ID is also more efficient.

We heard this strategy echoed by an executive director of an agency that primarily serves people with long-term substance abuse and mental disorders, and who are typically in poverty: "We have a vocational program, where we help people find jobs; and as a part of that, we inquire with all of them whether they are currently registered to vote, if they would like to. If they do, then we help them with that process." Sometimes these audiences do not have a picture ID because they don't drive, or simply don't know what the process of obtaining such an ID with a picture on it might entail.

Many nonprofits can become a "one-stop shop" in their local communities. One nonprofit employee in North Carolina mentioned how their staff mainly serve middle-income immigrants and refugees with immigration-related legal services but also provide social services in the community, such as assistance with employment, literacy, and housing. As a legal organization, "we are able to look at the right documents and ask the right questions and are culturally sensitive enough. . . . that's one thing we pride ourselves in doing." Knowledge of the local community and its demands is integral to adapting strategies and logrolling across the various issues manifest in a client's visit.

Working with federal rather than state documents helps in reaching out to citizens in particular places and spaces. An outreach coordinator from a nonprofit group in Kansas shared, "We do not use the state's voter registration form, we use the federal form which doesn't have the citizenship requirement. It's illegal to have a two-seated system [i.e., with a requirement to fill out two separate forms], so they [at elections offices] have to accept those forms; so, we have been using those instead to get people to register to vote." The coordinator also shared an example of how this method more successfully addressed voter documentation requirements: "When we were using the state form, we used to do voter registration at farmer[s] markets, and we used to get twenty to thirty a day. Or the library"—and "Community centers and fitness centers were also a great place." But the use of overriding federal forms in these local locations to meet the demands of new voter ID laws can be especially important due to a challenge we heard about earlier, that "people don't carry their passport or birth certificate" as they encounter voter registration drives. Ultimately, in doing outreach that piggybacks off places where people go, and by avoiding the vagaries of local or state forms, "Since we switched to the federal form, our numbers have gone back up."

Tailoring strategies to different populations remains essential to help-ing people with documentation problems. One of the more challenging populations to work with on this issue is the homeless. Sometimes act-ing as a simple intermediary between eligible citizens and some part of the system that can better serve them on voter ID is all that's needed. One nonprofit staff member who works with the homeless said:

> We do outreach in a soup kitchen that is a couple of miles down the road. We will do outreach there once a week and try to get clients there to get [the] benefits they need. . . . they either lose their documents or their documents get stolen. One of the places we do the outreach at, they have a specific program where they can help, it's a group of resources. One day a week there are different people who are there for different things . . . That is what one of the agencies does. Their sole mission is to provide those documents, so we partner with them. . . . We tell them to talk to this person, so it's a direct contact.

Populations such as the homeless often don't have access to resources that others take for granted, such as using the internet to set the process for documentation in motion. As the same nonprofit staff member told us, however, that's also a key part of the organization's strategies: "We provide them a computer center where they can go online and use those resources. I think it is mostly education; [we tell them] look, it is this easy to do it and this is why it is important." Having key personnel or volunteers available to do this work, and the equipment in place to do so, requires a conscious and dedicated effort.

Helping Immigrants with Documentation Issues

Working with and anticipating eligible-to-vote immigrants' challenges to voting goes hand in hand with identification requirements. A non-profit leader in Georgia said that their organization provides reminders to clients at every event about how the process of voting works and what types of documentation need to be brought to the polls. Partnerships with neighborhood associations and organizations working with diverse populations of immigrants (many of whom are undocumented and have children about to turn eighteen) can help fund these efforts; "when you think about the progression of the Latino community in Georgia, many of them actually are green card holders and could qualify to naturalize, become voters, [but] they just don't have the funding." Yet the organization had been successful in matching "50 percent of naturalization fees people face when it comes to the application."

Immigrants who are US citizens face many nuances around voter ID that others do not. The Mexican consulate helps immigrants in Georgia get certain IDs, although a law passed in 2011 banned many undocumented workers from receiving a driver's license and restricted the types of IDs they could receive, affecting how those eligible to vote feel about the nature and process of voting. Additionally, "Around 87 percent of all immigrants in Georgia speak a language other than English in their homes. If they misplace a document, often times they don't have time [to get a new one], they don't understand how to renew it, or quite frankly we have a lot of issues with transportation." They may have some documents, but not all that are needed, and "people are aware they have to bring documentation but sometimes they don't have clarity on what a voter ID means." Since many immigrant families are low-income, if a document is misplaced and a person can't drive, they face a situation in which no public transportation is available in most of the state. In fact, many immigrants rely on their children to drive them around. Immigrants who are eligible to vote often live or work with others who are not eligible, and parsing the differences between what one can and cannot do can be difficult when combined with the information, misinformation, and misconceptions available in one's family or community.

This is where local organizations can assist people by speaking to their fears about voting and overcoming other challenges such as not knowing what to do at a voting booth or dealing with translation or literacy issues. One of our interviewees shared: "A lot of our families don't have computers at home. They rely on smartphones to access the web, but then a smartphone is very different than a polling machine and you have hundreds of people looking at you and waiting for you." The more community-led these interventions, the better. Once again, we learned that addressing voter documentation requirements must be positioned within the web of barriers that people have with voting in general. Tugging on the voter ID string necessarily pulls so many other distinct challenges into this orbit.

Similar to the unique challenges immigrants face in Georgia, we also heard in North Carolina how transportation is a barrier for many immigrant populations:

> A lot of clients don't drive, and in states like North Carolina, having a car and driving is essential. So there are bus routes, but the times and so on, it's difficult for people to get where they need to be. So we, that's why we went to the church last Sunday, and we are going to communities themselves that predominantly host immigrants and refugees and other community members there, we plan on going out to them to get their registration done, because transportation is an issue, especially for the elderly. There's a lot of elderly . . . that are not mobile. Whenever they need to go out to register to vote, they will need a car, wheelchair-accessible, with ramps and all of that. So going out to their homes and knocking on their doors and speaking to them is also essential because they don't have the transportation to go out.

The sheer number of moving parts (visiting places of worship, having a car or van equipped with mechanisms for serving those with disabilities, etc.) necessary to pulling off such tasks goes well beyond a guiding assumption of so much public and governmental discourse about getting an ID.[22] It's not only the case that people need to quickly hop online to register to vote, or spend a few dollars on a quick journey to a local elections office; for many eligible-to-vote immigrants the costs, time, and labor involved with getting documentation together are only amplified by the costs, time, and labor that other people will also need to commit to helping with these acts. So, where hyperlocal, personalized strategies can help citizens get what they need to vote, this need can be drastically heightened for immigrant populations.

Similar sentiments were echoed in Wisconsin, where a nonprofit staff member related that some Latino and Hmong communities "need to be working with people that they trust a great deal. . . . what our strategy has been there is just trying to train people who work within that community to do the work that we do." Without cultural sensitivity and attunement to the unique needs of these populations, voter ID strategies could backfire or come across as tone-deaf. Yet, despite these hardships, that so many community organizations have found different ways to assist immigrants should give everyone hope.

Connecting with Government

Although this book has focused on the work of community organizations, it's clear that such organizations need to engage with the government in some capacity to do this work well. It's our belief that government organizations, in an ideal world, should be *solely* responsible for doing everything possible to help citizens to get what they need to vote. But until that ideal is realized, and while there is far too much variation and many people are not being served well by our voting system, organizations on the front lines of community service can still nudge and use the resources of government entities to advance voter registration and voting.

Nonprofits and other community organizations shouldn't feel as though they need to go it alone when helping citizens. Many participants in our research raised this need, with one founder of a nonpartisan research and election think tank stating the following:

> Our second primary audience is election officials. Election officials have an enormous amount of, of capability to make the process easier and also more inclusive. And probably surprisingly to many, almost all of them of both parties want to do exactly that, but they're looking for tools and they're working on limited budgets and they're working in partisan political environments that make that difficult at times. And so we work very closely with them to give them tools, with . . . proper evidence and support to document that these are tools that are not designed to create a political outcome. They're designed to serve . . . the voters where they live now.

The founder was in tune with helping both citizens and elected officials see that new technologies can facilitate easier communication than the traditional paper-and-pen formats that are still the staple of so many government offices. How nonprofits and community organizations frame their efforts can make all the difference when reaching out to government entities that want to help in these areas. It's not a hard case to make to elections offices that they should be willing to work with any organization that wants to facilitate easy access to voting for those it serves. Elections offices should welcome these organizations, especially now, when it is so difficult to follow through on the government's promise to implement voting easily and effectively.

One of the best ways to connect with government is to use a practice that many elections offices are already relying on around the nation. Although the laws around voter documentation changed in Kansas during our research (i.e., the state's proof-of-citizenship requirement was invalidated by the courts),[23] we learned from an expert that IDs were available at the county clerk's office, and on request the clerk's office would send a mobile unit to people's homes to prepare an ID for them. Because counties had different strategies for helping citizens, it's worth recognizing what the government already does and can do in these efforts in certain areas. In this county they had sustained "education efforts—mailers, postcards, social media, community events; [and] made info[rmation] available for candidates to forward," but were also ready to go directly to where people live or do business to close the gap between information and action.

A community relations director at a county record office and elections department mentioned that their efforts were all directed at an estimated "under one million eligible but unregistered voters in our county out here that we are attempting to go out and register." Giving people a ride is another strategy, as one of our participants told us: "We can pick them up and send them to the county office. The same thing with seniors in high schools. We do voter registration drives once a year in the local community. We usually do it at the fall festivals." One organizer in Wisconsin told us that, in connection with their voter ID coalition work, the city of Madison offered to give citizens free cab rides to a local DMV that had recently moved to an inaccessible location off the path of the city's bus lines. They saw an uptick in the use of these rides, demonstrating that building connections with local policymakers can make a difference when a nonprofit's resources are also spread thin. When giving people a ride and sending mobile units out become known strategies for multiple voting-related procedures within counties, an expectation that commonly denigrated government institutions (e.g., the

DMV) are now going the extra mile to make a difference in the lives of those they serve can be built.

Following the idea of helping immigrants with documentation, those assisting immigrants would do well to connect with the government, although trust remains a key factor. The director of a nonprofit with a focus on civic engagement and increasing voter participation among the Latino community in Wisconsin told us that many people they serve are well documented but not registered to vote. Many in the Milwaukee community, however, are reluctant to interface in any way with the government for fear that friends and family members will be deported. As a result, their organization dedicates time to work with Latino state legislators and alderpersons who do outreach in these districts to encourage people to get what they need and get registered to vote. Remarkably, in 2016 "the Latino district was the only district in Milwaukee that had a voter participation increase." These examples further show that nonprofits and other community organizations can use the government to help people get connected in their journey to the ballot box.

Part of the work that nonprofits and other community organizations can do is to make sure local officials know what's relevant to motivating these audiences. In general, the nonprofit director in Wisconsin told us, "there's just such a lack of outreach and education around the elections in general," so "why would you go and vote and why would you think to vote down ballot at all when there's no information being provided by the candidates, the organization, or whatever, to engage you and, and to make it relevant to the issues. It's really great that you want to talk about rural low-income health care when that has nothing to do with Latino issues in the south side of Milwaukee." Rather than focusing exclusively on the technical help needed to get an ID, local organizations can take a leadership stance by making links and filling the gaps between those at the periphery and those at the center of political processes.

Reaching People Online and via Mobile

We are in an age when most people live in two worlds: online and offline. In trends that show no signs of abating, these two worlds will only become further integrated.[24] Many groups hence use online tactics to address voter documentation requirements. The vice president of an advocacy group in Ohio, despite personally believing that documentation requirements are not a huge issue, told us that one key barrier is "that many of our voters move a lot. We believe that as many as 40,000 voters in Cuyahoga County are registered voters at the wrong address. So that becomes a challenge." Essentially, "If they go to the poll that matches their address, it's going to show that they are not registered at that location and they are either going to be told go to the one that you are registered in, which is technically not correct, or they are going to be given a provisional ballot." As such, the group is trying to use a program in which its volunteers can search online to see if people are at the correct location. Similarly, our interviewees often provided us with preferred sites for voter education and commitments, such as Vote411.org.[25]

Telling citizens to just go online for what they need is not enough in many situations. The internet may have put the world at our fingertips, yet the problem is no longer one of information, of which there's too much, but rather what exactly people should attend to in their everyday lives.[26] The use of an intermediary who understands what to look for via sites is a critical means of documentation assistance for many people. As online sites around voting burgeon, it can be hard to figure out which sites are the most useful and relevant to a person's needs. Those working in nonprofits and community organizations can, at a minimum, act as filters for sifting what's needed from what's not.

Social media plays a role in building trust with communities. A nonprofit staff member in Georgia told us, "Social media is huge here because the challenges in transportation and language access are real. So, a lot of people turn to Facebook and to WhatsApp to be able to connect. We are part of a support group for these communities along the corridors and highways." In essence, their nonprofit has hundreds of families that ask questions and need help in understanding various problems they face; thus, "It is a great way to communicate especially because eventually they learn to trust you. They see that you are constantly putting [out] information that is valuable for them." It's not just the use of these tools that matters, but a commitment to serving these communities repeatedly with useful information through trusted messengers.

Making the technology accessible and user-friendly can serve as a response to the inadequate and cumbersome processes of government websites. This matched our unexpected finding from the audits about the stark differences in websites across jurisdictions. A program director in Wisconsin emphasized, "You have to be able to prove your residence. The number of ways that you can prove your residence on types of documents are fairly restricted. The online voter registration system that they implemented is not an easy system to navigate if you do not have a Wisconsin driver's license or ID card." Even more frustrating is that these websites frequently require further resources, which "is particularly hard on college students and folks who might be moving often in terms of having to prove their residence."

Moreover, the annoying two-step process of filling out a document online and then having to print and mail it or drop it by a clerk's office can come into play. The program director summarized how for people who do so much business on their phones or online, it's strange to have to print out documents, creating a disconnect between "how the state is running the online voting registration system and how people actually engage with technology in real time and real life." Finding moments when eligible voters are in the process of using online software to sign up for or receive services of one type or another can be an initial step of commitment toward addressing voter documentation challenges head-on. These findings only underscore a need to connect with government and to do so in detailed and thoughtful ways with immigrant populations.

We learned that one organization uses software for Medicaid enrollment in Arizona, and "One of the last questions that is asked upon completion of enrollment, people are asked if they are registered to vote and they are also asked to register there in our office if they would like to." This tactic begs the question: Could something similar be used for harder cases where pre–voter registration issues arise? Helping people at the right place and time can likely extend to online tactics, even if the internet is only used as a transitional step to receive assistance.

In some cases, relying on the ad hoc nature of volunteering is not well suited to citizens' online and off-line experiences. The vice president of a voter advocacy nonprofit in Ohio told us that, in states such as Wisconsin, "We do have the legacy problem where people are still registered at the wrong address. That's why we are trying to train our volunteers on looking [them] up; all you need is a last name and a birth date of someone. We have been moderately successful in getting our volunteers to do it. I am sure that this is a nationwide issue." Yet thinking through volunteers' ability and resources to do this work is critical, since, at least in this case, the organization's volunteers are typically over seventy and not adept with technology, so they are "thinking about maybe getting a hotline where we can call a person who can check for them. We are working on that challenge. We don't have the answer yet. But we are trying." Perhaps more advanced trainings for volunteers would help, or working with high school students who could fulfill community service requirements through assistance with the technical aspects of voter ID and requisite community outreach.

Earned and paid media can contribute to these efforts, including funds put into digital communication. In Wisconsin a nonprofit director said that radio ads with involved legislators and representatives and through Spanish-speaking television, such as Univision and Telemundo, constituted part of its outreach strategies for voter turnout. By comparison, since using these methods, few field campaigns or traditional door-knocking campaigns have taken place, as modeled by the director's own choices: "I'm forty-one years old and you can't reach me unless you can get to me through my cell phone or my computer frankly."

Last, because not all uses of media are created equal, localized strategies are still a must when following these practices. In one county, there were no television ads (the county is within too large a media area for this to be meaningful or cost-effective), but "radio, local papers, campus newspapers covered ID info[rmation]." A clerk's office would make phone calls—sometimes even twice—to remind voters. And local nonprofit groups have taken people in buses to vote since the state did not have the staff or resources to do this. One nonprofit similarly has a "get-out-the-vote program closer to the Election Day" that used "phone banking and peer-to-peer text messaging" to rally people to come out and vote.

Create Accurate and Credible Voter Lists

To provide effective voter documentation assistance, it's imperative to use accurate and credible voter lists. This strategy partly addresses a concern about how to find people who might need help with IDs. A participant in our research highlighted how ERIC (http://ericstates.org)

can find eligible voters in one's community.[27] ERIC can serve as a helpful go-to site for nonprofits and community organizations interested in identifying and helping individuals within their service range. The participant explained:

> ERIC will take the entire motor vehicles file, excepting those who are on their face ineligible to vote. That would include, the biggest, the biggest group is people who are not eighteen yet. . . . it uses really sophisticated name matching and matches multiple, multiple data points. I'm very convinced that it's as accurate as we can get. And it'll come up with a list of people that we call EBUs, eligible but unregistered, who are not on the list. There is absolutely no consideration to any demographic statistics on those people. Either they're on the voter list or they're not. And now, now I will tell you, we know that that list will be more representative of the diversity of the population than the registered voter list because the registered voter list is not overwhelmingly, but it's still disproportionally, White, wealthy, and old.

On the whole, emerging technologies such as ERIC have advantages over the incomplete DMV lists (which the participant said accounts for about 90 percent of eligible voters) in having other data streams and sources that states contribute toward. As the ERIC site indicates, "ERIC also provides value by identifying out-of-date records found by comparing voter registration data between states, to motor vehicle licensing agency data, and to the Social Security Administration master death index list."[28] ERIC is a model for getting states to share information, dealing well with multiple registrations, when people move, and more.

Ultimately, as our respondent noted, inaccurate voter lists can have the effect of forwarding negative and false stories about voter fraud. If complete and accurate lists are available, "we may starve that narrative for fuel." As important as practical concerns remain, the moral lesson at stake here should supersede all others. For, "Even if there's one person who's eligible to vote, who gets turned away from the polls, we should be fighting for that person, even though it doesn't have any impact . . . on the election." Since many researchers have been measuring the impact of voter ID laws across the United States from a high-level perspective, this critical point shouldn't be lost: that any one person facing difficulties in getting what they need to vote should be cause for alarm.

Motivating messages acknowledging the use of credible, supported lists must be used to signal high standards and accountability. Matching the same concerns that surfaced in our MTurk surveys, we also heard how "people who want to improve the integrity of the elections aren't wrong. And we need to have a conversation and try to figure out how can we improve integrity while not diminishing the chances or opportunity for other people to vote." Those behind ERIC are continually working to integrate more accurate and up-to-date lists from non-voting-related sources into the program, like those from public assistance agencies.

The need for tools like these also became clear when we spoke with a participant from Wisconsin who is part of a voter ID coalition. She mentioned that the level of local knowledge necessary to pulling off the challenges of obtaining documentation or IDs can be extraordinary, and that sometimes even larger national organizations (such as Rock the Vote) have incorrect information on their websites, further confusing both staff and community members about what is right and what is not. It is not possible to help voters unless the information is correct to begin with, whether locally or nationally.

Support Election Integrity and New Developments

Related to online and social media strategies, and messages about the creation or use of accurate, credible lists, a theme from our literature review and MTurk surveys with community members in the strictest voter ID states was reinforced and expanded upon in the interviews. Namely, despite a lack of evidence for voter fraud nationwide, supporting election integrity remains critical to people's confidence in their votes and the voting system. Those working on voter engagement should be ready to answer a question that is on many people's minds: "How do we make sure that the possibility of fraudulent voting is minimized or eradicated?" For some, voter documentation requirements are perceived as wholly positive for keeping the integrity of an election system intact, so we would do well not to bifurcate this concern as irrelevant to the challenges that voter identification has also wrought.

To build credibility for new strategies in helping citizens get what they need to vote, it's important to stay on top of new developments around election infrastructure. One expert spoke about the use of blockchain technology for an app her organization is testing with overseas and military voters: "The blockchain is, it's an immutable distributed ledger," which "can guarantee . . . that your vote was cast as you intended and then counted as cast because you're . . . not able to change a vote that's been sent . . . you're able to trace votes back to that." Of the many reasons to shift toward these kinds of interventions:

> We just think we're living in an increasingly mobile world, and that election infrastructure is really archaic when you think about the shift in technology in the last decade, [the] machines people are voting on; the money was allocated in 2002 when the Help America Vote Act was passed. Right? And that was the first, so like a lot of the, almost all the machines that are, that we're currently voting on, are older than the first iPhone . . . we don't use any technology that's this old, like why is this industry so stubbornly in the past? . . . We have no intentions of removing polling stations, or trying to disenfranchise people who don't have mobile phones. . . . It's just we think that we're living in an increasingly mobile world and we should create another avenue for people with disabilities and working professionals and members of the military, really anyone who doesn't have a lifestyle that is, they're [not] able to leave to vote in person.

Although inspiration and a role for advocating for these changes could come from community organizations, it would take the government to scale such operations. To overcome citizens' states of confusion, more rigorous and coordinated efforts nationally have to be part of the picture. And these efforts can serve both ends: new tools can make it easier for citizens to vote while advancing an election infrastructure that is vastly improved and more able to support election integrity. As our participant told us, reflecting many similar sentiments from others, paper voting is not an inclusive strategy for the world that we're currently in and heading toward. The parallel for voter documentation is clear: having people bring paper forms of ID or other documentation to register to vote should also be seen as an increasingly outdated practice if the easy access afforded by the digital world is available.[29]

Contextual and Organizational Observations

Before addressing the question of what kind of organizational effort could best address voter documentation requirements, we want to highlight one noteworthy, dissenting viewpoint from the president of a New York nonprofit:

> I actually think that attacking the issue of voter documentation is a losing strategy. It's such a tiny strand of the efforts to make it more and more difficult to participate in this country. . . . I would look at the total issue of how do you make it easier for people to participate in our democracy? Documentation is a small part of that issue. If you only focus narrowly on the documentation issue, it is going to be very difficult to get traction and momentum. . . . I would go into it with [a] healthy respect that things are changing rapidly. There are lots of new conversations, lots of new players. Not to just put blinders on and focus on documentation, but really take on the whole field.

We believe this is a productive and provocative statement that goes beyond voter documentation but is critical to consider in framing overall, democratic solutions. From the research conducted for this project, we know that it's certainly worth addressing voter documentation requirements, but only as part of larger, systemic strategies and the networked efforts of many groups already in the voting space. Appeals about voter documentation shouldn't be made in isolation from other efforts. The president of the nonprofit mentioned numerous issues to contend with in this regard: places where there's no early voting or no mail-in voting, outdated voting methods, and potential problems with closed primaries in many states (e.g., "There are more Independents than Republicans in NYC. There are over a million just in the five boroughs. They are not allowed to vote in elections despite the fact that the primaries determine the outcome in 95 percent of the districts in NYC."[30] At the very least, this suggests that, where possible, if there are ways to address voter documentation *and* other issues at play that affect voter engagement, those paths should be taken.

The more we investigated voter ID, the more problematic aspects of the voting system nationally became apparent. As the president of the nonprofit additionally mentioned, "one of the dirty little secrets about American politics is that 50 percent of politicians in this country run unopposed. There is only one candidate on the ballot. So, when you look at participation being low, why would someone be so stupid to go vote in an election where there is only one candidate? So, competition is a big problem."[31] At the very least, voter documentation should be nested within these other structural and ongoing problems that citizens face, and the realistic objections they have to want to register to vote or vote.

We began this project with a question about whether new entities— particularly new nonprofits and community organizations that could expand the work of others already engaged with the issue—should be started to work exclusively on voter ID. Our hope was that answers to this question would point toward realistic solutions for voter ID while providing insights about what level of organizational or agency involvement might be needed to truly tackle the problem. We received a near consensus in responses: no, a national organization is not needed, but everything possible should be done to support and expand the efforts of those already working on voter documentation requirements in relevant areas.

We heard this response across different states. A data director for a state political party told us, for example, that "this structure [for helping with voter documentation requirements] likely already exists in Arizona. Increasing their capacity would be better than re-creating the wheel." A program director in Wisconsin answered, "Is there a need for a new nonprofit to work on these issues? No. Not in Wisconsin. We have this incredible table of organizations that already exist that are able to work on these issues and capable of working on these issues, that have been working on these issues . . . [in which] no individual players can easily navigate the system. Should there be more support for organizations like ours and others? Yes. Absolutely." The director explained, "One of the big needs here is [for] other folks to come in and say how can they support the work that is already happening. . . . support those who are already doing this work and allow them to expand their capacities as opposed to starting a brand-new organization." If there are funds available to support this work, it's best to spread them across already existing structures.

Forms of support are needed both locally and nationally. One interviewee working for a nonprofit dedicated to voting issues in Kansas stated: "No, we do not need a new national nonprofit. But we do need increased help [for] those at the national level and there are a lot of them. We should support them in what they are doing. That would be the better way to go." Another participant from Ohio also said that supporting existing entities doing this work would be best because "the more fragmented we are, the harder it is to do solid training." This comment about fragmentation highlights a need for some intellectual and practical cohesion among the disparate entities working on voter ID, one in which we hope this book can play a role.

Although voter ID remains a national concern, until and unless these laws are changed, one of the main reasons for choosing to work through existing entities concerns an ability to adapt well to the different requirements in each state. One respondent mentioned, "It would be a challenge because every locality is different; such an organization would get too specific or too vague to be helpful." This participant said that it couldn't hurt to attempt putting something together that could help people across different locales, though, since their county had to call "people in ID states to get guidance," including election centers and other voting organizations, just to get a handle on how to help people in each state with voter documentation requirements. That these informal learning exchanges are taking place underscores a need for a formal framework of knowledge about the issue and what to do about it.

Highlighting some of the organizations that surfaced in our background study, a senior legal director noted:

> There are a few organizations out there that are very good. I think building on that expertise . . . by giving them the opportunity to expand might be your rough bet. VoteRiders is an organization that has been focused on getting people voter IDs in particular, but I think that experience is pretty well applicable to the registration side too. There is an organization called Spread the Vote, [it] does the same thing. Having those organizations that have already built awesome expertise [and] have the opportunities to expand to cover the country more holistically would probably be the best way to go.

The organizations most in need of support were described as "on-the-ground," have "done the homework," and have "already organized." A staff member at a nonprofit further told us: "I just think that you should find one that already exists and see if there is a way to leverage what they already have happening."[32]

The last thing groups in this space need is to be competing with one another. If confusion is the reigning reaction with voter documentation, no one needs to add any more disorienting approaches to this mix by trying to draw boundaries between their work and the work of others. Whether working locally or nationally, collaboration rather than competition should be the focus to get citizens what they need to vote. A programs and outreach director for a national voting organization stated:

> I think with the proliferation of so many new groups, being interested in working in this space and doing important work and that has led to a severe, frankly shortage of funding, competition over very small pots of funding for this work. And we spend more time trying to carve out where we're unique from each other so that we can maybe get that small pile of grant funding than being able to effectively work together. . . . there are organizations like the League [of Women Voters], like NAACP, like [the] Advancement Project, like [the] Brennan Center. You know, there, there are organizations out in sort of the national playing field and certainly locally, which is even more important, where we need to support capacity and build up that capacity as opposed to entering in new, new spaces.

From their viewpoint, the local approaches of VoteRiders have been especially well received and trusted across different communities.

While national and local organizational strategies seem critical, there are tensions and trade-offs worth considering with blanket approaches. A nonprofit staff member in North Carolina described how her organization could address fear and distrust in a way that would be difficult for national and similar entities:

> Organizations like ours are already familiar with the communities. They know us. When they come to see us it's like one big family. It's coming to an organization where—the community knows us. You know, we interact

together well enough, there's been a long history of trust built in, and so if someone else comes and tries to do the same work, it might be a little bit difficult for that to be carried on because of someone new. . . . But I don't see a new organization, national organization, standing and calling people and them responding. I know how our community works, you know, who are you? . . . they know us on a first name basis. Oh, my child is having this. Oh, my mother is having this, you know? This or that issue, this is what's going on, they are familiar. So when we do pose a question or tell them about something new that may be beneficial to them, they are open to listening because we know their history. We are familiar with each other.[33]

Overall, people would prefer to come to nonprofits where they're already being helped rather than go to other organizations with which these connections haven't been well established.

At the same time, national entities can still play a critical part with assistance through their coordination, infrastructure, and useful resources. In Wisconsin, we heard that "the ACLU has been a huge advocate in our state for these voting rights issues. And I find that they do a wonderful job." As such, "We have a lot of the tools here already. It's a question I think of how can we best work together? I think there's a lot of people acting in silos . . . sometimes we forget we're part of the wider picture of things. So, I think sometimes we just have to work better on working among each other instead of starting something brand new the whole time every time. . . . we realize there are people out there that can help us make our message stronger." The response echoed the sentiments of many others—there's a lot of great work going on and much to build from, but more connections between organizations as they do the on-the-ground work could be helpful to systematically address voter documentation and ID challenges across the United States.

Finally, a nonprofit staff member in Georgia stressed the ideal of networked approaches for overcoming these challenges:

The best way is to support existing organizations because of a simple reason. National organizations have been here for a long time, they have become corporations in a way. They tend to not go out, and wait for the community to come to them. So, very little gets done. They rely on smaller organizations to do some of the work, do most of the outreach while they keep the money. I am a great supporter of instead funding a few organizations in partnership with a national organization, or for a national organization to come and do whatever they think we need and then leave, it's better to fund a network of organizations covering an issue. We don't have large organizations in Georgia, so the work gets spread out through a network. National organizations have a role when it comes to marketing materials, key talking points, but to drive the work it is important to have a network.

We received some different viewpoints on this question, however. One interviewee said, with some similarities to the network approach, "I think it would be good to have a dedicated agency [whose] sole goal is voter registration and [can] be a support system kind of like we are. They can in turn be with multiple agencies and hitting all their goals. They would know if it is done or not. Other agencies can rely on this organization, then it can be a smaller part that they would do." To formulate recommendations, these different perspectives provide glimpses of where opportunities to address voter documentation requirements lie. In the conclusion to this book, we'll offer an integrated look at and advice for the raft of knowledge provided by people all over the nation who had insight on the issue.

Before doing so, in the next chapter we arrive at the bottom of our funnel by exploring the stories of community members in strict voter ID states themselves trying to get a handle on what they need to be able to vote. These experiences of voter documentation challenges, and the many voting-related problems and forms of suppression surrounding it, offer a necessary look at the thicket of issues presented by voter ID.

5

Taking a Closer Look

Voter IDs in Everyday Life

If there's anything we've learned about politics in the United States, it's that there's an entire industry whose business model is built upon claiming to know and understand *others* better than they themselves do. Far too often, powerful media personalities and politicians reduce others to simplified caricatures, invalidate their experiences, or simply construct straw person arguments about them to easily knock down so that a manufactured, feel-good victory can be claimed.[1] When it comes to voter ID, no assertion has been too outrageous. Such figures will assert that without voter ID policies dead people and pets get to vote in every election cycle, that only lazy folks won't make the effort to meet documentation requirements, and that the future of civilization as we know it depends on these laws. To counter these unsupported claims that many citizens unfortunately believe are "common sense" about voting, our highest aspiration in this project was to hear from voters in different states to see what aligned with or diverged from these types of endlessly repeated narratives.

To understand ground-level impacts, this chapter elevates the voices of community members and their experiences navigating voter documentation requirements and related voting issues. The problems with voter documentation and similar issues that these citizens and others they knew face stunned us, from reasons for why a person would not even need an ID to what people undergoing identity transitions must deal with to meet different states' requirements. We carried out three focus groups in Ohio consisting of approximately thirty participants. To organize these groups, our partner organizations in Ohio included the League of Women Voters of Ohio, My Project USA, and Homeport, a nonprofit housing developer for low-income families. Each organization arranged one focus group composed of a specific demographic. The first group consisted of ten women of color who lived in a subsidized housing complex; the second included ten young voters, mostly college students; the third was composed of Somali and Ethiopian refugees who were US citizens and eligible to vote.

Through two nonprofit partners in Mississippi, One Voice and Mississippi Votes, we worked with another three diverse groups of about thirty participants that included rural Mississippians, returning citizens (i.e., those who had been out of state for a period and then returned) and those who were living in Mississippi but from other states, and queer and trans youth.[2] In these latter two groups, many participants also described themselves as students. As in chapter 4, here we move from a focus on the problems people experience to the solutions that might best address voter documentation requirements.[3]

Not Needing or Cannot Get IDs

Some people believe they simply don't need an ID. Often to their own astonishment, our focus group participants in Mississippi shared that, in contrast to the view that an ID should be an absolute necessity in contemporary society, they knew many people who would disagree. One focus group participant mentioned that, for a local candidate's election,

> We picked up a lot of people that didn't have IDs. And I was like, "Man, how do you all cash your checks and do everything without IDs?" They was like, "We go to the liquor store and cash our check, we don't need our ID." . . . I work at the different projects and housing, housing projects in this division. It was, it was amazing to me how many people didn't have voter ID. . . . One of the reasons I heard was their driver license was suspended and they couldn't go get another ID and that's why they didn't have an ID. And I, you know, that's the eligibility of being able to get an ID here in Yazoo City. It's a hardship when people get to Jackson, it might not seem like that, but it's a lot of people here that never been to Jackson, in Yazoo City.

We were astonished by this comment. For some people, an ID is not viewed as essential for local, daily activities. Moreover, if one of the main forms of voter identification (a driver's license) is withheld for any reason, it's a barrier to being able to get a different form of ID, in addition to traveling distances to other cities to coordinate such an effort.

We heard stories of losing IDs, temporary licenses that had expired, and the hassle of needing to add the procurement of an ID for voting to the list of life's demands. One person said, "I had lost my driver's license and, and they wouldn't let me vote," and, similar to others' responses, that voter identification requirements were a "burden." When we asked who did not have a US passport as an alternative, six participants in one focus group shared that they lacked this form of ID. The "circular traps" mentioned in our interviews also came up. One person mentioned needing to have a birth certificate (something that they didn't have) to get an ID. We also heard how, for one person, "he had the birth certificate but, the Social Security card was damaged, in order for him to get his state-issued ID, he needed his Social Security card. In order to get his Social Security, he had to have a state-issued ID." This clearly was a Catch-22 situation.

Even for those who wanted to get IDs amid all these obstacles, our focus groups manifest the confusion at the heart of voter identification challenges in the process of running the groups. During one focus group, one person said that they had gone to a local courthouse to try to get a permanent ID but were unable to do so. This led to a debate among three of the participants about whether a local courthouse could issue only temporary IDs, as opposed to longer-term forms of identification. We observed a lack of clarity about such issues performed in participants' very discussions.

Moving and Matching Address Changes

Moving from one place to another creates enormous challenges for citizens. Many of our questions centered on whether our participants had to show an ID in recent elections and what that experience was like. One focus group respondent told us, "You are required to show ID because I had moved, and I went to the same place that my sister went to. They told me that I had to go to a totally different area because I did not have my ID from my old address, it was my new address. Once I got it switched, I was able to go to the one my sister went to. They were very strict." Reflecting many of the earlier concerns we had seen in the literature and spoken about in our interviews with experts and practitioners, changing addresses is a major barrier in stories about voting.

In Mississippi, one participant ran into the challenge of trying to vote in a new county. If a person moves between counties they have to reregister in the state. Mississippi also does not have same-day registration (registration must be completed thirty days prior to voting), and people can only vote in their county. Additionally, one person was registered in another county and couldn't vote in one election; he asked for an absentee ballot but was unable to receive one. Again and again we heard that citizens simply fall off the electoral cliff when faced with even minor impediments.

Moving and matching address changes tie into other problems such as transportation. Another participant shared: "My current address didn't match the address on my license. Until this day, it still doesn't match. They told me I had to go to a whole other side of town to go vote. Now I moved again and would have to go again over there to go vote. They don't allow you to vote in the same area if you moved. They make it inconvenient for you to go to the place your license says to register and vote. If I bring proof of address, why can't I vote here? That was my only problem, and I still have that problem." Far from being an entirely new problem, we were shocked at the long-standing nature of these challenges for some participants.

Having an ID is a necessary but not necessarily sufficient condition for registering to vote or voting. In Mississippi, college students found crossing state boundaries and having address changes incredibly challenging. One college student said that she was a resident of Tennessee and discovered not being a Mississippi citizen confusing when it came to elections and address requirements. Since 2010, many states have put in place laws preventing students from voting in states that aren't the same as their parents, which some thought was unfair. At the same time, since college students tend to be a low-income population, the attendant expenses of dealing with obtaining an ID may serve as another obstacle.

Workplace Pressures

If the calculus that many citizens face requires choosing between work, a needed paycheck, and tolerance from their employers, as compared with taking time off work, losing money, and putting one's job in jeopardy, it's clear what road will be traveled. Obligations to one's workplace can impede voting-related procedures and voting. One respondent shared:

> At my workplace, there are older people who don't have cars and take public transportation for everything. They always complain that they don't have time to vote because no one has ever asked if our job would give us time off to vote, but we just think that they wouldn't. We have told them to go vote, but they say that they don't have time and can't afford to miss work. I had an issue where I couldn't afford to take off [time], also my boss didn't have enough people working so he told me he couldn't give me that time off. Even if he had given me the day off, he wouldn't be paying me, and I need that money.

Strategies to address voter documentation requirements and voting need to consider the significance of having to take time off from work. Just raising "awareness" or "educating" people about voting issues will not be enough to break through the understandable reasons why people may have higher priorities than voting.

In the United States, only half the population tends to vote in general elections (with some exceptions).[4] Many midterm, state, and other elections have far lower participation, following a long history of declining voting and election-related behaviors.[5] It's easy to attribute these problems to individual choices, such as voter apathy or laziness. But seen within the context of workplace pressures and the other forces at play (and since other countries declare their election days national holidays), many citizens make what they see as sensible choices, given their limited options.

All Documentation Is Not Created Equal

All forms of identification are not created equal across different state boundaries. A participant in Ohio provided this account: "I lived in Texas, so I have a Texas ID. I had to show that I was a resident, actually I think I ended up showing my military ID because I hadn't lived there that long. It was my first time voting, I'm going to say I showed my military ID and that's how I was able to vote."[6] It's interesting that the military ID was accepted, suggesting this process could be made easier for some populations by positioning voter documents in a hierarchy, with some sense of what should be prioritized, rather than through lists of documents that are clearly not all created equal when it comes to voter requirements in certain states (e.g., for those in the military, being able to use their military ID rather than worry about other forms).

Varying lists of requirements create confusion. Our participant explained: "They gave me a paper, because at first, they told me that I wasn't going to be able to do it because I had a Texas driver's license. So I wondered if, people move all the time, so there has to be another way. They had looked up in a book or something, they found a list of different things I had to bring in and show them in order for me to vote." As arose in our interviews with experts in this space, some of our focus group participants even found the idea of needing to vote in one polling place unjust. One person noted, "I would change that everybody can vote in any [polling] place they want because in the city they are not allowed to vote outside their district. Sometimes you are at work, far from home." In our computer age, one would imagine that polling places could be outfitted to accept ballots applicable to any part of a city, or even a state. There are still reasons for people to vote in a particular place because so much of representation is place-based, but expanding the availability of polling place options (and mail-in voting, which we explore further in the conclusion) would only help citizens. A place-based strategy to help people get what they need to vote, combined with accurate communication about the most essential documents, and an opportunity to cast votes in multiple sites that can accommodate a range of ballots for different polling places could all go a long way toward sorting out this confusing mess of requirements.

Unique Combinations of Material and Perceptual Challenges

We wanted to push beyond our immediate participants to see if others they knew had also been affected by voter documentation requirements. For one person, this immediately brought to mind "my grandmother. She doesn't know much about the internet. Even today, she struggles going to the DMV to renew her license. When it comes down to voting, she can't go. No one sits down and explains the system, goes through the things she needs to have to go vote." In fact, we were surprised by the breadth of challenges mentioned in the focus groups. Although there are many common barriers faced by citizens, sometimes it's the distinct combination of challenges that present the greatest problems (e.g., in this participant's example, skill with the internet, DMV renewals, possible transportation issues), and sometimes it's certain assumptions or information gaps that create hardships.

It's not only about keeping up with new requirements but knowing what old requirements are no longer in effect and having some sense of where to go to find the right, updated information. Another respondent noted, "With the older generation having . . . certain obstacles in order to vote, it is happening now with the felonies, when they are saying certain people can't vote because of their record, or they [laws] are passed and now there are new laws coming out overnight and it's hard trying to keep up to make sure that you are able to vote." Sometimes the barriers to wanting to get documents together to register to vote link with deeper concerns about the larger legal frameworks within which voting systems operate. For example, one person told us that once they found out about the Electoral College and how it worked, they gave up on voting because they were so distraught that the system would work in this way.

Although many voter documentation requirements are confusing enough for those born in the United States, for those from other countries, the challenges of adjusting to the norms of US election systems are even greater. A participant in our group from a refugee community commented, "There were two things that confused me about voting. I saw the people in line to vote, that was the time Bill Clinton was running for president. I didn't understand why people were in line since early in the morning, my country never did this. Didn't they have jobs? It was difficult to understand the time needed to vote, but when I became a US citizen, I learned how to do it." Among combined challenges that might be faced, in this example the refugee's learning curve is steeper for having to adapt to an entirely new context.

Time Needed to Get ID

Sometimes citizens' challenges primarily concerned the time it takes to obtain certain documents. In many states, receiving an ID is not solely a matter of going to a government office and immediately receiving the item. One person noted the confusing circumstances they faced in trying to get a new ID to vote:

> In the state of Ohio, they have this new ID thing [at the DMV], where they mail your ID, but [meanwhile] they give you a paper slip [a temporary ID]. I heard that you couldn't take your slip to places, and that no one would take it where you go. So, I had to vote provisional, because I didn't take it with me. I took my expired one, but they didn't take that one either. I was waiting for an ID that I didn't physically have, and I actually had my old one and you would think that that would be enough. Some people might not want to deal with it and simply not vote. There should be a better way to identify yourself. . . . When you go get your ID at the DMV, they allow different identifications and we should do something like that.

This situation suggests that attention should be paid to the mazelike situation in applying for and receiving IDs, depending on the rules for showing ID to cast provisional ballots in each state. Better and more uniform instructions would help eligible voters along these paths.

In our Mississippi focus group, one participant exclaimed that it should be easy to get a passport if you didn't have a driver's license. Others immediately pushed back by saying that it's not easy to get a passport and, at a minimum, that it would take seven to ten weeks for it to arrive. Some raised the possibility that the timing for getting a passport may have even changed. (And we'd add: during the COVID-19 pandemic, it changed a lot!). One person described how someone stole her driver's license and debit card a week before the election, and she was only able to vote in the election because she had a student ID that worked. She would not have been able to use her university address for getting a driver's license, however. Another participant said she was not allowed to use her student ID. And one election staffer gave one participant a lot of "crap" over her ID. Overall, the lack of clarity about deadlines (and a history of difficult interactions with election personnel) led to many misunderstandings.

Some expressed additional frustrations over DMV hassles and the "come back the next day" message they received. Participants would go to the DMV and be told that they would have to return another time, stalling their process. These challenges are magnified in places where transportation options such as Uber don't exist. Overall, someone asked why the process for voting isn't as stress-free as using one's Social Security number, which could be pulled up within systems easily, forgoing the need for deadlines and inordinate amounts of time spent waiting for documents.[7] The more we heard, the more we asked ourselves the same questions.

The System's Complexity and Inequalities

If there's any single roadblock that's undermining citizens' faith in registering to vote and actually voting, it's a bewildering complexity about the system and feeling isolated and "on one's own" in figuring out how to navigate the maze of voter ID requirements.[8] One of the focus group participants in Ohio shared the following:

> When I became a voter at eighteen, then and now, I don't feel like I have a solid understanding on how the system really works, how my vote matters, and what value it has. All the information that I do know about it, I had to seek myself. I was fortunate enough to have internet and have the resources to find that information. It's very frustrating to be uncertain. Why am I going to do this? And if it is such a hard thing to do, is the effort being used valuable? Are we doing it for a reason or does that vote even matter?

Examining this ambivalence, one can infer that voters need more help at all stages of this process, or at least more assistance than they are currently getting given changes in state laws, the complexity of the voting system, and what may seem like minor inconveniences to some but are major barriers for too many others. Sometimes the barrage of ads and the claims citizens hear create another level of perplexity. One participant mentioned: "Around election times, you see both sides release the same argument, but they are on opposite sides. You listen to their commercials, but it still doesn't make sense. You might look up their names and see all their beliefs. The hardest part is taking pieces and parts from everybody." Samuel Popkin describes citizens' attempts to comprehend

US campaigns and elections as a "drunkard's search" for information.[9] If it's hard enough making sense of the election system during these times, the problem is exacerbated by adding confusing voter documentation or registration requirements to the swirl, and conditions like those of the pandemic increase the confusion to an overwhelming degree.

Informational inequalities play into this entanglement. One of our focus group facilitators mentioned how in some jurisdictions, like New York, information packets about the candidates and issues are sent to voters. One participant reacted by saying:

> It should be the government's responsibility to make it easier. Even if the government sent us those packets they send y'all, if you really believed in who you are voting for, then you probably would go all out, put more effort to vote. But if you are just going in there, and you don't know who you are voting for, you are waiting for the list like. When I first used to vote, they would just give me the list and say just vote all Democrat or vote all Republican. So, if you don't even know who you are voting for, if you don't even know what they do, then you are probably quicker to not even go.

People need to feel some agency about voting. Having basic information should be within the reach of all. And, as one person from another country shared, this "is important especially to us who are immigrants." The deterrence to voting that arises for those facing unfamiliar jargon, convoluted language, or a lack of translation can't be separated from a generalized need to be informed. According to another participant: "My problem is how they word things. I cannot understand what they are talking about, so, how can I read what they say and then go try and talk to them about the topic. I only know how to say it my way. I don't know how to do it their way." Furthermore, one person in Mississippi said that he was overwhelmed about voting for anyone beyond the presidential candidates. Even in states where getting an ID for voting is easier than in others, confusion permeates thoughts about voting and elections in general, marked by a transference of negative feelings that overshadow every part of the process.

Geographic inequalities loom large, creating unequal access to voting. One person noted how "there is only one place in Franklin County to early vote. And that is up in the north side. It shouldn't be that way, they should have voting in north, south, east and west. There should be one center downtown because that is where the courthouse is, but [there should] also be one for people to have access, able to get on the bus lines and go and vote." Some individuals lack their own transportation, and local buses don't reach where many of them live. Whoever is helping a citizen or citizens to register to vote should take the additional step, if possible, to follow up to make sure that the voter both became registered and is clear on how to vote in their respective district.

As much as data tell us that voter ID problems affect huge numbers of people, this issue must be considered within a larger context. The title of Jim Hightower's book *If The Gods Had Meant Us to Vote, They Would Have Given Us Candidates* rings true here: the whole system is rigged against populations, down to the nitty-gritty fact that obstacles including campaign finance, lobbying, and all types of systemic issues prevent people in the United States from having meaningful elections all the time. Who can even effectively run for office is a matter of tremendous weight. Add to this a lack of decent education generally, the conditions that people live in because of low wages and having to worry so much about missing a day's work or not being able to pay the rent, and the disparate impacts of health provisions and forms of health insurance in the United States that physically hamper some populations from voting on a given occasion. All this is to say, people must make unconscionable choices and are not irrational when they weigh the pros and cons and conclude not only that is it hard for them to vote, but also that voting has not gotten them anything they need.

Lost Faith versus Responsibilities Owed

At the heart of many community members' beliefs about elections and politics lies a striking, actionable paradox. During our focus groups, we heard about the general loss of faith many people had in the voting system in general. With two presidential elections in memory that led to the candidates with the most votes losing the election due to the Electoral College system (but also involving hotly contested vote counts, as in Florida in *Bush v. Gore*), one participant of a focus group in Mississippi elaborated, "It's like every election, it makes a lot of people lose confidence in the system." This lost faith in the election system bears on how active and motivated citizens feel about engaging with the government at any level.

At the same time, this loss of faith is juxtaposed against an opposite belief with a moral pull: that people have given their lives for the right to vote, and their sacrifice should be honored through one's own obligation to vote. Several Black participants in our Mississippi focus groups shared that their ancestors had died for voting rights; as one of them explained, "We need to pick up what was, with what they left behind." This suggests that when voters express malaise about the election system's inadequacies, it could be critical for government institutions, nonprofits, and other community organizations to communicate about a shared past, responsibilities, or other ways that everyone has an obligation to pay forward what individuals and groups have inherited.

Redistricting, Hours of Operation, and ID

One problem related to timing and geography concerns a lack of knowledge about redistricting. People often end up at the wrong polling place because they were not aware of changes made to their districts (or perhaps through their own failure to take seriously what they get in the mail) or because of their lack of knowledge or comprehension. In an election in Mississippi's Hinds County, one person noted how "we had a problem with the supervisors [who] had changed the, they changed the, redistrict. . . . And they didn't . . . notify the public that there had been redistrict[ing]. And when the people showed up to the precinct that they had been voting in for years, they . . . couldn't vote." The significance of this problem shouldn't be lost, as it reinforces a theme that runs through this project—getting voter identification prior to an election constitutes one hurdle to cross, but showing up at the polls the day of the election, or even knowing how to fill out a ballot once you get there, can create other politicized and racialized hurdles.

If one's identification is not valid at a polling place within an area that has been redistricted, many citizens quite reasonably wonder if their local system even represents them anymore. As the same participant shared with us, the story did not have a happy ending: "And no one told [people], exactly, where to go to vote and they just went home." To a possible objection that all people need to do is find the correct polling place and go there once they learn that they're at the incorrect location, participants in a Mississippi focus group made clear that any additional impediment put in place at the polling station is enough to make possible voters give up.[10] One person highlighted, "A lot of people will just, if they get turned around at the polls, they'll just go back to work or, you know, they only have a small time to be off and they don't wanna run all over town trying to figure out where they can vote." Many people have neither the time nor the interest to sustain much more attention within already finite periods and with limited resources.

This again brings into focus how work hours can compete against voting hours. As one respondent said: "All right, if you show up at the polls and you ain't got but an hour and they tell you, 'Well, you don't vote here.' By the time you get ready to find out . . . it should be, it's almost too late. I mean, you can get there just in ten minutes before, I mean, and still can, you can get in. But if it's a line outside there, then . . . you're done." Government incompetence plays a part in these events. But not everything is attributable to government failure. What these comments reveal is that there are hosts of systemic problems that converge or even conspire to keep people from voting, and that need to be addressed before we can get to a truly even playing field with voting and, ultimately, democracy.

Provisional and Other Ballots

One common bar to voting arising from the failure to have the "right" ID is a lack of understanding about how to cast a vote when ID is insufficient at the polling place. The differences between various types of ballots can hinder voting. In the Mississippi focus groups, some of our participants talked about what it meant to complete an affidavit in support of a provisional ballot, while others talked about how complicated they found the distinctions between voting on a machine or filling out a provisional paper ballot. People need help to walk through an unfamiliar process. But during that process, additional hindrances may arise that are often too late to address. One participant said she ran into problems when trying to cast a provisional vote—with the help of a poll worker—with having two different addresses, and eventually it became too late to complete an affidavit after she had been sent to three different locations. As a result, she was unable to vote. The difference between provisional and absentee ballots was especially unclear, including how many days one would have to procure and then show an ID to support these types of ballots.

Another person shared a story about how all had been fine until there was a subsequent runoff election. He discovered that he couldn't vote— although he had completed a provisional ballot, it arrived at the Board of Elections too late to be counted. Others also were unable to vote in runoffs. One participant said she had an Indiana driver's license, and when she gave it to a poll worker, "she looked at it for five minutes" and said, "Well, you can't vote." An argument ensued. This participant would have been sent away, but she knew the laws and her rights and was able to vote. As mentioned earlier, one person talked about getting temporary IDs at a courthouse (these IDs lapse after thirty days) and then not being able to get another temporary one. This comment evoked much discussion among the other focus group members about whether these types of IDs could be renewed, revealing more voter confusion. The problems with runoff elections or poll workers' lack of training on ID add to this mix.

The distinctions between different kinds of ballots involve more than legal technicalities. One respondent said that it feels like "they're trying to silence us." One person shared that Black people are the most oppressed and that it can still feel like slavery when fraud against the Black population occurs, especially with a rare but recent example of election fraud in North Carolina in the background.

On the other hand, as one person shared, having a candidate that an individual can't wait to vote for can provide the motivation to want to undertake a provisional or absentee ballot process. Participants were asked whom they would turn to or call if they weren't sure how to cast a particular kind of ballot. A majority said they would know where to go, but others did not. One person expressed that knowing about the presence of organizations such as Mississippi Votes would obviously help.

One staff member told one of the groups that you can definitely show your state ID when you go vote, or a driver's license from a different state, and that if you get denied that right, it's likely illegal voter suppression and time to call the ACLU or an election protection hotline.[11]

Overall, *that so much needed to be understood in our focus groups itself was telling.*

Name and Identity Marker Transitions

Going into this research, we knew that some people have had problems with voter identification requirements due to name changes. Both the hassle and the timing of receiving new IDs can affect an individual's ability to vote after major life events, such as a marriage. But this problem runs deep for other populations as well. In our Mississippi focus groups, some participants shared how they couldn't have any ID at all during their sex/identity transitions. Changing a name and changing one's identity marker are two different factors with their own hurdles.

Several groups have been trying to help trans Mississippians with this, but there are still problems, depending on where you live and in which county. One transgender participant shared how he had gone through the process of getting an ID but knew others who had not been able to change their name or their gender marker. He believed he was privileged by being born in Massachusetts and had a head start given that state's more accessible requirements. In Mississippi there have been many more obstacles, however, and people are told not to vote, or the poll workers just don't know what to do because it is so difficult to get an ID that accurately reflects specific identification markers.

Is this a niche issue with a negligible election impact? The Williams Institute at the UCLA School of Law has estimated that there are seventy-eight thousand trans people across eight states who currently require photo ID.[12] According to a survey conducted across the United States by the National Center for Transgender Equality, out of approximately twenty-eight thousand trans respondents, "only 11% of respondents reported that all of their IDs and records listed both the name and gender they preferred, and rates were lower for certain populations. . . . More than two-thirds (68%) reported that none of their IDs or records had both the name and gender they preferred."[13] One person in our group said that there are fifteen thousand trans people in Mississippi, and two-thirds do not have ID. There are regulations governing name changes, and the process both involves money out of pocket and for some people can be too difficult to wade through. Overall, the situation demonstrates how voter identification affects people unequally in both its features and its functions, resulting in the exclusion of populations of voters from the franchise.

The Influence of One Person, Family, and Friends

We wanted to find out from our focus group participants what might best help them procure voter documentation and engage in processes that lead to registration and voting. The influence of one person or organization figured prominently in their answers to these questions; as one person told us: "Having an office where people can get the information from the beginning and then hav[ing] someone . . . come out to the community" could help get what's needed in an election cycle.

Some other ideas included "Have a little daycare at the sites so moms can take the time to vote, help those who can't see well," and "Me, as a millennial, I voted and everything, and after that whole process, they still had to explain it to me. I'll go to older people, my family, for them to fully explain, to know about the Electoral College and the popular vote. . . . So it was a little confusing for the most part." Consistent with our MTurk surveys, the reliance on family and others within one's network became instrumental to better understanding voting.

The importance of local, influential others shouldn't be lost here, especially for their possible impact on the thinking or habits of voters. In Mississippi, one person told us that they had been instrumental in helping their son with voting, while another shared about assisting a brother through the process. Consistent with the influence described in these families, but with the opposite effect, a participant in Ohio commented, "My grandparents yelled at us for not voting. My parents didn't vote so I didn't want to vote and that triggered all my siblings to not vote at all too." Even in the span of a single generation, election-related practices can become solidified.

When those whose first language is not English try to figure out how to navigate the political system, friendship plays a critical role, as the same participant further explained: "I have a friend of mine that lived here longer than me. He taught me. That is what we do. When I went to orientation I didn't know how to speak English. Orientation was given in your language. There was a video that we were shown but I couldn't understand. But my friend taught us a lot." When the system puts up obstacles, people naturally turn to those they know and trust to mediate these experiences.

In Mississippi, we heard from community members that people are used to voting based on relationships. That is, "people like from the hood and family know 'em." People in local churches or other places of worship, locations where people who know each other gather regularly, can and do speak to the importance of voting. Six participants in one focus group had received help with voter documentation from people close to them. Many expressed how they knew others who needed birth certificates, suggesting that people are often one degree removed from those who need assistance. Some said that having someone come to schools would further help, or at least having someone like a speaker at a local community venue who could answer questions or having someone to follow up with them on these matters.

One person told us that she consults her mother, who does work at the polls and oversees her family's taxes and thus is considered well educated on bureaucratic processes. Another said she talks to her father because he's well-informed. He was described as watching CNN and other channels to stay on top of what's happening in politics and elections. Some said they have the CNN app and that they go on social media to find out information. Family conversations are a big part of all of this—there's an online/off-line interaction to how people process elections and figure out what they need to do, or even if they don't need to do anything at all.

Similar to what we heard from experts and practitioners during our interviews, we learned from other individuals in our focus groups that the idea of having volunteers to guide voting processes is fundamental to outreach. One person who organized volunteer efforts shared: "If you feel like you don't understand all the issues, that is fine, there are folks who can help you in that case. We have done voter registration in the past and it was picking people up from their homes and driving them to the election to get them registered to vote during business hours. It was a volunteer who helped bring mail-in votes to everyone. Then that same volunteer secured internet registration." A consistent use of volunteers or others who can close the gaps individuals uniquely face can go a long way toward addressing voter ID challenges.

Organizational Expectations

People want more organizations to engage in voter documentation assistance. To our inquiry "The fact that all these organizations are helping folks, do you think that there needs to be more organizations?" one person answered, "Yes. Definitely so. More so, so they can explain to the voters that are coming of age, and they can fully learn the process, and then they aren't confused on what their vote is going to." Like others, this respondent explained, "Right now, they [the respondent's peers] are not believing in the voting process. Because it kind of let us down, a lot of [us] who did vote, we knew what we were voting for, and then for the turnout to be different. There seems to be a lack of communication when it comes down to the voting process. . . . But if we had more organizations in our community, to reach out and explain what is going on," that would only help.

When we asked our focus group participants to name organizations they thought helped with voting, one person in Mississippi shared (specifically to the prompt of who they thought could get them help with a birth certificate), "We don't know of any." The general feeling was that going to Jackson (the closest big city) would be necessary to get organizational help—yet, at another point in the focus groups, two participants expressed that there was no bus to the city. Another person in Ohio shared, "I don't know of any organizations specifically, but I do know that it has become more frequent, you are seeing things like commercials, social media, and things like that." These types of responses suggest that getting clearer about what organizations are available to help would prove beneficial.

The invocation of the US military and how it works with voter registration was also seen by one participant as a bright spot in efforts to get diverse people registered to vote. Campuses were a good source for voting, said another: "They make sure that you go out and vote and have the proper stuff. On campus, there is one [information resource] for transgenders to get registered and anyone in the LGBT community, they help them register, they give them the information that they need. Some will actually go with you and help you register to vote." Moreover, "My campus sets up a table outside; it's a small school so they know everyone. It would take like twenty minutes, and if you didn't want to do it, then they give you a paper to do it online. They have shuttles to and from the voting location." Instrumental to this design were dedicating time and resources to make sure everyone could get what they needed, and assuming that the challenges would not all be created equal.

The people doing the public-facing work on behalf of such organizations should take heed of citizens' organizational expectations. Our focus group participants discussed what it would take to motivate eligible or previously eligible voters to get the process moving, and especially the roles that could be played by educational institutions. In a series of comments, one participant said:

> I think you should start with before the actual age that they can vote. To me, in high schools, assemblies really stood out. If you get somebody energetic, somebody that is really passionate about voting, that knows the history, especially if you are talking to minorities, go in there. In the assembly for ninth grade, tenth grade, and make eleventh and twelfth grades together, then maybe they will be a little more serious. I don't know how you would break it up, but if it was somebody passionate; you could go to different schools, major schools, and start educating them. . . . Somebody that isn't [going] to go in there and sound boring and lame. Somebody that really knows history, really knows the battles that people face, like police brutality, whatever would make somebody feel safe. This person really wants to help the community. This person really wants to see a hospital built over here for kids that are dying, like in Chicago. They have a major area where they don't have a hospital, so by the time people who get shot make it to another area, they're dead. So that would be something major for me, if I lived in Chicago, when is that hospital getting built? Who wants to see the hospital get built? That would be who I'd vote for if I lived in Chicago.

In this example, the participant places significant emphasis on the messenger, their manner, and the connections with local issues. One focus group member further shared that the best way to encourage those who haven't registered to vote (or at least start the process toward this end) was to ask them why they haven't voted and if there are any issues that keep them from voting. At that point, a person could let them know what they would get out of voting or adapt their strategies accordingly.

Building Trust through Repetition

From citizens' stories, the importance of repetition within communities of influence stood out. Community organizations can build trust through repeated communication in helping people get what they need to vote. This strategy flies in the face of voter registration focused on one-shot efforts. It also accords with literature highlighting how assistance shouldn't be a single event that fails to see people through the whole process.[14] At the same time, having some sense that one's peers would be involved in these repetitions was, according to our participants' accounts, a sensible way forward. One person summed this up for us:

> I talked to my nephew this morning, and I grew up in the church, he said that he was incarcerated, and he really didn't believe in a higher power, but a guy came to him every day and talked to him. Man, come on, man. He said that he kept coming. If you have a person like that, a friend or whatever, look at this video, look at what they went through. To take that extra mile, to be an exception to the rule. If [only] we had more people like that. There is a lack of communication when it comes to their age groups. There is no one there, they don't have no one to give them information. Or to even tell them about the voting process. . . . have someone in their age group be the ones that invite them, tell them about the voting process, then they will listen to those people. But now they are like, "Oh, my God, here we go." Once you start talking to them it goes through one ear and out the other. But their age group, they might listen to them.

While these types of strategies may seem difficult for community organizations such as nonprofits to accomplish—given the non-voting-related work on their dockets and a lack of resources—they more than make up for these limitations with the repeated encounters they have with clients. Overall, as is clear from our participants' accounts, people and organizations that go that "extra mile" will make all the difference between voting and not voting.

We also heard about a different kind of experience having to do with reliability. One person talked at length about how they had contacted a local council member to help with problems in their apartment complex.

After hearing gunshots in the area, this person recounted, "I was wondering about my kids' safety. He listened to me for like an hour, then he was like there is somebody else I want you to talk to. Those people never got back to me." A year later, some children in the area ended up getting shot. With horrifying experiences like this in the background, it's critical to cultivate sustained, trustful relationships between local organizations, government entities, and citizens as part of a central strategy for voting. A one-time interaction with no follow-up can leave citizens with a sour taste that takes years to shake off.

Indeed, the strategy of providing reliable supports is well known to many organizations. One member of a voting rights organization told us how, in recent years, its strategies have had to change from simply getting everyone they can registered to vote to a broader message asking citizens to check that they are registered to vote on a regular basis, to make sure there are no impediments and that they are still eligible.

A participant who was in the US Army said that, because of not knowing if their votes were being counted, many personnel lost trust in the military postal system. For some in the military, there was no way of knowing if their votes had left their base or the country they were in. This comment raised the need for citizens to know that the actions they have taken count, so perhaps some kind of postvoting verification at all levels of voting—from marking that the correct ID was in place to postregistration postcards affirming that everything needed to cast a ballot has been received—could build further trust among constituents. In today's world, tracking mail or packages via the internet has become standard operating procedure. Presumably local government could adopt this approach for mail-in ballots, and some have already done so.[15]

Whom and what to trust online and off-line also stood out among participants' comments. The discussion manifested a sense of not knowing where to turn for good information, given all the misinformation and bias on the internet. One person noted:

> Anyone can make a website on the internet. You have to sift through information. It is a lot to go through and one wonders who can they trust? If I contact an organization that supports certain views, would I [be] getting biased information? [It's] questionable to get information that

isn't influenced by somebody else's opinion . . . on different social media and the news. Everything is tilted in some kind of way. You would have to have time and want to sift through all the information. I have my mom and I'll ask her but sometimes she doesn't even know.

A participant further shared, "In my day, I felt that the newspapers and news were more real than today. It's all jumbled up. You don't know what to believe anymore." This leaves room for organizations perceived as fair and neutral to break through individuals' distrust of the voting process.

That being said, a deficit emerged in these responses. While local "others" were most trusted, they were not necessarily always seen as the most knowledgeable about what citizens need to vote. One focus group member related: "I use my phone for anything. I usually go online and do the research. You could go ask someone, but they are going to tell you that they don't know." With both a desire to use their phones and go online to do the research (while knowing that it's hard to navigate through information that might or might not be credible) and to speak to friends, family, or others about voting issues (but with the expectation that they might not be the preferred source of knowledge, given the wealth of information and expertise available via the internet/mobile), it was difficult to know who or what to turn to for trusted information.

Advocacy for Streamlining Processes

Depending on their bandwidth, community organizations might take another approach. One focus group participant provided a solution that would require more attention to voting structures and processes:

No one has time to go to the DMV since it takes a lot of time for everyone in there trying to get something too. I'd rather it be "here is my last four numbers of my social, I'm here to vote." Make it easier for those at work or who have lost their license. Why can't they take your picture when you register to vote and then they automatically have your picture? A lot of places where you get an ID, they take your picture, your phone number or full name. They can pull it up and see your information. At the hospital, I didn't have identification on me, but they had already had me in the system and just requested personal information to access it. We can't use our expired IDs but why would they give it back to us? They also wouldn't take a damaged ID even though it could be scanned from the back.

This comment suggests that local organizations could advocate for the streamlining of such processes, within the constraints of whatever laws exist in each state. At the very least, acting as an advocate on behalf of eligible citizens can be integrated into this work.

One participant in a Mississippi focus group shared a novel idea for decision makers in this area too, stating, "Elderly, sixty-five and older, they shouldn't have, have to have an ID because, like I said, it's a hardship for somebody, especially in these areas, to get to Jackson and get a ID." Perhaps after a certain number of years and because the elderly may be slowing down or have difficulties with transportation that they may not have had earlier in life, or because they are far less likely than other people to even need an ID anymore, there could be a blanket policy solution for not needing an ID given conditions such as a regular record of voting or upon applying for and receiving Social Security benefit payments at a certain age.

One other policy recommendation involved the rights of people convicted of felonies. Participants in our Mississippi focus group wanted to talk about what makes someone convicted of a felony less eligible to vote than people who are, for example, ignorant. The group imagined how many more votes there would be if all people serving time for felonies (and presumably ex-felons) could vote. A facilitator shared that the state of Vermont allows prisoners to vote. The other participants found this surprising and wanted to know more. Another person stated that people who have served time for felonies, having been in the government system, know more about it than others and so should have this right restored. One person said that his father was a felon, and that he's working and paying taxes but not getting his right to vote restored in return. This issue has been at the center of many voter eligibility debates, with more permissive laws being set and then severely limited in states like Florida, where former felons in theory have the right to vote. But in practice that right is now conditioned on the payment of court fees, fines, and restitution.[16] Advocacy for streamlining voter identification processes must be considered in multiple contexts, with population categories affected differently in their capability or eligibility to cast a ballot. We'll return to these connections in the conclusion to this book.

Motivation for Getting Assistance

As a final point worth underscoring: people are generally motivated to get assistance with voter identification requirements, whether through help with making the process of procuring a driver's license easier or another procedure. One person in Mississippi mentioned that political science professors would be good to talk to about voting because they're well-informed. Another participant built on that remark by saying one professor per department should be identified on every college campus throughout Mississippi to be a "go-to" person on issues like these. A focus group member said, "We need more educators who will teach on this exact topic in every public school at least." One person mentioned that having information that is hard to obtain is itself a form of voter suppression.

The importance of being able to obtain assistance locally through educational and other institutions was seen as a high-stakes matter. One person said that the idea of not voting is basically voting—it's casting a vote for someone who could harm them, and that's enough motivation to vote. Community members also mentioned wanting to pay attention if there are particular ballot measures supported by candidates.

People are willing to receive assistance wherever it may be had to pursue one of their most basic rights. The focus groups showed that people want not just education but also help in the face of a continually shifting, confusing environment that creates challenges at each turn. In the next chapter, we turn to ways that the United States can get out of this awful mess of preregistration, registration, and voting requirements with voter ID. In the conclusion to the book, we'll connect the voter identification crisis to relevant issues at play nationally, with a focus on what might be done to make voting the easy, accessible, and inclusive act that it should be.

6

How to Fix the Problem

Implementing Realistic Solutions

The story that emerges from our study of voter ID requirements in the United States is that the players, organizations, and government offices involved with this issue present a confusing morass of deterrents for too many people to get what they need to vote. Indeed, among the many issues highlighted, helping citizens escape the paradoxical "circular traps" of needing an ID but not having the requisite documentation to obtain one puts civil society in a double bind. That citizens in one state have different, inequitable experiences in getting what they need to vote compared with citizens in other states makes little sense.

Following what we heard from people across the United States in this project, this chapter focuses on specific recommendations for policy-makers, community organizations, and others for helping eligible citizens get what they need to vote. Our suggestions are supported by the evidence analyzed in previous chapters.

While our focus is mostly on what local organizations can do to help citizens get what they need to vote, we first lay out a call for the federal government to create a uniform policy regarding voter documentation requirements to the greatest extent that the US Constitution permits. In their current form, voting processes belong almost exclusively to matters of state law and policy. This isn't to say that the states should not be involved with voting, but rather that without some national alignment and correction to the "states of confusion" status quo—precisely the kind of national, uniform expectation put into play by the former preclearance requirement of the Voting Rights Act—the variegated US voting system will continue to fail democracy.

Based on the findings from this project, we maintain that voter ID laws are deeply politicized and racialized. There are many politicians and other decision makers who promote these laws based on uninformed rationales about election integrity and the prevention of voter fraud that do not have a basis in fact. Some likely do not know about the unintended consequences of these laws on populations of the elderly, young people, marginalized communities, and others.[1] Regardless of these laws' intent, we join with others in calling for an abandonment of the existing, confusing, inequitable approaches to voter ID in favor of designs that can preserve the integrity of state and national elections without disenfranchising voters in the process.

In the absence of national, standardized (whether mandated or recommended) guidelines for making voting easier, or given that voter ID is here to stay, we present our conclusions from what we learned about how citizens can best be helped with voter documentation requirements. Overall, our solutions are offered in the hope that we can either eliminate, or greatly diminish, the widespread confusion, inequities, and resulting injustices at the core of voter ID challenges.

A National Call for Easy, Accessible, and Cost-Free Voter ID Uniformity

Using what we learned in this project, we want to make an unequivocal point for overcoming the challenges many citizens face with voter ID and related issues. All the challenges we've analyzed here point toward a conclusion that getting citizens what they need to vote is ultimately the government's function as one part of administering elections. The states themselves can make voting, voter registration, and any documentation required much easier, more accessible, and cost-free.

Yet Congress also has a role. A national, blanket policy, supported with federal financing for states' underfunded election administrations, could put changes into place and would do more to address voter ID problems than any other single solution. While the states have significant autonomy in the administration of elections, Congress has the power to govern a wide arena of election matters, particularly when violations of the Fourteenth Amendment are implicated, as we argue is the case with the strict ID voter requirements.[2] Ultimately, our voting system should not have to rely on private citizens, nonprofits, or other community organizations to close the gaps between citizens and systems. When state governments' voting systems are underfunded, understaffed, or otherwise deficient in so many ways (e.g., as we found in an Arizona county, only a few election personnel were responsible for millions of voters), it is no surprise that so many citizens do not vote, given the failures of bureaucracy. Boards of elections especially need sufficient federal funding and resources to carry out their work well.

Policymakers need to supplant, amend, or build on previous federal law, such as the Voting Rights Act, the Help America Vote Act (which, despite its name, did much to put the impediments we describe into effect), and the original vision of the National Voter Registration Act (whose main purpose was to make voter registration easier).[3] To date, state policymakers have created election administration laws that are not easy to implement and are applied in ways that run counter to espoused desires for election integrity. These laws, well-intentioned or not, have left extraordinarily wide room for disparities in their application, including human error, a variability of standards, and, most important, negative impacts on marginalized communities.

What would this uniform policy look like? First and foremost, it would replace current state documentation for registration or voting across the United States by providing a federal voter ID, as is provided in other countries that can act as models.[4] This ID would be easily obtained or preferably provided by the government to US citizens upon birth or naturalization, and a national database could be developed for this purpose. Credible platforms such as ERIC could be used as a foundation, using automated data matching of information from the states.[5] This proposal will no doubt be met with opposition,[6] but for voting purposes its value should outweigh grounds for disagreement. For individuals who lack standard documentation such as driver's licenses or birth certificates, they could provide their age,[7] and a signature or sworn statement that they are citizens of the United States[8]—with further supporting attestations from the hospital, city, and state in which they were born. We also argue that if a person has ever legitimately registered to vote in any state, and has cast votes, they should be retroactively maintained in the voting system without the need for documentation not previously required by law.[9] It is worse than unfair to people who have voted—many of them older people who have done so for their entire adult lives—to see their voting rights taken away by new laws that call for additional documentation.[10]

Elections generally need, very simply, verified name, age, citizenship, and residency.[11]

As much as is feasible, we urge the standardization of voter registration deadlines across states. It's time to make voting-related deadlines as uniform as possible.[12] Same-day registration should be available across all states, giving people as much time as possible to get the required type of ID. As the participants in our research pointed out, waiting seven to ten weeks for a passport to arrive alone demands that as much time as possible be allowed for voters to register while they juggle all of life's other needs.

Second, uniform policy and practice would do much to highlight what verification is needed. One of the ironies of current voting laws, especially those that prohibit inclusive documentation, is that they require forms of identification that in their formation had nothing to do with voting (e.g., Social Security number, driver's licenses). We don't think this bind can necessarily be solved quickly, but it should remain at the forefront of thinking through any proposed solutions. We suggest that people without traditional residency provide a verification in the form of swearing that one lives in a certain area or on a reservation, having attestations from neighbors, by providing latitudinal and longitudinal coordinates, through a wide net of inclusive IDs, or similar means.

The obvious entities to alert voters regarding alternatives for certain kinds of documentation are the local boards of elections. In the same way that voters are alerted about their polling places, dates of elections, and other voting-related matters, they should be made aware not just of the opportunity to vote but also how they can show their eligibility to vote. This doesn't need to be complicated. There are good reasons to require a specific location if a person requires voter ID, of course, such as voting for one's local congressperson by jurisdiction. Across the nation, our research participants amply described how documentation requirements necessarily disenfranchise the homeless, many Native American communities, and those who find themselves transient for any number of reasons. As in the case of Native American communities, one may not live at a traditional address or location, and so there should be a special accommodation for voters in various circumstances. Similarly, when five college students share an apartment but only one of their names is on the lease, it's regressive and disempowering to require a narrow proof of residency that could preclude four of these five people from voting. And, as mentioned to us during this project, when someone is new to the country, their address can change repeatedly in short periods of time. Residency proof must be of a kind that reflects instability in living circumstances to avoid the inequity created by particular types of documents needed to establish residence. Any state that prioritizes driver's licenses to vote over other forms of evidence of eligibility to vote creates another, similar imbalance. Neither being the one person whose name is on a lease nor having passed a driver's test should be a precondition to voting.

Additionally, the government should establish uniformity in ID requirements. When citizens are told that a student ID will work for voting in one state but not in another, the lists of what can and can't be used become selective and exclusionary. This should also mean making it easier to get truly "free" voter IDs. The government should verify that citizens have what's needed and provide a means of confirming that their vote was counted. In contrast to the ways states have implemented selective documentation for voter ID policies, some federal government practices could be a guide here. For example, for citizens to get passports, the US State Department's Bureau of Consular Affairs provides "secondary citizenship evidence" that, in the absence of a birth certificate, can be used to attest to one's status via baptismal records, early school records, doctor's records, and more.[13]

One great challenge is to get states to cooperate with each other in keeping voter information up to date. ERIC has been successful in getting more than thirty-one states and the District of Columbia to cooperate for this purpose.[14] Instead of leaving nonprofits and other organizations to fill these gaps, a national, nonpartisan agency that supports and administers this uniformity would help with implementation of more accessible IDs.

Third, at every level, elections offices need uniformity within their own bureaucracies. When calls to elections offices show that not everyone is on the same page, or that issues such as voter documentation requirements are in the hands of one person rather than known to others in the organization, policies and practices must be developed with uniform expertise and training in mind. The citizen experience proves most telling. When state and county offices present such variation on their websites, via phone numbers, and in general information sources that creates confusion or makes the experience of procuring an ID or other documentation harder than it needs to be, citizens can slip through the cracks.

Broadcasting positive evaluations of election integrity will remain critical for combating so many current attempts to undermine citizens' confidence in government and in election results. Requiring uniform policies and procedures helps achieve that goal. If a government office seems disorganized when citizens approach it for voting help, perceptions of integrity necessarily fall flat. With so many misconceptions, misinformation, and misleading sources abounding, the standardization of "go to" sources and "official" accounts makes even more sense. Add to those structural issues, such as any negative or unsatisfactory interactions with poll workers, and civic engagement becomes even harder. Having easy-to-understand, field-tested literature for diverse audiences and simple instructions for the illiterate (available via audiovisual and similar materials) to receive help should be foundational and standard.[15]

We also need to make voting easier for voters who have personal circumstances that make travel and waiting time prohibitive. Any one additional, tangible obstacle to understanding the process for voting should require government offices to take proportionally more accessible and uniform steps with voters. This includes situations such as runoff elections that require people to take further steps to vote, a compounding difficulty if one's ID expires between the primary day and the date of the runoff.

Last, as the most radical but, in our estimation, most needed change to make to the voting system given the previous points, we advise that automatic voter registration be implemented across all US states. As we learned from our participants, voter registration itself continues to constitute the biggest barrier to voting in the United States. If you can no longer pull off a voter registration drive outside of a supermarket because people understandably don't bring their birth certificates with them to get groceries, the process has gone horribly awry. Having demanding voter documentation requirements further creates misunderstandings about what's needed for voter registration and the different items that may be needed to vote at the polls. Some citizens' difficulties in understanding temporary IDs and whether those IDs can be renewed show the layers of technicalities that only cause more and more confusion about voting. These complications compound to create a much greater, tangled web than the sum of their individual, discouraging parts.

Like Illinois and other states already committed to this policy change,[16] with automatic voter registration voting can become an "opt-out" rather than "opt-in" process. A Brennan Center report titled "Automatic Voter Registration Works Everywhere It's Been Implemented" demonstrates the results of this approach.[17] Behavioral economists have promoted the virtues of public services that operate on the basis of "opt-out" choices for years,[18] so it is time to bring our voting system more fully into the present. Although this may be jarring to many people who believe that ID is essential, the fact remains that many citizens simply don't need ID for day-to-day activities (e.g., they cash checks; can no longer drive and don't need to, or live in a place with adequate public transportation options; have lost or had their driver's license suspended; don't need a passport for any reason; have real difficulties with lost or stolen documents), but still want to vote. These citizens prove the need for more inclusive voting policies. One way to accomplish this is to automatically enroll constituents in whatever system is needed or provide them with the ID that would be similarly, automatically available from birth, or the moment US citizenship is granted, and let individuals decide whether they want to vote.[19] No enrollment would be necessary. Eliminate the need for citizens to have to travel anywhere for ID or related documents: anything that is needed should be mailed directly to people and/or made available electronically.[20] As a starting point, the government can put a plan in place to provide automatic registration to babies born in the United States or upon a minimal showing of being born abroad or, for example, on a US base abroad, which is accepted as a basis for US citizenship.

Such approaches would eliminate, or at least substantially reduce, the need for provisional ballots that are so vexing and leave many voters wondering whether their votes will count.[21] Provisional ballots are one answer to preserving citizens' votes when there are problems at the polls about showing ID. As an aid to new systems for voting, all US high school juniors' and seniors' curricula could include key information that prepares them for voting. And, as mentioned earlier, anyone who, as of a certain date, voted in the past under whatever regime existed, should be able to vote forever after. The terrible stories of older people who have voted all their lives and who find that suddenly they are disenfranchised by newly enacted voter ID laws justify this approach. This includes many who lived at times when birth certificates were not necessarily routinely recorded. Most elderly people are already in government and electronic systems, so there should be ways to confirm identity that do not require additional documentation.[22]

In sum, the government should automatically issue ID, registrations, or anything else needed to make these processes easier. In a comment we heard repeatedly from citizens, in our digital age there's an expectation that electronic systems can simply pull people's pictures or be connected to the last four digits of a Social Security number.[23] Government institutions need to link with the state of current technology and mobile use for voting, or by surveying and applying emerging and supported digital methods that some participants raised in our research. Using distributed and decentralized security measures to maintain citizens' privacy and curb governmental overreach would make election integrity a hallmark of government processes, creating uniformity in both process and outcome, rather than constantly shifting the burden to citizens to get it right.

When someone dies, the speed with which interconnected electronic systems now update that information so that, for example, Social Security payments are cut off, credit cards are halted, and bank accounts are frozen is generally rapid and efficient.[24] When there's money at stake, there's a great deal of incentive to get a citizen's status right, in real time. The technologies for making these types of updates are already there. And for those concerned about election integrity, most advances in security measures are being made on these fronts.[25]

There are many parts of the US government that already have a good administrative record, such as Social Security and Medicare. Our voting systems, requiring the clunky implementation of voter documentation requirements, voter registration, and voting at the polls, stand opposite the efficiencies of these other systems. Voting could be made more like one-click online shopping than having to navigate through the host of sites, places, and people that is now the case.[26]

Toward Realistic Local Assistance in the Interim

Due to indifference, polarization, or other factors, policymakers may shy away from the sweeping changes with voter ID that we recommend, and such changes will in any event take time. But since the stakes for elections couldn't be higher, this is no time to give up on election reforms. Based on the insights of many participants throughout this project, and building on the burgeoning efforts already underway, there are many strategies that nonprofits, community organizations, and anyone else interested in advancing secure and inclusive elections can implement now to ensure that eligible people are enfranchised.

Working in Coalitions

No one individual or organization must go it alone. We heard repeatedly, across many sources, that building a coalition to help citizens with voter ID is a solid strategy. Working in coalitions increases credibility, expertise, and resource sharing for providers. A local nonprofit place of worship or a community group may be more influential for a particular citizen than any government or private entity, as these organizations have spent years building trust with their constituents. Local strategies can include support with technological needs, response to confusion about unusual address challenges, messaging alignment, and directing tasks and concentrating expertise efficiently.

The more nonpartisan signaling the coalition can do with the help of trusted individuals and institutions, the better. Coalitions need to represent a broad spectrum of people and institutions to help voters get what they need to vote and cast a vote. The following are among the many strategies coalitions can employ and have already had success with. We have put them in a roughly chronological order, following a general timeline for a voting cycle:

- Start early by working on ID issues in off election years so that these demands for documentation don't become rushed. Everyone who has a voice must press legislators, executives, and other decision makers to support general assistance for local boards of elections, which are notoriously underfunded and understaffed. Without monetary support from the federal government, there is little chance that we can improve the efficiency of our voting process.

- Organize to share resources based on expertise and reach (e.g., one centralized entity that might be available to help people with provisional ballot processes).
- Connect local organizations with pro bono immigration attorneys, attorneys who know about voters' rights, or knowledgeable people who can help with basic voting information.
- Identify experts who can be present at schools, naturalization ceremonies, and other similar venues or events.
- Build a shareable hierarchy of documentation to pursue (i.e., certain forms of ID may be easier to procure, so a visual hierarchy for each state would make it easier to understand what to get, when to get it, and what to do to ensure accessibility for eligible citizens).
- Translate the content and form of sometimes incomprehensible government documents into terms and languages that can be understood by as many people as possible.
- Identify who lacks ID through wide reach, prioritizing, for example, farmers markets, libraries, community and fitness centers, and soup kitchens, while partnering with neighborhood associations.
- Piggyback off other places or points in life for which people need ID (e.g., Medicare enrollment).[27]
- Use ERIC to match voter rolls and enhance voter confidence with accurate lists.
- Prepare promotional materials to get the word out about obtaining voter documentation to priority audiences, reaching potential voters through local television, radio, print, online news, or relevant media.
- Orchestrate transportation for individuals such as the elderly who cannot or do not want to drive anymore.
- Take people to the local Department of Motor Vehicles or any other agencies they need to visit to get registered.
- Follow up with eligible voters to make sure key deadlines are met.
- Use repetition through text message reminders (especially from peers, if available) for key deadlines.
- Use WhatsApp and Facebook or other apps or social media sites to foster a sense of community, snowballing outward to find people who may lack what's required to vote.

- Track who has received help in a central repository. Once an organization within a coalition has helped a particular individual or individuals, they can be listed in a shared electronic Excel document or Google doc, with details such as the day and time assisted, what documents were gathered, and any remaining steps to helping that citizen get what they need to register to vote or vote.

Local coalitions can also join with national entities that would support their work. Whether it's the ACLU, the United Way, the Andrew Goodman Foundation, or another national entity, coalitions can benefit from resources and connections with these institutions. At the same time, national organizations will always have a hard time being as contextually and culturally sensitive as a local coalition, so these larger entities also stand to benefit from the local learnings and applications coalitions can in turn provide.

Individual and Organizational Strategies

Short of working in a coalition, the efforts of one person or organization can also make a significant dent in helping citizens overcome the challenges of voter documentation requirements. For example, the one-to-one pairing strategy already in use by Spread the Vote has been successful. Volunteers dedicate their time to make sure that each eligible citizen who does not have the requisite documentation is taken through the complete process for what they need. Voter documentation requirements cannot be addressed in a vacuum. The core need is to identify or create launching points for helping citizens work through all levels of the voting process.

For this book's purposes, it is useful to summarize some further promising practices for organizations and people in this challenging and ever-changing field. These can be consulted to begin addressing the deficiencies in our voting systems. Again, these are arranged in a roughly chronological order, following a general timeline for a voting cycle:

- Begin connecting voters with organizations like Spread the Vote (spreadthevote.org) and VoteRiders (voteriders.org), which will get citizens on the right path. VoteRiders' "chatbot" program, through which citizens from any state can text or communicate via Facebook messenger or website chat (in English or Spanish), is a novel way for people to find out what is needed in any one state to vote.[28]

- Act as conduits for voter guides and informational resources that would be helpful to those served. Awareness does not equal behavior, though. Additional steps such as helping people considerably ahead of time with where to go for documentation, registration, or voting—or aiding with applications—increase the probability that needed actions will be taken.

- Act as a filter for getting people to websites such as turbovote.org, vote411.org, usvotefoundation.org, and votingrightslab.org. If local people affected by voter documentation requirements are known to use Facebook pages or groups, nonprofit staff can join and use these forums for sharing about assistance programs. Encourage peer-to-peer communication through social media and take advantage of interpersonal dynamics that are influential in decision-making about voting.

- Use place-based strategies, going to where people are at, thinking about where citizens are in their everyday lives to increase the likelihood that they will follow through. Having monthly birth certificate clinics (or other documentation clinics) at a nonprofit or community institution can build a systematic expectation that challenges can be tackled.

- Apply personal, localized, and motivating strategies. Put out information that's valuable to people to build trust. For those who have lost faith in the government and elections, communicating about a shared past and the responsibilities owed (e.g., paying forward the hard-won battles for voting rights by one's ancestors or community) can make a big difference. Since many people don't understand how much their vote matters, personal messages that connect public issues and the services that people receive are important. For others, emphasizing the closeness of many elections may be the right message at the right time to get them on the path to action.

- Highlight the successful stories of peers who have overcome a challenge—a time-tested, research-backed strategy.[29] Local organizations have the advantage of identifying those most influential in the lives of their priority audiences. Practitioner literature refers to the need to think seriously about "influential others" in creating strategies that increase the likelihood that behaviors will happen.[30] The example from our research of immigrants' children driving them around and playing such a large role in their parents' lives comes to mind, as does the influence of family and friends in general.

- Make sure to address falsehoods, such as a belief that registering to vote means that one will get called for jury duty.
- Act as advocates with eligible voters' employers. (A phone call to let an employer know that you're helping the employee and that they'll need time off work to make this happen could be helpful.)
- Build community service requirements for juniors and seniors in high schools. Educational institutions have a natural audience for civic-minded action. High school juniors and seniors could be trained on all the steps in the voting process and use their knowledge to help others connect in a meaningful way and become invested in government and local issues.
- Have one voting advocate, such as the head of student life, a participant in student government, or an instructor on every university campus who knows the system, to help build a sustained civic structure in higher education too. This can be mirrored for high school students. Civic education needs to be emphasized to make sure those who are coming of age to vote understand its importance and how it is done.

Even in the absence of a coalition, nonprofits, community organizations, local officials and representatives, and individuals can advocate for many of the ideas described here, especially in streamlining processes. Some of the best work we observed linked nonprofits to county or city election-related offices. Local advocates can highlight the stories and experiences of their clients to deal with voter ID and related issues. They can address the burdens on those living with disabilities or convey what happens when someone comes up against the barriers of time, cost, and transportation issues in procuring documentation to register to vote.

Voting Plus

In researching these local strategies and tactics, one theme we heard across this project is worth underscoring. If there's one action that individuals and government or nonprofit staff should engage in, it's what we call "voting plus." This means doing what's needed not only to make sure you are personally registered but to help at least one other person who may have a harder time registering to vote and ultimately voting, in contextually and culturally sensitive ways. It may be people in community groups proximate to an organization, or even one's neighbor, for instance. The local Rotary Club, YMCA, places of worship, or other organizations may have members who could use help themselves or know others in their groups who would benefit from some one-to-one attention in this area.

Going the extra mile and calling people twice with reminders about registration deadlines or the need to gather documentation, if they have the bandwidth, can make a difference. Because many citizens remain fatalistic about voting, initiatives must go beyond educational efforts that fail to speak to the true benefits and barriers people have to getting started. Nonprofits and community organizations can connect people with elections offices to help those with disabilities and others who would benefit from mobile offices coming to them. Additional help for people who have moved even within one state can be part of this effort. See appendix D for further election-related resources for nonprofits and community organizations, many of which have been successful, as highlighted in this project.

Depending on the languages spoken in an area and the communities involved, even seemingly neutral, innocuous-sounding terms such as "documentation" may come loaded with unintended associations for many eligible voters. For some immigrants the term can evoke distress, so one-to-one attention can focus on translation or assistance with such terms. Sensitivity about how language is perceived is needed in every aspect of this work, particularly because rhetoric about voter ID comes wrapped in legalese. And that is also how it functions to disenfranchise: it doesn't look or sound like politicized and racialized machinations. It's a discourse of procedure and election technicalities.[31] No language is value-free, as all terminologies ask us to look to selected aspects of the world to the exclusion of other ways of looking.[32] It's important for implementing realistic local strategies to take control of the language best suited to the people and groups being assisted. In these hyperpartisan times, language must be used to support the legitimacy of nonprofits and other community organizations by conveying what voter ID does or does not do to prevent deceit, on the one hand, and to enable voting, on the other.

Most people in the United States believe that election integrity is important, and they should not be ignored. Attempts to build connections with governmental stakeholders should emphasize how this work is about creating legitimate, fair elections, while registering to vote and voting can be patriotic commitments.[33]

Participants in this research project showed us that solutions can be maximally engaging. In a nation where civic education and engagement are sorely lacking, we hope that the approaches described in this book can contribute to the future of voting in the United States. Let's finally turn to a bigger picture for voting, integrating these concerns with other high-stakes issues that are playing out nationally, with an eye toward how roadblocks between citizens and voting can be dismantled.

Conclusion

Closing the Gap between Citizens and Voting

The right to vote is the most fundamental right in our democratic system of government because its effective exercise is preservative of all others.
—US Congress, Committee on the Judiciary[1]

The hard truth of the US election system is that it is failing its citizens. Different from explicit past attempts to diminish voting, the recent increase in states' demands for obtaining voter documentation is remarkable for its subtler form. Mundane lists and bureaucratic paperwork don't present themselves to voters as evil schemes. Yet, in their design, new voter ID laws create haphazard and byzantine expectations for some voters that clearly serve to suppress votes.

By far the greatest concern is with recent changes in some state election laws, with more in the pipeline, to reconstruct local processes for voting and counting votes that have, until now, been expected to be overseen and performed by boards of elections, state employees, and secretary of state offices. Several state legislatures have shifted accountability so that the legislatures themselves will have the power to oversee and even overturn election results with which they disagree. This has been happening in Republican states where, because of gerrymandering, most representatives are Republican, even though the voting population is majority Democratic.[2]

We must keep putting these disturbing developments out in the open. Nowhere did policymakers' desires to quash votes surface more overtly than when the COVID-19 pandemic swept across the planet, rupturing our social and economic systems in unimagined ways. Our calls for the US government to relax or amend voter documentation requirements and voter registration have been heightened by election difficulties during a worldwide crisis. With numerous offices closed, in many cases the possibility for people to get documentation was made impossible. Polling locations shut down (poll workers tend to be sixty years of age, on average, and feared catching the virus, while many voters were afraid of going to the polls). Already onerous hours of waiting in line at the polls became longer (mostly affecting minority populations), machines broke down, and explicit forms of suppressing the vote went public, such as Oklahoma's attempt to retain a requirement that absentee ballots be notarized during a global health crisis.[3]

Some states had to turn away from in-person polling sites and toward more mail-in voting to make it easier for people to vote. Research confirms that mail-in voting has neutral partisan effects and increases voter turnout.[4] Yet false assertions, uneven policies, and a lack of will to implement mail-in voting during the pandemic showed that the differences in voting practices from state to state are a major factor that pushes people out of the electoral process just because they have moved. Why should citizens face a different election expectation for mail-in from one state to another?[5] At the same time, recent hopeful turns toward mail-in voting in places like Kentucky, largely due to bipartisan agreement about the pandemic emergency, show that a collective determination to make the system work for as many people as possible is not beyond politicians' grasp.[6]

Better choices must be made. While observing the grave, antidemocratic deficiencies in the current voting landscape while working on this project, we also observed some reasons for optimism. Many people have clearly had enough with the current system and want to make a difference. Based on the outstanding work of individuals and institutions in the voting arena, we have proposed a road map for making more citizens' voices count.

In this conclusion, we zoom outward by connecting this book's main themes with looming policy initiatives such as REAL ID, concerns about absentee voting, attention to how other countries deal with voter ID and elections, and other links between this project and emerging work, all focusing on ways to confront the United States' voting crisis. Positioning new voter ID laws with redistricting, reducing and altering census practices, and other means of limiting the power of targeted populations' votes, we note Spencer Overton's timely thesis that, contrary to politicians' pronouncements about voters' choices in a democracy, what we have is a system in which incumbent elected representatives, political party officials, large donors, lobbyists, and elites who influence those representatives get to choose their voters.[7] This leads us to examine what is possibly the most wide-ranging change: the recent introduction of a federal REAL ID, which will likely place extraordinary roadblocks in front of millions of people.

What about REAL ID?

Many concerns in this book implicate controversies about REAL ID. To reiterate our policy recommendation, we believe that a uniform federal voter ID that is cost-free, easily or automatically accessed, and meets many of the criteria described in the previous chapter could eliminate the states of confusion eligible voters experience across the United States with voter ID laws. Unfortunately, in the guises it has taken, REAL ID does not meet these ideals and instead promotes the types of disparate impacts we have detailed throughout this book. There are many aspects of REAL ID beyond this book's scope, but some quick background is necessary to bring these challenges into view.

The REAL ID Act was passed by Congress in 2005, based on "the 9/11 Commission's recommendation that the Federal Government 'set standards for the issuance of sources of identification, such as driver's licenses' with minimal standards prohibiting federal agencies from accepting non-conforming driver's licenses or other ID."[8] For most people, these standards will most commonly apply for boarding commercial aircraft. Effective May 2023, no one will be permitted to move beyond airport security gates in the United States without a form of REAL ID or a passport to show US citizenship. Non–U.S. citizens will be able to go through security only if they have documentation such as a foreign passport or other evidence of lawful presence within the United States (such as a permanent resident card). According to the US Department of Homeland Security, "The purpose of REAL ID is to make our identity documents more consistent and secure."[9] For our purposes, what's most relevant is that REAL ID was never developed or intended to be a form of ID for voting. And, as often happens, trying to transform a process that has one purpose to serve another is a tricky proposition.

When it comes to the practice of procuring a REAL ID and its implementation across all US states, many of the same problems identified in this book might prevent citizens from getting, or even applying to get, a REAL ID. For one, citizens are instructed, "Visit your state's driver's licensing agency website to find out exactly what documentation is required to obtain a REAL ID."[10] The same difficulties caused by current requirements for Voter ID exist for REAL ID.[11]

With implementation on track, REAL ID stands to exacerbate rather than solve the states of confusion already at play throughout the United States. REAL ID brings into view the government's trade-offs in purportedly balancing "national security, the public outcry for protection of civil liberties, and the installation of technological safeguards to ensure data integrity and security."[12] But we should recognize that these types of initiatives must also accord with the United States' changing demographics. REAL ID comes at a time when White politicians have attempted to create new systems that exclude non-White people from the voter rolls and many other benefits. These include trying to abolish or limit the Deferred Action for Childhood Arrivals (DACA) citizenship status that has been subject to ongoing court challenges.[13]

If REAL ID created equitable, cost-free, and inclusive uniformity that wasn't tied to the selectiveness of driver's licenses or state ID cards, the expense of passports, or the added layers of complexity documentation requirements already present—if it simply made citizens' lives easier—we'd be on a path to the types of solutions outlined in this book. As is, however, REAL ID looks to pile another load onto many eligible voters.

Absentee Voting in a COVID-19 Era

No discussion of closing the gaps between citizens and voting would be complete without a further acknowledgment of how the COVID-19 pandemic posed vexing dilemmas for voters. These challenges bring into view absentee voting solutions that connect with our recommendations. The infrastructures in place (or that were removed) to respond to the virus run parallel to the obstacles created by the strict requirements of voter ID laws. Voters were faced with the danger of going to the polls during a pandemic, and thus likely exposing themselves to a deadly virus and to long lines due to the need for social distancing. Even more than that, polling places were not as open or available as in the past, among hosts of other problems, including risks for poll watchers and other election administration employees. The failure in many jurisdictions to relax requirements for the submission of absentee ballots in a coronavirus world made voting especially difficult.

A pandemic election further opened the door to politicized changes in the rules governing and implementation of voting processes. Some failures were exacerbated by technical, bureaucratic, and resource gaps. Even open polling places were inadequately prepared and understaffed. We observed the failure of voting machines, of providing an adequate number of machines, and of offering sufficient provisional ballots in cases of malfunctioning (or nonexistent) voting machines. The Vote4DC Mobile App was one example. Voters either could not use the app on their phones, complete their ballot request, or follow its status, adding to already long lines and to the discouragement voters would observe in conditions unfavorable to voting.[14]

One might have expected that absentee voting would be made immediately available as an alternative to in-person voting during this time. Even during the height of the pandemic, at its onetime epicenter (New York City), prospective voters, like those in many states, had to mail in an application requesting a mail-in ballot.[15] The response by the states to making absentee voting a practical option was mixed, at best. The situation was sufficiently dire that some five hundred election law practitioners and professionals, as well as public health and political science experts, signed an open letter calling on Congress and the states to take steps to ensure a safe and secure election during unprecedented times.[16]

All states have provisions for voting by mail, particularly for absentee voting.[17] A number of states, including Colorado, Hawaii, Oregon, Washington, and Utah, have successfully provided for statewide mail-in ballots for many years, without any meaningful voter fraud.[18] Twenty-eight states and the District of Columbia have "no excuse necessary" requirements for voters to vote absentee, while seventeen states allow for voters to get absentee ballots for specific reasons, such as an illness or being out of state.[19] Yet during a time of crisis, and now being used to making their own policies for voting absent federal oversight, the states scrambled (some more energetically than others) to give voters who feared coming to the polls the option to vote by mail.[20]

Some policymakers declined to make any special efforts, or did so only under immense public pressure.[21] Unfortunately, egregious and explicit attempts to accomplish voter suppression by making absentee voting even more difficult were in full force.[22] While some new requirements were blocked by the courts, new ones can easily come in their place.[23] The Supreme Court offered no relief, effectively blocking expanded voting by a 5–4 decision running along conservative/liberal lines.[24] Ironically, demonizing the vote-by-mail process could actually end up harming its opponents in the long run.[25]

We observed inexcusable breakdowns in primary races when, for example, Georgia voters waited hours in line to vote at a reduced number of polling places, in the face of failures of new voting equipment that left some polling places without any working voting machines, and a lack of provisional voting ballots available for citizens when machines were not available or not working.[26] Some voting machines never made it to the polling places at all. Thousands of voters gave up and went home. Turnout nonetheless tripled compared with that for the 2016 election: 960,000 people cast a vote compared with 310,000 in 2016—a testament to voters' commitment in a crucial election period to overcome life-threatening conditions to exercise their most basic right.[27]

Kentucky approved mail-in ballots for all its voters in 2020, but those ballots had to be formally requested, and the state made no provision for alerting voters to this option. Moreover, despite a bipartisan push to increase the number of voting locations to curtail the virus's spread, the state limited the locations to one per county, resulting in lengthy waits in long lines with little social distancing, adding to an increase in the risk of being exposed to COVID-19.[28] In a troubling change, a number of jurisdictions delayed their primary elections.[29] Delaying an election is a matter of significant public policy—even the Civil War did not stop the presidential elections from taking place, and President Lincoln took office as scheduled.[30]

Despite these conditions, states' efforts to continue enacting stricter voter identification laws show no signs of abating: "As a consequence of this new skepticism about the security of absentee ballots, several Republican-controlled legislatures have increased identification requirements for mail ballots—in many cases adding them when they had previously been nonexistent. Examples of laws passed early in 2021 were those enacted in Georgia (SB 202), Florida (SB 90), and Montana (SB 169)."[31] There are ways to make voting easier, but at every juncture the dizzying array of different state-by-state requirements has turned the United States into a country where the burden is placed on eligible voters to jump over unnecessary hurdles.

We highlight these developments because they tie so strongly to this book's argument in favor of uniform law and practice with respect to voting. Absentee ballot arrangements vary widely from state to state, in the same way that voter ID laws vary from state to state, and this lack of uniformity exacerbates the inability of election officials, even if they are so motivated, to implement absentee ballot practices and other measures in a way that will alleviate burdens on voters. Laws in effect in some states with statewide absentee ballot experience provide models for other states, and best practices have been identified that can support the changes necessary for successful implementation.[32] Other models for improving US elections can also be found through a comparative perspective.

Voter ID in Other Countries

No final thoughts on voter ID would be complete without some attention to what happens in other countries. Two key questions must be asked: What improvements might the United States adopt considering other democratic countries' successes in executing the function of voting without the difficulties we experience? And why does the United States make it so much harder than other democratic countries to vote with an ID? It is rare to hear that other countries with largely democratic traditions have voting crises revolving around registration and voter ID.

The state-based voting system in the United States in effect creates not just fifty different systems but more than three thousand systems, as voting is largely implemented by the states, which in turn give counties the primary role in running elections.[33] In the United States, each county may design its own ballots, use its own machinery, have different counting and audit systems, and handle almost everything about voting as a local matter. The chaos this creates (such as in Florida 2000, *Bush v. Gore*),[34] and what it means for establishing uniform systems throughout the three thousand–plus counties or even the fifty states in the United

States have been at the core of our findings about new voter ID laws. Nothing, however, prevents the states from voluntarily creating uniform systems, and it is possible that the federal government could require or at least encourage uniformity, for example, by funding the resources to accomplish this.

With that backdrop, one answer to the question of why other democratic nations have an easier time with running elections is that they tend to have a national registry or national ID cards that can be used for many purposes, including voting.[35] In Finland, for instance, a newborn is registered with the government and given an identity code, so that registration is accomplished for later in life, with adequate documentation to vote.[36]

In some countries, such as Japan, the government sends each voter a ticket to show when they should vote. No additional ID is required. But if the voter does not have a postcard with them, they can use a national ID card or a driver's license.[37] In some nations that require ID to vote, citizens may bring different kinds of documentation to vote. In Canada, there are dozens of acceptable types of ID, and in the absence of any ID, another person assigned to the same polling place can "vouch" for one other voter who does not.[38] In light of these examples, what reason is there for US states to not allow various, inclusive forms of ID to qualify to vote, except for the baseless claim that there is rampant voter fraud afoot in US elections—a claim that clearly masks an intention to limit the voting population. As in other countries, implementing voting rights should be directed at including eligible voters, not preventing their votes.

Other governments bear the responsibility for keeping registration up-to-date and encouraging citizens to vote. In addition to creating a single, nearly automatic registration process, they conduct censuses and keep registration current by requiring residents to update addresses when they move.[39] Some also cross-check lists with various government services agencies to keep registration lists accurate. In the latter case, some nations send a notice to their voters when the agencies update an address based on government information. Great Britain, among other international jurisdictions, has relied on canvassing and enumerations to ensure that voter rolls are correct. Some even have government staff go from door to door for this purpose.[40]

Voting in many other countries takes the form of "opt-out" rather than the maze of "opt-in" requirements across many US states. We note an extensive report by Harvard University's Kennedy School of Government recommending the need for the United States to adopt "universal civic duty voting" that requires participation in elections, on a par with the civic obligation of jury duty.[41] Although controversial and likely subject to objections on the basis of constitutionality, we support in principle attempts to create a sense of civic responsibility that would both encourage voting and serve the purposes of our primary recommendation for national uniformity with voter ID, by putting responsibility on the government to make voting as easy as possible for everyone.

We recognize that factors vary from jurisdiction to jurisdiction, some distinctive to the United States as compared with other countries, that can affect turnout and are related to controversies regarding voting. For example, traditions in a given foreign jurisdiction, the homogeneity of a population, the form of government, the strength of political parties, and laws exist that are different from those of the United States. These differences would impede or even prevent change here. Yet a general point is hard to miss: that so many other countries have inclusive and effective ways of implementing voter ID and running elections confirms what is and can be possible.

Other Ways Forward

What else can be done? First, while zooming in on the challenges of voter documentation requirements, it's equally important to zoom out on the connected storm of voting problems that call for systemic changes, national solutions, and vigorous litigation. We cannot lose sight of the web of influences creating forms of voter suppression at every level. These issues also follow our states of confusion theme.

One critical, related issue is improper purges. Indeed, "between 2014 and 2016, states removed 16 million voters from the rolls," with states such as Texas erasing approximately 363,000 more voters from the rolls since the federal preclearance requirement of the Voting Rights Act was eliminated—and Georgia purging twice the number of voters between 2012 and 2016 as between the four years prior, according to one report.[42] Like voter documentation requirements, "no uniform approach to voter purges exists."[43] And there is the advance of voter deception through online, social media, and mobile architectures that are unraveling basic norms for truth-telling, fact-checking, and the credibility of political claims of all types. We're now in a time when it isn't just citizens but also public officials who routinely misinform, lie, and gaslight the public, with few mechanisms for accountability.[44]

Felon disenfranchisement further influences elections. As another way in which states of confusion play out, if you were an ex-felon in one state who is fully reenfranchised, but move to a different state for the purposes of, say, employment, you may find yourself disenfranchised again under that new state's laws. At issue are the voting rights of mostly minority populations who as a group could overturn many of the state-level and national results we've seen in the past two decades. As two contrasting examples, in Rhode Island and Florida efforts have been made to restore voting rights to ex-felons. In both cases, the expansion of voting rights was accomplished by referendum. In Rhode Island, the proposal to restore voting rights for felons on probation and parole was on the ballot and won by more than 51 percent.[45] In Florida, a ballot initiative was adopted to restore ex-felons' voting rights, with some qualifications, and subject to administrative processes to vet applications from prospective voters. Later, however, the Florida legislature adopted a requirement that ex-felons pay outstanding fines, fees, and restitution before they could have their voting rights restored. This has effectively prevented reenfranchisement for many individuals.

Despite the fact that the citizens of Florida in 2018 voted to reenfranchise 1.4 million of the state's citizens (about 10 percent of its population) with felony convictions via a constitutional amendment that passed with 65 percent of the vote ("the largest expansion of voting rights in a half-century"), "the legislature has contravened the will of the people, once again disenfranchising hundreds of thousands of returning citizens through a bill that imposes an antiquated poll tax on them in the form of court fees."[46] The fees requirement found its way through the courts.[47] The US Supreme Court declined to lift a lower court order invalidating much of the payment requirement, putting the votes of ex-felons in jeopardy.[48] Until more federal or national progress can turn these forms of suppression on their head, millions of eligible voters will continue to be knocked off the voter rolls in different states. A grand contradiction running parallel to our voter ID themes must be surfaced by individuals and organizations: Why does an ex-felon in one state get to vote in the national election while another in a different state does not, as a separate and decidedly unequal status? And can any national election ever call itself "national" under these conditions? We think not.

Second, although it's beyond the scope of our topic, we find Heather Gerken's idea persuasive: that states should adopt a "democracy index" that would give them incentives to bring about election reforms and make voting as easy and accessible as possible.[49] Efforts to improve citizens' experiences with voter ID could be nested within this larger initiative, motivating states to address these challenges in pursuit of improving their elections and avoiding poor performance marks when compared with other states. Ideally, the federal government could provide funding for improvements in voting processes or could withhold funding until certain benchmarks that enhance improvements in a state's voting processes are in place. Similarly, to hold policymakers accountable, in a compelling overview of one way to frame changes to policy and decision makers, Joshua Geltzer says that the crisis of voter identification requirements and other policies that are making it difficult to vote need to be placed in constitutional terms:

> The U.S. Constitution is famously short—a mere 7,591 words, including its 27 amendments. That makes it all the more remarkable that 110 of those words have been, in effect, lost to the ages. These forgotten words form Section 2 of the 14th Amendment, which was designed to guard against the infringement of voting rights. The lost provision is simple: States that deny their citizens the right to vote will have reduced representation in the House of Representatives. . . . The Amendment's framers worried, in particular, that recalcitrant states would respond to the formal expansion of the vote by devising new ways to abridge that vote. Section 2's second sentence would be a powerful threat, saying that, should a state dare to try that, it would have to reduce its number of representatives in the House proportional to the vote infringement carried out by that state. . . . [This] may well be the Constitution's most important lost provision.[50]

There has never been a more important time to refer to this. One strategy could be to mandate by law that the Census Bureau find out who has been subject to voter infringement via surveys. According to Geltzer, "This would be the first word, *not* the last word: Self-reporting surely would demand follow-up investigation rather than serving, on its own, as the basis for calculating the proportion of a state's citizens—now to include all of its voting-eligible citizens—whose right to vote has been infringed." As a realistic way forward, Geltzer points out that this kind of research is something the Census Bureau already handles all the time.[51]

Third, the use of voter impact statements could at least be reviewed at the state level, whereby offices of secretaries of state or attorneys general would be required to examine any legislation potentially impairing citizens' right to vote. Such statements would let people know when voting changes are made and allow for comment periods—putting the burden on policymakers rather than on citizens to prove impact.[52] Although this is a reduced version of the former federal preclearance requirements of the Voting Rights Act, and still would leave the "states of confusion" problem in play, it would establish some minimal level of oversight within states, putting a brake on the hodgepodge, "anything goes" voting systems now in place.[53]

Last, we stand with the Brennan Center's prescriptions for allowing registration through Election Day, increasing the number of voting locations, expanding early voting, relaxing deadlines for mail-in ballots to be requested and returned, and making mail-in voting available and free to all as an alternative to in-person voting. As the center advises, expanding options for requesting, receiving, and returning mail ballots, requesting that mail ballots should be available not only via mail, but also by phone and via the internet, and returning ballots at, for example, specially designed drop-off boxes with security or verification cameras would help. Improvements in processing and counting mail ballots should further be made by "election canvassing and certification deadlines [that] should be extended to account for delays in receiving and processing mail-in ballots, and ballot processing times should be adjusted."[54] Everyone should also receive paid time off to vote, since election days are not holidays, nor are people compensated for the sometimes many hours they must stand in line to practice their most basic societal right.[55] Other reforms outside this book's scope are central to accomplishing progress, such as stronger ethics rules and campaign finance reform to rein in the huge sums of contributions and independent expenditures in US campaigns, creating more confidence in candidates and elected officials and an even playing field for those vying for public office. These are challenging arenas to address but must be included in any ultimate success for democratic elections.

Even structural solutions cannot fully deal with human deficiencies. The problem of the "the fox guarding the henhouse" is a mighty one,[56] whereby politicians and partisan officials make election rules that suit their interests. The unwillingness of the players to operate in good faith, according to established norms that promote democracy, through the lines of gerrymandering, a takeover by the state legislatures of their elections process on a partisan basis to preserve single-party power, and more, raises questions about the very possibility of shared ground for a fair and integrity-driven election system. If, for example, legislators are willing to pass laws that allow a party-ruled legislature to change the outcome of an election, and we have a Supreme Court willing to live with that, the very possibility of meaningful democracy may be damaged beyond recognition. This is precisely why every type of voter suppression needs to be tackled before each retrogressive step creates "death by a thousand cuts."[57] In whatever form they take, the more that any ideas and policies would reduce voter documentation requirements to the very minimum needed, the more citizens will be on the path to an operating democracy that has meaningful elections.

Toward an Inclusive, Democratic Voting System

Having taken a deep and broad assessment of voter ID problems in the United States, we believe the experiences and stories of what it's like to face these challenges at the level of everyday life are the most telling. At present, due to voter documentation requirements and other forms of suppression, many elections in the United States simply do not matter. Everyone likes to say that they care about the right to vote. Yet, assuming the most generous laws and regulations and templates for best practices, the actual effect of administrative acts, such as requiring strict voter IDs or limiting absentee balloting—even if well-intentioned, which often they are not—is to undermine the administrative implementation of processes that should be straightforward.

Unlike the polarizing messages of government representatives, people in the US citizen population have a bipartisan supermajority in agreement about many basic subjects relating to health care, immigration, and other critical issues.[58] But we have an election infrastructure that elects officials who too often work counter to this reality.

We urge readers of this book to rid this nation of disenfranchising documentation requirements. When access to voting is difficult or even insurmountable for large numbers of people, those responsible must be held accountable. This can start by simply finding out what documentation requirements are in effect in your town, your county, and your state, especially as they affect marginalized and disadvantaged communities.

This project uncovered the extent and magnitude of problems related to voter documentation requirements across more states than we had expected. The number of different requirements and expectations in various states, the limitations on the reach and funding of organizations trying to tackle this issue across states, and the disconnects between citizens, community organizations, and institutions such as election offices (including information deficits and administrative failures) lead us to believe that a national organizing government agency, or at least one that sustainably funds local efforts that include elements recommended in this book, is sorely needed, especially since there are so many places with a cash-strapped board of elections.

In a speech to the nation on protecting the right to vote, President Joseph Biden asserted, "This isn't about Democrats and Republicans; it's literally about who we are as Americans. It's that basic. It's about the kind of country we want today, the kind of country we want for our children and grandchildren tomorrow."[59] The importance of voting is directly related to every other policy and practice of national and local governments. For citizens to get what they really need or want from government—whatever that might be—their first step should be in the arena of elections. We are reminded of the late US representative and civil rights hero John Lewis's statement: "Freedom is not a state; it is an act."[60] Indeed, freedom cannot be found in the states of confusion brought on by new voter ID laws. Instead, starting now, we must all commit to actions that will build a more fair, inclusive, and democratic future for every participant in the political life of this country.

ACKNOWLEDGMENTS

Our gratitude first goes to Viktoriia Chubirka, who, as our primary research assistant on this project, exhibited an unfailing commitment, stellar organizational skills, and an outstanding ability to talk to people across the United States in the pursuit of making votes count. Keeping several professors and an entire team on task, you are a superstar, through and through. Our thanks also go to the rest of our research team and graduate assistants, who helped us with gathering a broad range of viewpoints and information on voter documentation requirements, including Gaurav Bawa, Daniel Randall, Erika Smithson, Korenet Brown, Michal Borusiewicz, Shana Kieran-Kaufman, and Andrew Tomassi. We are indebted for the advice and assistance of Nedra Kline Weinreich and Caitlin Donnelly. We are also grateful for the institutional support provided by David Shanton, James Krauskopf, Hector Cordero-Guzman, Cristina Balboa, and the Center for Nonprofit Strategy and Management at the Marxe School of Public and International Affairs. Special thanks to Irv Yoskowitz for bringing the crisis of voter identification to our attention and supporting research that served as the basis for this project. Finally, we would like to take note of the courage, tenacity, and importance of the late John Lewis to the fight for voting rights in the United States. He is one of our heroes, and Sonia was honored to call him a friend.

APPENDIX A

Strict Voter ID States Documentation Requirements

TABLE A.1. Voter Documentation Requirements

State	Acceptable Forms of ID	Voters without ID
Arizona	- Valid Arizona driver's license - Valid Arizona non-driver identification - Tribal enrollment card or other form of tribal identification - Valid US federal, state, or local government-issued identification - Utility bill dated within 90 days of the election - Bank or credit union statement dated within 90 days of the election - Valid Arizona vehicle registration - Indian census card - Property tax statement - Vehicle insurance card - Recorder's certificate	An elector who does not provide the required identification shall receive a provisional ballot. Provisional ballots are counted only if the elector provides identification to the county recorder by 5:00 p.m. on the fifth business day after a general election that includes an election for federal office, or by 5:00 p.m. on the third business day after any other election.
Georgia	- Georgia driver's license, even if expired - ID card issued by the state of Georgia or the federal government - Free voter ID card issued by the state or county - US passport - Valid employee ID card containing a photograph from any branch, department, agency, or entity of the US government, Georgia, or any county, municipality, board, authority, or other entity of this state - Valid US military identification card - Valid tribal photo ID	A voter without one of the acceptable forms of photo identification can vote on a provisional ballot. He or she will have up to three days after the election to present appropriate photo identification at the county registrar's office in order for the provisional ballot to be counted.
Indiana	Specific forms of ID are not listed in statute. ID must be issued by the state of Indiana or the US government and must show the following: - Name of individual to whom it was issued, which must conform to the individual's registration record - Photo of the person to whom it was issued - Expiration date (if it is expired, it must have an expiration date after the most recent general election; military IDs are exempted from the requirement that ID bear an expiration date) - Must be issued by the United States or the state of Indiana	Voters who are unable or decline to produce proof of identification may vote a provisional ballot. The ballot is counted only if (1) the voter returns to the election board by noon on the Monday after the election and: (A) produces proof of identification; or (B) executes an affidavit stating that the voter cannot obtain proof of identification, because the voter: (i) is indigent; or (ii) has a religious objection to being photographed; and (2) the voter has not been challenged or required to vote a provisional ballot for any other reason.

TABLE A.1. (*Cont.*)

Kansas	The following forms of identification are valid if they contain the name and photograph of the voter and have not expired. Expired documents are valid if the bearer is aged 65 or older. - Driver's license issued by Kansas or another state - State identification card - Government-issued concealed carry handgun or weapon license - US passport - Employee badge or identification document issued by a government office or agency - Military ID - Student ID issued by an accredited postsecondary institution in Kansas - Government-issued public assistance ID card	A voter who is unable or refuses to provide current and valid identification may vote a provisional ballot. To have his or her ballot counted, the voter must provide a valid form of identification to the county election officer in person or provide a copy by mail or electronic means before the meeting of the county board of canvassers.
North Dakota	Identification must provide: - Legal name; - Current residential street address in North Dakota; and - Date of birth A valid form of identification is: - Driver's license - ID card issues by the North Dakota Department of Transportation - ID issued by tribal government to a tribal member residing in the state If an individual's valid form of ID does not include the required information or the information is not current, the identification must be supplemented by one of the following that provides the missing or outdated information: - Current utility bill; - Current bank statement; - Check issued by a federal, state, or local government; - Paycheck; or - Document issued by a federal, state, or local government	If an individual is not able to show a valid form of identification but asserts qualifications as an elector in the precinct in which the individual desires to vote, the individual may mark a ballot that must be securely set aside in a sealed envelope designed by the secretary of state. After the ballot is set aside, the individual may show a valid form of identification to either a polling place election board member if the individual returns to the polling place before the polls close, or to an employee of the office of the election official responsible for the administration of the election before the meeting of the canvassing board occurring on the sixth day after the election. Each ballot set aside under this subsection must be presented to the members of the canvassing board for proper inclusion or exclusion from the tally. The following forms of identification are valid for individuals living under special circumstances who do not possess a valid form of identification: - For an individual living in a long-term care facility, a long-term care certificate prescribed by the secretary of state and issued by a long-term care facility in this state; - For a uniformed service member or immediate family member temporarily stationed away from the individual's residence in this state, or a resident of the state temporarily living outside the country, a current military identification card or passport; and - For an individual living with a disability that prevents the individual from traveling away from the individual's home, the signature on an absentee or mail ballot application from another qualified elector who, by signing, certifies the applicant is a qualified elector.

(Continued)

TABLE A.1. (*Cont.*)

Ohio	- Current and valid photo identification, defined as a document that shows the individual's name and current address, includes a photograph, includes an expiration date that has not passed, and was issued by the US government or the state of Ohio - Current utility bill - Current bank statement - Current government check, paycheck, or other government document	A voter who has but declines to provide identification may cast a provisional ballot upon providing a Social Security number or the last four digits of a Social Security number. A voter who has neither identification nor a Social Security number may execute an affidavit to that effect and vote a provisional ballot. A voter who declines to sign the affidavit may still vote a provisional ballot. Voters who cast a provisional ballot because they did not provide acceptable proof of identity must appear in person at the board of elections to provide such proof within the 10 days immediately following Election Day.
Tennessee	- Tennessee driver's license - Valid photo ID card issued by Tennessee - Valid photo ID license issued by TN Department of Safety - Valid US passport - Valid US military ID with photo - Tennessee handgun carry permit with photo	If a voter is unable to present the proper evidence of identification, then the voter will be entitled to vote by provisional ballot in the manner detailed in the bill. The provisional ballot will only be counted if the voter provides the proper evidence of identification to the administrator of elections or the administrator's designee by the close of business on the second business day after the election. However, "A voter who is indigent and unable to obtain proof of identification without payment of a fee or who has a religious objection to being photographed shall be required to execute an affidavit of identity on a form provided by the county election commission and then shall be allowed to vote."
Virginia	- Valid US passport - Valid Virginia driver's license or ID card - Valid Virginia DMV-issued veteran's ID card - Valid tribal enrollment or other tribal ID issued by one of 11 tribes recognized by the Commonwealth of Virginia - Valid student ID card from within Virginia if it includes a photo - Any other ID card issued by a government agency of the Commonwealth, one of its political subdivisions, or the United States - Employee ID card containing a photograph of the voter and issued by an employer of the voter in the ordinary course of the employer's business	Any voter who does not show one of the forms of identification specified in this subsection shall be offered a provisional ballot marked ID-ONLY that requires no follow-up action by the registrar or electoral board other than matching submitted identification documents from the voter for the electoral board to make a determination on whether to count the ballot. In order to have his or her ballot counted, the voter must submit a copy of one of the forms of identification to the electoral board by facsimile, electronic mail, in-person submission, or timely US Postal Service or commercial mail delivery, to be received by the electoral board no later than noon on the third day after the election.

TABLE A.1. (*Cont.*)

Wisconsin	
- Wisconsin driver's license - ID card issued by a US uniformed service - Wisconsin non-driver ID - US passport - Certificate of naturalization issued not more than 2 years before the election - ID card issued by a federally recognized Indian tribe in Wisconsin - Student ID card with a signature, an issue date, and an expiration date no later than 2 years after the election - Photo ID card provided by the Veterans Health Administration All of the above must include a photo and a name that conforms to the poll list. If the ID presented is not proof of residence, the elector shall also present proof of residence.	An elector who appears to vote at a polling place and does not have statutory ID shall be offered the opportunity to vote a provisional ballot. An elector who votes a provisional ballot may furnish statutory ID to the election inspectors before the polls close or to the municipal clerk no later than 4:00 p.m. on the Friday following Election Day.

Source: Wendy Underhill, "Voter Identification Requirements | Voter ID Laws," National Conference of State Legislatures, May 31, 2018, www.ncsl.org/research/elections-and-campaigns/voter-id.aspx.

APPENDIX B

Examples of Costs

How much does it cost to get a passport in Arizona and Kansas? Table B.1 shows the prices for a first-time passport applicant, according to the US Postal Service.

TABLE B.1. Prices for First-Time Passport Application

Product	Form	Application Fee	Execution Fee
Passport book	DS-11	$110	$25
Passport card	DS-11	$30	$25
Passport book and card	DS-11	$140	$25

Table B.2 shows the prices for an adult passport renewal, according to the US Postal Service.[1]

TABLE B.2. Prices for Adult Passport Renewal

Product	Form	Application Fee
Passport book	DS-82	$110
Passport card	DS-82	$30
Passport book and card	DS-82	$140

1. How much does it cost to get a copy of your birth certificate in Arizona and Kansas? (It is different in every state.) Arizona is $20 according to the Arizona Department of Health Services.[2]
2. Kansas is $15 according to the Kansas Department of Health and Environment.[3]
3. How much is an ID in Arizona and Kansas? In Kansas standard ID cards are available at a price of $22, which includes a photo fee

of $8 and a license fee of $14. Note that applicants with disabilities and seniors older than sixty-five can obtain a state ID card at the total cost of $18.[4]

4. In Arizona the cost for an original, duplicate, or replacement Arizona ID card is $12, but the cost can be waived for those who are either sixty-five years old or older or receiving Supplemental Security Income disability payments from the federal government.[5]

APPENDIX C

Research Instruments

We're looking to build a research network of nonprofits interested in helping eligible citizens with voter documentation requirements (i.e., to assist with voter ID laws that require different documents such as birth certificates to register to vote). We would also like to explore the possibility of providing a small grant to your organization in exchange for participation in this project. To determine your potential eligibility and interest in this project, leading to a follow-up phone interview, please answer the following questions.

1. Given your state's requirements for documentation to register to vote (i.e., voter ID law that requires forms of documentation such as birth certificates, etc.), how often would you say voter documentation problems arise for the people your organization serves?
   a. Often
   b. Occasionally
   c. Rarely
   d. Never
   e. Not sure

2. If you answered a, b, or c to question 1, briefly describe any ways that your organization handles voter ID issues, if applicable. For example, what do you do to assist eligible voters with documentation requirements?

3. Name of organization: _____

4. Location of organization:
   a. City:
   b. State:

5. Focus of organization:
   a. Community health center
   b. Food pantry
   c. Family services
   d. Community development corporation
   e. Youth
   f. Education
   g. Health-related (not community health center)
   h. Civic and community engagement
   i. Advocacy
   j. Religious organization
   k. Political party
   l. Other: _____

6. Who are your organization's primary clients/constituents? (check all that apply)
   a. Adults
   b. Youth
   c. Seniors
   d. Women
   e. Men
   f. LGBTI
   g. Specific racial/ethnic groups
   h. Low-income populations
   i. Other: _____

7. Is your organization currently involved in any kind of voter registration and/or voter engagement efforts?
   a. Yes
   b. No, but we plan to become involved
   c. No, and we do not plan to become involved

8. If yes, what aspects of voter registration and/or engagement do you address?
   a. Registering eligible voters
   b. Educating eligible voters about the process of registration and voting
   c. Advocating for particular policies and/or candidates
   d. Arranging debates or educational forums
   e. "Get out the vote" efforts
   f. Other: _____

9. As mentioned, in exchange for a small grant, we're looking to build a research network of nonprofits interested in helping eligible citizens with voter documentation requirements. Would you (or the appropriate person at your organization) be willing to participate in a phone interview to help us learn more about how your organization and the people you serve have been or could be involved in assisting eligible citizens with voter documentation requirements?
   a. Yes
   b. No
   c. Maybe—I need more information

10. If yes or maybe, please provide the following information:
    Name:
    Title:
    Email:
    Phone (if preferred):

NONPROFIT STAFF PHONE INTERVIEW GUIDE
Name:
Position:
Organization:
Phone Number:
Date:

Introduction:
Hi, thanks for agreeing to talk with me today as part of our research on nonprofits and voter documentation requirements. I'm a researcher

working with Baruch College, City University of New York on this project.

Is it okay if I record our call today? It will only be for my reference for purposes of this research so I don't have to frantically take notes while we speak. Everything you say will be confidential, and your name will not be attached to our results. Our conversation will last about 20 to 30 minutes, and I very much appreciate your time and input. After we speak, I'll tell you a bit about the nonprofit research network we're putting together and the incentive grants we have for participation.

Do you have any questions before we get started?

Questions:
1. Tell me briefly about what your organization does and what your role is there.
2. Tell me about the types of people your organization serves. Do you focus on specific populations . . . or are there characteristics that tend to distinguish the community members you work with?
3. How has your organization been involved in voter registration or documentation work?
4. Has voter documentation been a problem for the people you serve, as far as you know? Can you tell me about any specific cases you know of, just to give me an idea?
5. Do you know of anything that your state or county is doing to help previously registered to vote or eligible voters secure a voter ID? Is there anything the state or county does that makes it hard for potential voters to secure a voter ID?
6. Based on your experience, what do you think are the main barriers that get in the way of your community members voting?
7. What do you think are the main reasons why your community members would be likely to want to vote?
8. What has worked in the past when you have tried to engage with community members? For instance, are there particular times, locations, messages, and/or channels for communication that have worked well for engaging your community members on issues related to voting?
9. What do you think about the need for a new nonprofit specifically to address voter documentation issues? Or would it make more

sense to support existing nonprofits to take on this issue? What incentives would be motivating to a nonprofit such as yours?

10. We're putting together a research network of nonprofits to help us with recruiting (and the necessary logistics to speak with) community members. We're offering a small grant in exchange for participation. Might your organization be interested in being involved?

11. Before we wrap up, do you have any other thoughts on the topic that we haven't covered or things that you think I should know?

Thank you so much for your time and assistance!

COMMUNITY MEMBERS FOCUS GROUP / INTERVIEW DISCUSSION GUIDE [MIXED VOTER ID EXAMPLE]

Welcome and thank you for coming to our session today. My name is _____, and I am working with Baruch College, City University of New York to conduct this focus group / interview related to voting issues. We are a nonpartisan organization and not affiliated with any political parties or advocacy groups.

Focus groups / interviews are a research method that will help us to better understand what you think and do related to the elections process. [For focus groups: They are like an opinion survey, but rather than asking questions of one person at a time, we bring a group of people together to discuss a particular topic].

[For focus groups: I'll be asking you questions to generate discussion, but there are no right or wrong answers, just differing points of view. Please feel free to disagree with one another—we would like to have many points of view. Keep in mind that we're just as interested in negative comments as positive comments, and sometimes the negative comments are the most helpful. But we're not here to talk about politics, so let's try to keep away from specific discussions on that topic].

Before we begin, let me explain the ground rules. We're recording the discussion because I don't want to miss any of your comments. All of your comments are confidential and will be used for research purposes only. We'll be on a first name basis today, and in our reports there will not be any names attached to comments. [For focus groups: I want this to be a group discussion, so you don't need to wait for me to call on you. But please speak one at a time, so that the microphone can pick up everything. (Assistant moderator name) [if applicable] will be assisting me].

We have a lot of ground to cover, so I may change the subject or move ahead to the next question abruptly. Please stop me if you want to add something. Our discussion will last about one–two hours [for interviews: 30 to 60 minutes], and at the end you will receive your appreciation gift.

[For focus groups: First of all, let's just go around the room and introduce ourselves. Please give us your first name, and how about your favorite thing to do in your spare time? I'll start . . .]

I. LEVEL OF INTEREST IN VOTING

1. Let me start by asking, what do you think about voting in general? Is it something you think is important? Is it worthwhile? Irrelevant?

2. How many of you have ever registered to vote? [for interviews: have you ever registered to vote?] (Show of hands and verbal confirmation). How long ago was that? What was that process like for you? How did you do it? Did you get help from someone else or an organization?

II. VOTING EXPERIENCES

3. Assuming you were eligible to vote, how would you make the decision of whether you'd want to vote in a particular election or not? What factors go into it? (Probes: Who the candidates are? What the measures on the ballot are? Whether you're available that day?)

4. If you've voted in the past, or tried to vote in the past unsuccessfully, think back to the last time you did so. What was that experience like? What went smoothly? What maybe didn't go as smoothly?

5. [If not mentioned previously] Has anyone [or have you ever] had a problem voting because you didn't have the right kind of identification or documentation to prove you were eligible? What happened? How did that affect you?

III. VOTER DOCUMENTATION KNOWLEDGE AND ATTITUDES

6. What can you tell me about the requirements to vote in this state? (Probes: Federal laws—e.g., age, citizenship, non-felon, etc., state documentation laws—what IDs are acceptable?)

7. How do you feel about the voter documentation requirements in this state? Are they a good idea or a bad idea? Why?

8. If you didn't have a driver's license or U.S. passport, or one of the other types of documents we've already mentioned, how do you think you would go about getting an ID you could use for voting? How difficult of a process would it be?

IV. INFORMATION AND HELP SEEKING

9. Do you know of any organizations that might provide assistance to people who need help with getting a voter ID or getting their documents in order, such as tracking down a copy of a birth certificate? How would you try to find an organization like that if you needed it? Are there specific types of organizations that would be most convenient for you, or that you trust the most?

10. Have you ever received assistance yourself from an organization or individual in obtaining your voter ID documentation? Who were they? What was that process like? If you don't have a voter ID, would you be open to that type of assistance if you needed it?

11. When you have questions about how to take care of government-related business, such as voting, filing taxes, or getting specific services you're entitled to, what do you usually do to try to get answers to your questions? (Probes: Google? Call or stop by the government office? Ask a knowledgeable friend? Hire a professional to help?)

12. Where do you get most of your news and information that informs you about elections or political issues? (Probes: TV? Talk radio? Facebook? Friends and family? Get as specific as possible.)

13. Finally, I want to open it up to find out if you have any other comments or suggestions about voting-related issues (especially related to voter documentation requirements) that we haven't touched on yet.

We have reached the end of the session. I want to thank you so much for your time and valuable insights. Please be sure to sign out with (Assistant Moderator) [if applicable] before you leave to get your appreciation gift. Thanks!

ELECTIONS OFFICE AUDIT
State:
Government office contacted:
Phone Number:
Date:

Call introduction:
"Hi, I'm calling to find out what is needed to vote in the next election?"

Voter ID

1. Mentions voter ID (unprompted)	Yes	No
If doesn't mention voter ID, ask "What about ID?"		
2. Mentions voter ID (when prompted)	Yes	No

Valid Forms of Voter ID

3. Describes valid forms of voter ID (unprompted)	Yes	No
If no description, ask "What kinds of ID do you accept?"		
4. Describes valid forms of voter ID	Yes	No
5. Types of ID mentioned:		
Driver's license	Yes	No
State identification card/non-driver ID	Yes	No
US passport	Yes	No
Student ID card	Yes	No
Tribal ID card	Yes	No
Utility bill/property tax statement	Yes	No
Other:_____	Yes	No

No ID

Ask: "What if someone doesn't have any of those IDs? How can they vote?"

6. Mentions provisional ballot	Yes	No
7. Describes how to obtain valid ID	Yes	No

Wrap Up

Ask: "What days and hours is your office open?"

_____

Say: "Thank you for your help." And hang up.

Additional Items of Note from Call:

MTURK SURVEY OF COMMUNITY MEMBERS

We care about the quality of our survey data. For us to get the most accurate measures of your opinions, it is important that you thoughtfully provide your best answers to each question in this survey.

Do you commit to thoughtfully provide your best answers to the questions in this survey?
   a. I will provide my best answers
   b. I will not provide my best answers
   c. I can't promise either way

1. Are you a registered voter in your state?
   a. Yes
   b. No
   c. Not sure

[If No, skip to Question 4.]

2. Did you vote in the most recent presidential election (2016) or any other state or local elections in the past two years?
   a. Yes
   b. No
   c. Not sure

[If No or Not Sure, skip to Question 4.]

3. Why didn't you vote in any of the elections in the past two years?
   (select all that apply)
   a. Not interested in the candidates or issues
   b. It was inconvenient
   c. I did not have the correct voter identification to be able to vote so did not bother going to the polls
   d. I did not have the correct voter identification to be able to vote so I was turned away at the poll when I tried to vote
   e. I wanted to make a statement by not voting
   f. I didn't know there was an election
   g. I forgot to vote

h. I didn't think my vote would make a difference
i. Other: _____

4. Does your state have specific requirements regarding showing a form of identification in order to be allowed to vote?
   a. Yes
   b. No
   c. Not sure

5. Do you have identification documents that you could use to prove your identity if required for voting purposes, such as a driver's license, state-issued ID card, US passport, or other official photo ID card?
   a. Yes
   b. No
   c. Not sure

[If Yes, skip to Question 7.]

6. Why have you never received an identification document such as a driver's license, state-issued ID card, US passport or other official photo ID card? (select all that apply)
   a. I never needed one
   b. It's too much of a hassle
   c. I don't have the necessary documentation
   d. I'm not a citizen
   e. It costs too much money
   f. I would rather not be part of the "official" system
   g. Other: _____

7. Have you ever sought help or received help in obtaining identification documents from any of the following? (select all that apply)
   a. Government agency
   b. Nonprofit organization
   c. Religious organization, such as a church, mosque or synagogue
   d. Political party
   e. Voter registration workers

    f. Family

    g. Friends

    h. Other: _____

    i. I never sought nor received help

8. Would you be interested in receiving free help from a nonprofit organization or other type of organization to obtain official identification documents?

    a. Yes

    b. No

    c. Not sure

9. Do you know of other people (not including yourself) who have not been able to vote because they did not meet voter identification requirements?

    a. Yes, 3 or more people

    b. Yes, 1 to 2 people

    c. No

    d. Not sure

10. Please indicate your level of agreement with the following statements (1 = strongly disagree, 2 = disagree, 3 = neither agree nor disagree, 4 = agree, 5 = strongly agree):

    a. Everyone who is eligible should vote in public elections.

    b. The requirement to show identification before voting is important to prevent voter fraud.

    c. Voting is not worth the effort.

    d. I value my right to vote if I choose to do so.

    e. It's easy to obtain photo identification that can be used as proof of eligibility to vote.

    f. I would be proud to vote in the next election.

    g. I don't care very much about politics.

    h. Voting is for other people, not me.

We're almost done! Please let us know a bit about yourself.

11. In which state do you currently reside? [Dropdown list]

12. Age as of your last birthday: _____

13. Sex:
    a. Male
    b. Female

14. What race or ethnicity do you consider yourself? (choose all that apply)
    a. American Indian/Alaska Native
    b. Asian/Pacific Islander
    c. Black/African American/Caribbean
    d. Hispanic/Latino
    e. Middle Eastern/North African
    f. White/Caucasian
    g. Other

15. What is your current approximate annual household income?
    a. Less than $25,000
    b. $25,000–49,999
    c. $50,000–$99,999
    d. $100,000 or more
    e. Decline to state

16. What is the highest level of education you have completed?
    a. Did not complete high school
    b. High school
    c. Some college
    d. College
    e. Post-college studies, graduate or professional degree

17. Politically, which party do you identify with the most?
    a. Democrat
    b. Republican
    c. Independent
    d. Other
    e. None

18. You made it to the end! Do you have any comments or feedback for us about the survey so we can improve the experience in the future?

We thank you for your time spent taking this survey.
Your response has been recorded.

Your MTurk completion code is:
[random 8-digit code]

VOTER DOCUMENTATION PHONE INTERVIEW GUIDE FOR EXPERTS
AND PRACTITIONERS
Name:
Position:
Organization:
Phone Number:
Date:

Introduction:
Hi, thanks for agreeing to talk with me today as part of our research on voter documentation issues. I'm a researcher working with Baruch College, City University of New York on this project.

Is it okay if I record our call today? It will only be for my reference for purposes of this research so I don't have to frantically take notes while we speak. Everything you say will be confidential, and your name will not be attached to our results. Our conversation will last about (10 to 60 minutes) [note: choose the time limit accordingly, some may not have much time to speak with us, but at least 10 minutes seems warranted], and I very much appreciate your time and input.

Do you have any questions before we get started?

Main Questions:
1. Tell me briefly about your organization and what your role is there.
2. Tell me about the types of people your organization serves. Do you focus on specific populations . . . or are there characteristics that tend to distinguish the community members you work with?
3. How has your organization been involved in voter registration or documentation work?

4. What can you tell me about the voter documentation requirements or voter ID laws in your state?
5. Has voter documentation been a problem for the people you serve, as far as you know? What are the main issues that have come up? Can you tell me about any specific cases you know of, just to give me an idea?
6. What does your organization do to help individuals who experience voter documentation problems? What about on a larger level in the community?
7. Do you know of anything that your state or county is doing to help previously registered to vote or eligible voters secure a voter ID? Is there anything the state or county does that makes it hard for potential voters to secure a voter ID?
8. Based on your experience, what do you think are the main barriers that get in the way of your community members voting?
9. What do you think are the main reasons why your community members would be likely to want to vote?
10. Are there any particular times or places that you think we could best reach your community members, where they'd be more likely to pay attention to our messages or be interested in being able to vote? What about specific communication methods that might be particularly effective to reach them?
11. What do you think about the need for a new nonprofit specifically to address voter documentation issues? Or would it make more sense to support existing nonprofits to take on this issue? What incentives would be most motivating to offer?
12. Do you know of other experts on the topic of voter documentation who you would recommend we speak with? Do you have their contact information?
13. Before we wrap up, do you have any other thoughts on the topic that we haven't covered or things that you think I should know?

Thank you so much for your time and assistance!

Additional, Optional Questions (to ask in whole or part if relevant to the work of the individual being interviewed):
1. What are the number of individuals and percentage of the state population that your [or others] organization[s] serves?

2. What are the demographics of your population? [or the population of others you know who work in this area?] (i.e., breakdown by party membership, race/ethnicity, gender/sex, socioeconomic circumstances, etc.)

3. Can you quantify the success of your efforts [or of those you know who have been doing work around voter documentation requirements] in order to determine best practices? (i.e., how many people in numbers and percentage of the population you or others serve)

4. How many of those you [or others] serve were self-educated about voter ID requirements? Turned out to vote? Were unable to cast a vote? Had to cast a provisional ballot? Successfully voted?

5. How many of those you [or others] serve were educated by your [or others] efforts? How many were helped to obtain the ID that they needed as a result of your [or others] efforts?

6. How many people obtained IDs as a result of your [or others] education and other assistance? How many people went to vote as a result of your [or others] education and other assistance?

7. How many of these people had trouble voting at the polls or through other means because of documentation or ID issues? What kinds of problems did they run into? Why?

8. What methods do you believe were/are most helpful in educating people, helping them obtain ID, and/or turning out to vote?

9. What do you know about voter suppression efforts related to voter ID? What form did they take? (e.g., literature sent out suggesting negative consequences of attempting to get voter ID or to vote; advertisements to the same effect; door-to-door engagement with voters discouraging them from voting; something other than these?)

10. Do you have written materials that are helpful on any of the above? If so, where can we find these?

11. Do you have data (e.g., de-identified, longitudinal data) on any of the above? [note to IRB: if the data is de-identified, we will collect and use in our research; if they offer data with identifiers, we will seek IRB approval before using for research purposes]

APPENDIX D

Election-Related Resources for Nonprofits and Community Organizations

Advancement Project: Fair Elections
www.advancementprojectca.org

American Association of People with Disabilities: Voting Resource Center
www.aapd.com

American Civil Liberties Union Voting Rights Project
www.aclu.org

American Constitution Society
www.acslaw.org

America Votes
https://americavotes.org

Asian Americans Advancing Justice: Voting Rights
www.advancingjustice-aajc.org

Best Colleges: Student Voting Guide
www.bestcolleges.com

Black Votes Matter
www.blackvotersmatterfund.org

Brennan Center for Justice: Ensure Every American Can Vote
www.brennancenter.org

Campaign Legal Center
https://campaignlegal.org

Campus Vote Project
www.campusvoteproject.org

Common Cause
www.commoncause.org

Democracy Initiative
www.democracyinitiative.org

Demos
www.demos.org

Election Protection
https://866ourvote.org

Fair Elections Center
www.fairelectionscenter.org

Fair Vote
www.fairvote.org

Federal Voting Assistance Program
www.fvap.gov

HeadCount
www.headcount.org

Hip Hop Caucus
https://hiphopcaucus.org

Latino Justice
www.latinojustice.org

Lawyers' Committee for Civil Rights under Law
https://lawyerscommittee.org

Leadership Conference Education Fund
https://civilrights.org

League of Women Voters: Expanding Voter Access
www.lwv.org

Let America Vote
www.letamericavote.org

Mexican American Legal Defense and Educational Fund
www.maldef.org

Movement Voter Project
https://movement.vote

National Association of Latino Elected Officials
https://naleo.org

National Election Defense Coalition
www.electiondefense.org

National Woman Suffrage Association
www.crusadeforthevote.org

New Florida Majority
https://newfloridamajority.org

Nonprofit VOTE
www.nonprofitvote.org

Project South
https://projectsouth.org

Project Vote
www.projectvote.org

Rock the Vote
www.rockthevote.org

Southern Poverty Law Center: Voting Rights
www.splcenter.org

Spread the Vote
www.spreadthevote.org

Texas Civil Rights Project
https://texascivilrightsproject.org

Verified Voting Foundation
www.verifiedvoting.org

Vote411
www.vote411.org

VoteRiders
www.voteriders.org

Voter Participation Center
www.voterparticipation.org

When We All Vote
www.whenweallvote.org

NOTES

PREFACE

1 Dylan McGuinness, "San Antonio Leaders, Residents Outraged after Former Mayor Lila Cockrell Isn't Allowed to Vote," MySA, May 31, 2019, www.mysananto nio.com, par. 1.

2 McGuinness, par. 5.

3 David Griggs, "Supporting Voters in States with Voter ID Laws," Nonprofit VOTE, April 18, 2019, www.nonprofitvote.org.

4 Russell Contreras and Stef W. Kight, "Dozens of States See New Voter Suppression Proposals," *Axios*, February 10, 2021, www.axios.com. Throughout this book, we will use the US Census Bureau's nomenclature for racial and ethnic categories, "About," US Census Bureau, October 16, 2020, www.census.gov.

5 Maya King, "How Stacey Abrams and Her Band of Believers Turned Georgia Blue," *Politico*, November 8, 2020, www.politico.com.

6 Nathaniel Rakich and Elena Mejía, "Where Republicans Have Made It Harder to Vote (So Far)," May 11, 2021, FiveThirtyEight, https://fivethirtyeight.com. In mid-2021, "17 states have enacted nearly 30 laws to make it harder to vote. . . . legislators across the country, overwhelmingly Republican, have introduced nearly 400 bills to restrict the vote." Michael Waldman, "Voter Suppression's Death by a Thousand Cuts," Brennan Center for Justice, July 20, 2021, www .brennancenter.org, par. 3. The Voting Rights Lab provides a tracker of these bills and their current status here: https://tracker.votingrightslab.org. A snapshot of legislation can also be found here: https://tracker.votingrightslab.org and here: www.ncsl.org. See also Alexa Corse and John Kamp, "States' New Voting Laws: What You Need to Know," *Wall Street Journal*, July 30, 2021, www.wsj.com.

7 Pam Fessler, "The Legal Fight over Voting Rights during the Pandemic Is Getting Hotter," NPR, May 2, 2020, www.npr.org, par. 12.

8 Kim Chandler, "Lawsuit Challenges Alabama Voting Rules during Pandemic," *Daily Mountain Eagle*, May 2, 2020, http://mountaineagle.com, pars. 1–4. Rebecca Seung-Bickley also highlights that in past elections, "one of the most obvious ways officials have attempted to suppress the African American vote is by imposing a requirement that voters have one of a limited set of forms of photo ID, while, at the same time, making it more difficult to obtain photo ID by closing 31 driver's license offices in counties—including every county in which African Americans are 70 percent or more of the population." Rebecca Seung-Bickley, "Alabama's Effort to Suppress Black Vote Couldn't Prevent Huge Turnout," Common

Dreams, December 15, 2017, www.commondreams.org, par. 4. Ironically, the Alabama governor herself voted by mail. Mike Cason, "Alabama Gov. Kay Ivey's Stance on Absentee Voting Criticized," *AL.com*, March 26, 2020, www.al.com.

9 Bruce Schreiner, "Kentucky Lawmakers Override Veto of Voter ID Measure," *PBS News Hour*, April 14, 2020, www.pbs.org; Amanda Terkel, "Kentucky Republicans Pass Voter ID Law in Midst of Coronavirus Pandemic," *HuffPost*, April 15, 2020, www.huffpost.com. The issue also played out in Missouri. "Missouri Mail-In Curbs Head to State's Top Court as Governor Mulls Exemption," *The Fulcrum*, May 21, 2020, https://thefulcrum.us.

10 Zach Montellaro and Quint Forgey, "Trump Misstates Michigan Mail-In Ballot Policy, Threatens Federal Funding," *Politico*, May 20, 2020, www.politico.com; Carrie Dann, "Two-Thirds of Voters Back Vote-by-Mail in November 2020," *NBC News*, April 21, 2020, www.aol.com/article/news; Matthew Rosza, "Tucker Carlson: 'Radical Expansion' of Voting by Mail Championed by Obama Would 'Destroy' Democracy," *Salon*, April 15, 2020, www.salon.com.

11 Marianna Spring, "'Stop the Steal': The Deep Roots of Trump's 'Voter Fraud' Strategy," *BBC News*, November 23, 2020, www.bbc.com. Trump did not let go of this assertion, leading to legions of supporters following along and most Republicans believing that the presidency was stolen well after the election. Rick Hasen, "Convention Circuit of Delusion Gives Forum for Election Lies," *Election Law Journal*, June 19, 2021, https://electionlawblog.org.

12 Eliza Sweren-Becker, "Florida Enacts Sweeping Voter Suppression Law," Brennan Center for Justice, May 6, 2021, www.brennancenter.org. As one example, for a breakdown of the timeline regarding the postelection Maricopa County audit in Arizona, including details supporting the election's integrity and countering the false claims of voter fraud on which it was based, see Ralph Neas, Richard A. Gephardt, Timothy E. Wirth, Gary Hart, and Anthony Essaye, "How the Arizona Senate Audit in Maricopa County Is an Assault on Voting Rights," The Century Foundation, July 1, 2020, https://tcf.org.

13 Darlene Superville, "Michelle Obama Group Backs Expanding Voting Options for 2020," *PBS News Hour*, April 13, 2020, www.pbs.org; Eli Hager, "The 470,000 Potential Voters Most Likely to Be Disenfranchised Next Election," The Marshall Project, April 24, 2020, www.themarshallproject.org. Some civil rights groups have made clear that options for in-person voting should also be extended, so that disenfranchised groups who may have a difficult time with voting by mail, or could benefit from same-day registration and voting, can do so. Joey Garrison, "Amid Vote-by-Mail Push, Civil Rights Groups Say In-Person Voting Still Needed during Pandemic," *USA Today*, April 20, 2020, https://news.yahoo.com.

14 "It's Official: The Election Was Secure," Brennan Center for Justice, December 11, 2020, www.brennancenter.org, par. 2; Jen Kirby, "Trump's Own Officials Say 2020 Was America's Most Secure Election in History," *Vox*, November 13, 2020, www.vox.com; David E. Sanger, Matt Stevens, and Nicole Perlroth, "Election Officials Directly Contradict Trump on Voting System Fraud," *New York Times*,

November 12, 2020, https://advance-lexis-com. See also "Factbox: Trump's False Claims Debunked: The 2020 Election and Jan. 6 Riot," Reuters, January 6, 2022, www.reuters.com.

15 See, for example, US Constitution, Article I, Section 4, Clause 1; Article II, Section 1, Clauses 2 and 3.

16 "Oppose Voter ID Legislation—Fact Sheet," ACLU, n.d., www.aclu.org.

17 Theodore R. Johnson and Max Feldman, "The New Voter Suppression," Brennan Center for Justice, January 16, 2020, www.brennancenter.org, "Erecting" par. 6.

18 Johnson and Feldman, "Meet," par. 1.

INTRODUCTION

1 All information in this paragraph is detailed in Wendy Underhill, "Fraud Fighter or Ballot Blocker?," NCSL, September 1, 2014, www.ncsl.org, pars. 33–35.

2 Suevon Lee and Sarah Smith, "Everything You've Ever Wanted to Know about Voter ID Laws," *Propublica*, March 9, 2016, www.propublica.org, par. 4.

3 Richard Sobel, "The High Cost of 'Free' Photo Voter Identification Cards," Charles Hamilton Houston Institute for Race and Justice at Harvard Law School, 2014, http://charleshamiltonhouston.org.

4 "Voter Identification Requirements | Voter ID Laws," NCSL, May 21, 2021, www .ncsl.org, par. 1; "Voter Identification Laws by State," *Ballotpedia*, 2021, https:// ballotpedia.org.

5 William D. Hicks, Seth C. McKee, Mitchell D. Sellers, and Daniel A. Smith, "A Principle or a Strategy? Voter Identification Laws and Partisan Competition in the American States," *Political Research Quarterly* 68 (2015): 18; "Voter Identification," MIT Election Data and Science Lab, 2021, https://electionlab.mit.edu, par. 25.

6 Kettering Foundation, www.kettering.org.

7 Three decades ago, Linda Alcoff pointed scholars toward "the problem of speaking for others." In this book, we attempt at every opportunity to conduct analyses that bring to the fore others' voices from different viewpoints. See Linda Alcoff, "The Problem of Speaking for Others," *Cultural Critique* 20 (1991): 5–32.

8 See Alcoff.

9 Molly McGrath, "Fighting Voter ID Laws in the Courts Isn't Enough: We Need Boots on the Ground," *Los Angeles Times*, February 21, 2017, www.latimes.com.

10 Heather Ann Thompson, in *Voter Suppression in U.S. Elections*, ed. Jim Downs (Athens: University of Georgia Press, 2020), 70. In short, voter documentation requirements are overly burdensome, unjust, and inequitable by design, supporting what is ultimately an antidemocratic and "minoritarian rule." Thompson, in Downs, *Voter Suppression*, 70. It's worth asking if the United States can reasonably be called a democracy by any measure if these trends continue, where, by 2040, "70% of Americans will be represented by just 30 senators, and 30% of Americans by 70 senators. That has lots of implications, such as for the Senate filibuster, where a party that represents a shrinking minority of voters can block almost all

major legislation." Mara Liasson, "Democrats Increasingly Say American Democracy Is Sliding toward Minority Rule," NPR, June 9, 2021, www.npr.org, par. 9.

11 Griggs, "Supporting Voters in States with Voter ID Laws." Some 25 percent of these voters are African Americans who lack government-issued photos IDs such as passports, driver's licenses, or military IDs; 16 percent of Latinos and only 8 percent of White voters face the same problem. Gilda R. Daniels, *Uncounted: The Crisis of Voter Suppression in America* (New York: New York University Press, 2020), 88.

12 Don Waisanen, *Political Conversion: Personal Transformation as Strategic Public Communication* (Lanham, MD: Lexington, 2018). Frames can shift when an individual has repeated confrontations with anomalies that don't fit. For instance, writing about police violence against people of color, and trying to find ways to work beyond reactionary impulses in the face of widespread evidence, Mimi Onohua states, "By considering the vast context and evidence present in the nation's history, we can save ourselves from tacitly reinforcing the idea that structural violence matters only when it can be compressed into a form that fits what we recognize as evidence. And, in doing so, we give ourselves new frames for thinking about the many people who have died at the hands of brutality and whose deaths were not recorded. As we find a fluency in addressing the greater mass of life that is lived outside of our data, we can begin, finally, to fully address the living." Mimi Onohua, "When Proof Is Not Enough," FiveThirtyEight, July 1, 2020, https://fivethirtyeight.com, par. 19.

13 See Michael Wines, "How Charges of Voter Fraud Became a Political Strategy," *New York Times*, October 16, 2016, www.nytimes.com. The effect of this decades-long narrative has been substantial. In the 2016 election, for instance, "Trump capitalize[d] on the widespread distrust of the election process. Likely voters who lack confidence that votes will be counted accurately back him over Clinton by 63–18 percent. He has a similar 61–22 percent advantage among those who think voter fraud happens somewhat or very often." Julie Phelan, "Pessimistic or Optimistic? Election-Wise, It Matters," *ABC News*, September 15, 2016, https://abcnews.go.com, par. 7. The veracity of these claims has been fact-checked repeatedly. "US Election 2020: Fact-Checking Trump Team's Main Fraud Claims," *BBC News*, November 23, 2020, www.bbc.com; Nick Corasaniti, Reid J. Epstein, and Jim Rutenberg, "The Times Called Officials in Every State: No Evidence of Voter Fraud," *New York Times*, November 10, 2020, https://advance-lexis-com. A half year after the 2020 US general election, fewer than two dozen cases of voter fraud had been charged (without conclusions) to that point, or only about one in ten million in terms of votes cast. Philip Bump, "Despite GOP Rhetoric, There Have Been Fewer Than Two Dozen Charged Cases of Voter Fraud since the Election," *Washington Post*, May 4, 2021, www.washingtonpost.com. With both data and examples, Amber Reynolds and Charles Stewart III write, "Widespread calls to conduct the 2020 elections by mail, to protect voters from COVID-19 exposure, are being met with charges that the system inevitably would lead to massive voter

fraud. This is simply not true. Vote fraud in the United States is exceedingly rare, with mailed ballots and otherwise. Over the past 20 years, about 250 million votes have been cast by a mail ballot nationally. The Heritage Foundation maintains an online database of election fraud cases in the United States and reports that there have been just over 1,200 cases of vote fraud of all forms, resulting in 1,100 criminal convictions, over the past 20 years. Of these, 204 involved the fraudulent use of absentee ballots; 143 resulted in criminal convictions. Let's put that data in perspective. One hundred forty-three cases of fraud using mailed ballots over the course of 20 years comes out to seven to eight cases per year, nationally. It also means that across the 50 states, there has been an average of three cases per state over the 20-year span. That is just one case per state every six or seven years. We are talking about an occurrence that translates to about 0.00006 percent of total votes cast." Amber Reynolds and Charles Stewart III, "Let's Put the Vote-by-Mail 'Fraud' Myth to Rest," *The Hill*, April 28, 2020, https://thehill.com, pars. 1–4. The Heritage Foundation website—linked to by the White House during the Trump administration—can be found at www.heritage.org (with the corresponding link at www.whitehouse.gov). As in Reynolds and Stewart's analysis, a quick look through these sites shows that these instances are one-off, a collection of many years and many states' small events, and often actually not about a person attempting to be someone else via an absentee ballot. For example, we searched on the Heritage site only for cases having to do with fraudulent absentee ballots across all fifty states. Here is what we counted: in 2020, 2 cases; in 2019, 4 cases; in 2018, 7 cases; in 2017, 14 cases; in 2016, 7 cases. This is the equivalent of zero. Voter fraud is not accomplished by absentee ballots and would require multitudes of people to be a part of a conspiracy to do so. Successful fraud to affect an outcome in an election is more likely to arise from corruption via the administration of the voting apparatus. For example, it is widely accepted that Lyndon Johnson's victory against Coke Stevenson in 1948 for Senate was accomplished in this way. Martin Tolchin, "How Johnson Won Election He'd Lost," *New York Times*, February 11, 1990, www.nytimes.com; Robert A. Caro, *The Years of Lyndon Johnson: Means of Ascent* (New York: Vintage, 1991).

14 Alejandro de la Garza, "President Trump Tweets Misleading Claim about 'Rampant' Texas Voter Fraud," *Time*, January 27, 2019, https://time.com, par. 2. To be clear, "Voter fraud is one of the oldest charges a politician can level in American elections—though no president in modern times has done so with such frequency, and so little evidence, as President Trump." In recent history, "the topic has been a staple of coverage on Fox News going back to the 2000s, when hosts like Bill O'Reilly spread exaggerated stories about immigrants who were voting illegally, campaigns that paid people for their votes and community groups like ACORN whose employees had submitted fraudulent voter registrations. (The ACORN employees, who were also the subject of an attack ad that John McCain's campaign ran against Barack Obama in 2008, did not appear to be attempting to influence voting, but rather to get paid for voter registration work they hadn't

actually done.) Claims of voter fraud have often involved absurd and far-fetched scenarios—dead people, dogs, busloads of people of color—which is another way they live on in the public imagination. In recent years, conservative activists have pushed unverified reports that buses full of illegal voters showed up at polling places from California to Wisconsin." Jeremy W. Peters, "Claims of Voter Fraud Are Common. It's the Fraud That's Rare," *New York Times*, November 16, 2020, https://advance-lexis-com, pars. 4, 8–9.

15 Carol Anderson argues that many forms of voter suppression in current US politics stem from what happened after the Fifteenth Amendment guaranteed the right to vote for former slaves, and the Mississippi Plan of 1890 that was generated by the state's legislature as a way of preventing Black people from voting without having a discriminatory, overt law in place. In Downs, *Voter Suppression*, 23. As Frank Palmeri and Ted Wendelin put it, "The South may have lost the Civil War militarily, but it won politically. For most of United States history, laws and policies that favor the South have prevailed," especially from the Southern Compromise in which the South was able to count each slave as three-fifths of a person in population counts, giving the South a third of congressional seats and electoral votes, while carrying out a "legal regime of racial apartheid" after the war. To a common refrain that liberals put in place some of the most oppressive slave laws and norms from the past, it's also worth highlighting the following points by Palmeri and Wendelin: "Southern hegemony returned with the electoral 'Southern strategy' pursued by Richard Nixon and subsequent Republican national candidates. The seventies saw a mass exodus of Southern [W]hites and Southern politicians from the Democratic Party to the Republican Party, and that party moved further and further to the right, refining its use of racial code words to appeal to [W]hite voters centrally but not exclusively in the South. The Republican National Committee admitted the strategy of exploiting racial antagonisms and apologized for it to the NAACP in 2005; yet the party still pursues this path energetically, and the . . . Republican President [Donald Trump] has attracted and not disavowed the enthusiastic support of neo-Nazis and former Klan members in the South and in other regions." Frank Palmeri and Ted Wendelin, "The Long and Despicable Roots of Voter Suppression and Similar Tactics," History News Network, April 22, 2018, https://historynewsnetwork.org/article/168634, pars. 1–5, 11. See also Eoin Higgins, "It's 2020 and Florida's Supreme Court Just Ruled in Favor of a Poll Tax," Common Dreams, January 16, 2020, www.commondreams .org; Dara Kam, "Florida Judge Refuses to Put Felons Voting Rights Decision on Hold," *Tampa Bay Times*, June 15, 2020, www.tampabay.com; Matt Steib, "Federal Judge Overrules GOP Poll Tax for Ex-Felons in Florida," *New York Magazine*, May 25, 2020, nymag.com; Spenser Mestel, "Amid Accusations of Violence, Some Say National Guard Should No Longer Staff Voting Stations," *The Guardian*, June 17, 2020, www.theguardian.com; Fred Hiatt, "Why the Republicans' 2020 Strategy Is to Keep as Many People as Possible from Voting," *Washington Post*, June 14, 2020, www.washingtonpost.com. The candid words of Paul Weyrich, summed up by

Ari Berman, identify this modern strategy: "Republicans have long tried to drive Democratic voters away from the polls. 'I don't want everybody to vote,' the influential conservative activist Paul Weyrich told a gathering of evangelical leaders in 1980. 'As a matter of fact, our leverage in the elections quite candidly goes up as the voting populace goes down.' But since the 2010 election, thanks to a conservative advocacy group founded by Weyrich, the GOP's effort to disrupt voting rights has been more widespread and effective than ever. In a systematic campaign orchestrated by the American Legislative Exchange Council—and funded in part by David and Charles Koch, the billionaire brothers who bankrolled the Tea Party—38 states introduced legislation this year designed to impede voters at every step of the electoral process." Ari Berman, "The GOP War on Voting," *Rolling Stone*, August 30, 2011, www.rollingstone.com, par. 2; Michael Wines and Fausset Richard, "North Carolina's Legislative Maps Are Thrown Out by State Court Panel," *New York Times*, September 3, 2019, www.nytimes.com; Jesse Jackson and Daley David, "Voter Suppression Is Still One of the Greatest Obstacles to a More Just America," *Time*, June 12, 2020, https://time.com.

16 In Downs, *Voter Suppression*, 24.

17 Daniels, *Uncounted*; Carol Anderson, *One Person, No Vote: How Voter Suppression Is Destroying Our Democracy* (New York: Bloomsbury, 2018). See also Zachary Roth, *The Great Suppression: Voting Rights, Corporate Cash, and the Conservative Assault on Democracy* (New York: Crown, 2016).

18 Daniels, *Uncounted*, 206, 2. The crisis of voter identification laws can't be disconnected from the ongoing battle to restore voting rights to ex-felons. For an overview of the issues at stake with ex-felons' challenges and voter ID, see Nicole Lewis, "They Got Their Voting Rights Back, But Will They Go to the Polls?," The Marshall Project, August 13, 2019, www.themarshallproject.org.

19 See, e.g., *Harper v. Va. Bd. of Elections*, 383 U.S. 63, 667 (1966).

20 David Daley, "Republicans Have a New Plan to Thwart the Will of the People," *New York Times*, May 21, 2020, www.nytimes.com.

21 Vann R. Newkirk II, "How Shelby County v. Holder Broke America," *The Atlantic*, July 10, 2018, www.theatlantic.com.

22 In Downs, *Voter Suppression*, 32.

23 Carol Anderson in Downs, *Voter Suppression*, 27; Daniels, *Uncounted*, 34.

1. ON THE GROUND

1 Sobel, "The High Cost," 3.

2 Paul S. Martin, "Voting's Rewards: Voter Turnout, Attentive Publics, and Congressional Allocation of Federal Money," *American Journal of Political Science* 47 (2003): 109–127.

3 This story comes from Christina A. Cassidy and Ivan Moreno, "In Wisconsin, ID Law Proved Insurmountable for Many Voters," AP, May 14, 2017, https://apnews.com, pars. 14–17.

4 Cassidy, pars. 14–17.

5 Keith G. Bentele and Erin E. O'Brien, "Jim Crow 2.0? Why States Consider and Adapt Restrictive Voter Access Policies," *Perspectives on Politics* 11 (2013): 1088. See also Daniel R. Biggers and Michael J. Hanmer, "Understanding the Adoption of Voter Identification Laws in the American States," *American Politics Research* 45 (2017): 560–588. For a sweeping history of voting in the United States, see Alexander Keyssar, *The Right to Vote: The Contested History of Democracy in the United States* (New York: Basic Books, 2009). For a closer look at voter suppression in the United States, see Tova Andrea Wang, *The Politics of Voter Suppression: Defending and Expanding Americans' Right to Vote* (Ithaca, NY: Cornell University Press, 2012); Michael Waldman, *The Fight to Vote* (New York: Simon and Schuster, 2016); and Caroline Fredrickson, *The Democracy Fix: How to Win the Fight for Fair Rules, Fair Courts, and Fair Elections* (New York: New Press, 2019).

6 "Federal Elections 2000," Federal Election Commission, June 2001, www.fec.gov.

7 See 531 U.S. 98, 121 S. Ct. 525 (2000).

8 Data in this paragraph are from Daniels, *Uncounted*, 31–32. See also Mark Louis Latour, *American Government and the Vision of Democrats* (New York: University Press of America, 2007), 25.

9 Daniels, *Uncounted*, 64–65.

10 Keyssar, *The Right to Vote*, 284.

11 *Shelby v. Holder*, 133 S. Ct. 2612 (2013); Jenée Desmond-Harris, "Why Is Section 4 of the Voting Rights Act Such a Big Part of the Fight over Voting Rights?," *Vox*, February 14, 2016, www.vox.com.

12 Desmond-Harris. These practices were identified in a dozen states or parts of states. For an extensive history of the Voting Rights Act, the electoral successes it set in motion, and the counterrevolutions against it, see Ari Berman, *Give Us the Ballot: The Modern Struggle for Voting Rights in America* (New York: Farrar, Straus and Giroux, 2015). For vivid details about the impacts of the first five years of the Supreme Court decision, see Anderson, *One Person, No Vote*. Gilda Daniels argues, "If Selma, Alabama, serves as the birthplace of the VRA [Voting Rights Act], Shelby County, Alabama, could certainly serve as its resting place." Daniels, *Uncounted*, 45. See also Jennifer L. Patin, "The Voting Rights Act at 50: The Texas Voter ID Story," Lawyers Committee for Civil Rights under Law, August 6, 2015, https://lawyerscommittee.org; "An Assessment of Minority Voting Right Access in the United States," US Commission on Civil Rights, 2018, www.usccr.gov; Lawrence Goldstone, *On Account of Race: The Supreme Court, White Supremacy, and the Ravaging of African American Voting Rights* (Berkeley, CA: Counterpoint, 2020); Jesse H. Rhodes, *Ballot Blocked: The Political Erosion of the Voting Rights Act* (Palo Alto, CA: Stanford University Press, 2017); Terry Smith, *Whitelash: Unmasking White Grievance at the Ballot Box* (New York: Cambridge University Press, 2020). The requirements also applied in some surprising places. While the preclearance process was directed at protecting the Black vote in jurisdictions having a history of racism, New York City was subject to preclearance for different groups "because New York State had passed a law in 1921 requiring an

English literacy test to vote. This was mostly an anti-immigrant move, following on the heels of other anti-immigrant election bills that first required voters to register every year and then moved election day to Saturday—the Jewish Sabbath. The people most hurt by the English literacy test? Puerto Ricans, most of whom were educated in Spanish-speaking schools on their home island at the time. In 1968, Latino voter registration was so low that Manhattan, Brooklyn and the Bronx became covered jurisdictions under the Voting Rights Act. Voter suppression of various minorities was working so well that fewer than half of voting-age people voted." Jennifer Vanasco, "Explainer: 'The Supreme Court, Voting Rights and New York,'" WNYC, June 25, 2013, www.wnyc.org, pars. 13–15.

13   Ari Berman, "Why the Voting Rights Act Is Once Again under Threat," *New York Times*, August 6, 2015, www.nytimes.com, par. 4; Ana Marie Cox, "The Supreme Court Guts the Voter Rights Act . . . Since Racism Is Over," *The Guardian*, June 25, 2013, www.theguardian.com; Newkirk, "How Shelby County"; Nancy Abudu, "Seven Years after Shelby County vs. Holder, Voter Suppression Permeates the South," Southern Poverty Law Center, June 25, 2020, www.splcenter.org.

14   Downs, *Voter Suppression*, 10–11. As an example of purges, Anderson highlights that in 2000, "The St. Louis Board of Elections had purged some 50,000 names from the voter rolls, primarily in key Democratic precincts. And it had failed to notify the people who had just been stripped of their vote, as the law required. So when those voters showed up to cast their ballots, they were told they were no longer registered." Carol Anderson, "The Republican Approach to Voter Fraud: Lie," *New York Times*, September 8, 2018, www.nytimes.com, pars. 11–12. Voter purges are founded on a proposed need to remove felons, the mentally incompetent, and dead voters from the rolls, but they have the effect of removing people of color disproportionately, with many documented mistakes. Daniels, *Uncounted*, 122.

15   All information in this paragraph comes from Carol Anderson in Downs, *Voter Suppression*, 43–44. Daniels adds the illuminating fact that "the cost of a driver's license may seem minimal, unless, like 25 percent of African Americans in Georgia, you do not own a car." Daniels, *Uncounted*, 70, 72.

16   "Election 2016: Restrictive Voting Laws by the Numbers," Brennan Center for Justice, n.d., www.brennancenter.org.

17   "Fish v. Schwab (Formerly Fish v. Kobach)," ACLU, 2020, www.aclu.org.

18   "Fish v. Kobach," ACLU, April 18, 2018, www.aclu.org, par. 1. In the United States, many states require documentation of citizenship, whether for voting or, in some cases, for driver's licenses. This documentation usually takes the form of a birth certificate. This can be a hardship not just because it may cost money and take a lot of time to obtain a copy of one's birth certificate but because there are people born in the United States who, for various reasons, may not have one, or the likely repositories for birth certificates (like hospitals) have not maintained their files. An additional story and details about policies covering documentation, citizenship, and voting reveals these problems: First, "in 2008, as the state of Missouri

was poised to adopt a constitutional amendment to require documentary proof of citizenship of every person wishing to register to vote in the state, the New York Times and other media outlets reported on the story of Lillie Lewis. The 78-year old Ms. Lewis, an African American Missourian, was born in Mississippi and had voted in every presidential election she could remember but had no documentary evidence of her U.S. citizenship. As the Missouri amendment was being debated, she wrote to the vital records office in Mississippi seeking a copy of her birth certificate. In response, she received a letter stating that the state had no record of her birth. After decades of voting, she effectively became a non-citizen, excluded from engaging in the voting process that defines a democracy. Although the amendment failed a vote in the Missouri Senate, a number of other states have passed similar laws demanding that citizens produce documentary evidence of citizenship in order to register to vote." Second, "States already ask for evidence of citizenship. Since states began requiring voters to register prior to voting, every state has required individuals wishing to register to sign a statement under penalty of perjury affirming that they are citizens and that they meet all of the state's other voter eligibility requirements. The federal form also requires such a statement and additionally states that non-citizens who register may be criminally prosecuted and deported. Statements under penalty of perjury are acceptable evidence in courts of law, and for many decades every state in the nation accepted them as evidence of citizenship for voter registration purposes. What is new is that a handful of states are no longer accepting such statements and are demanding that voters instead provide documentary evidence of citizenship, such as birth certificates, naturalization cards, or Native American tribal documents. These states insist that requiring such evidence is necessary to ensure that non-citizens do not fraudulently register to vote. . . . documentary proof-of-citizenship requirements do no more to prevent voter registration fraud by non-citizens than the threat of criminal prosecution and deportation has done ever since states began registering voters. Preventing legitimate voters from participating in our democracy is an unacceptable price to pay for stopping at most a tiny number of fraudulent voter registrations." Stuard Neifeh, "How Do Proof-of-Citizenship Laws Block Legitimate Voters?" Demos, August 25, 2014, www.demos.org, pars. 1–2, 6–8. Additional issues include how, "given America's highly mobile work force, many individuals do not live in the city or state in which they were born, and most vital records offices require individuals to appear in person or to already have another form of government-issued identification to order a birth certificate online or by telephone. Even those who do have a birth certificate may not be able to use it to establish their citizenship. For example, many married women do not have a birth certificate that reflects their current name." Neifeh, "How Do Proof-of Citizenship Laws Block Legitimate Voters?," par. 10.

19 Nina Totenberg, "The Supreme Court Deals a New Blow to Voting Rights, Upholding Arizona Restrictions," NPR, July 1, 2021, www.npr.org, par. 13. Rick Hasen writes, "We've seen a sea change in the Republican Party's attitude

towards the Voting Rights Act" because it is now "reliant on [W]hite voters, it has less of an incentive to support any renewed voting rights protections." Totenberg, par. 24.

20 "Citizens without Proof: A Survey of Americans' Possession of Documentary Proof of Citizenship and Photo Identification," Brennan Center for Justice, November 2006, www.brennancenter.org, 3, 1; see also Matt A. Barreto, Stephen A. Nuno, and Gabriel R. Sanchez, "The Disproportionate Impact of Voter-ID Requirements on the Electorate—New Evidence from Indiana," *PS: Political Science & Politics* 42 (2009): 111–116; Gabriel R. Sanchez, Stephen A. Nuno, and Matt A. Barreto, "The Disproportionate Impact of Photo-ID Laws on the Minority Electorate," *Latino Decisions*, May 24, 2011, www.latinodecisions.com.

21 Keesha Gaskins and Sundeep Iyer, "The Challenge of Obtaining Voter Identification," Brennan Center for Justice, July 29, 2012, www.brennancenter.org, 1.

22 Ian Vandewalker, "Analysis: The Effects of Requiring Documentary Proof of Citizenship to Register to Vote," Brennan Center for Justice, July 17, 2017, www.brennancenter.org, 4. Native American and other groups continue to challenge North Dakota's voter ID requirements as reaching beyond their original intent to suppress votes. "Federal Judge Won't Delay North Dakota Voter ID Ruling," Associated Press, May 1, 2018, https://newsok.com.

23 As cited in Richard L. Hasen, "Softening Voter ID Laws through Litigation: Is It Enough?," *Wisconsin Law Review*, September 20, 2016, https://wlr.law.wisc.edu, par. 43.

24 Vanessa M. Perez, "Americans with Photo ID: A Breakdown of Demographic Characteristics," Project Vote, February 2015, www.projectvote.org, 1. Another report again states that some 25 percent of African Americans 18 and over do not have a government photo ID, as compared to 8 percent of White people. Jenée Desmond-Harris, "If Voter ID Laws Affect Everybody, Why Are They Seen as Discriminatory?," *Vox*, February 14, 2016, www.vox.com, par. 2.

25 Perez, "Americans with Photo ID."

26 Jessica A. Gonzalez, "New State Voting Laws: A Barrier to the Latino Vote?" CHCI, April 2012, www.researchgate.net.

27 See Genya Coulter, "Identity Crisis: What Happens When Nobody Knows Who You Are Anymore?," U.S. Vote Foundation, 2018, www.usvotefoundation.org.

28 "Issues Related to State Voter Identification Laws," US Government Accountability Office, www.gao.gov. Although Stephen Ansolabehere concluded in 2009 that "voter ID does not appear to present a significant barrier to voting," this was prior to the passage of many states' strict voter ID laws from 2011 forward. Stephen Ansolabehere, "Effects of Identification Requirements on Voting: Evidence from the Experiences of Voters on Election Day," *PS: Political Science & Politics* 42 (2009): 129. See also Jason D. Mycoff, Michael W. Wagner, and David C. Wilson, "The Empirical Effects of Voter-ID Laws: Present or Absent?" *PS: Political Science & Politics* 42 (2009): 121–126. Additionally, many previous studies focused on self-reports rather than actual turnout. Zoltan Hajnal, Nazita Lajevardi, and Lindsay

Nielson, "Voter Identification Laws and the Suppression of Minority Votes," *Journal of Politics* 79 (2017): 365–366.

29 Jan E. Leighley and Jonathan Nagler, *Who Votes Now? Demographics, Issues, Inequality, and Turnout in the United States* (Princeton, NJ: Princeton University Press, 2013); Sidney Verba, Kay Lehman Schlozman, and Henry E. Brady, *Voice and Equality: Civic Voluntarism in American Politics* (Cambridge, MA: Harvard University Press, 1995).

30 Richard Hasen, *The Voting Wars: From Florida 2000 to the Next Election Meltdown* (New Haven, CT: Yale University Press, 2012), 97.

31 John McCormack, "The Election Came Down to 77,744 Votes in Pennsylvania, Wisconsin, and Michigan," *Weekly Standard*, November 10, 2016, www.weeklystandard.com.

32 Eric Ortiz, "North Dakota, Native Tribes Agree to Settle Voter ID Lawsuit to Combat Voter Suppression," *NBC News*, February 14, 2020, www.nbcnews.com, par. 24.

33 Vandewalker, "Analysis," 1.

34 Vandewalker, 1.

35 R. Michael Alvarez, Delia Bailey, and Jonathan N. Katz, "The Effect of Voter Identification Laws on Turnout," *California Institute of Technology Social Science Working Paper* 1267R (2008): 1.

36 Vandewalker, "Analysis," 3.

37 "Voter ID Study Turnout Effects in 2016 Wisconsin Presidential Election," September 25, 2017, University of Wisconsin–Madison, https://elections.wiscweb.wisc.edu.

38 Kenneth R. Mayer and Michael G. DeCrescenzo, "Voter Identification and Nonvoting in Wisconsin—Evidence from the 2016 Election," Midwest Political Science Association conference, April 5–8, 2018, Chicago, IL, 1.

39 Rachel Treisman, "'Based on a Lie'—Georgia Voting Law Faces Wave of Corporate Backlash," NPR, April 1, 2021, www.npr.org.

40 M. V. Hood III and Charles S. Bullock III, "Much Ado about Nothing? An Empirical Assessment of the Georgia Voter Identification Statute," *State Politics & Policy Quarterly* 12 (2012): 394. Georgia has been at the center of related forms of suppression. In the 2018 midterm elections, "In addition to voter ID laws, Georgia had implemented a program called 'exact match' that a judge had previously ruled was racially discriminatory but was, nonetheless, reborn with all of its defects by the Georgia legislature and in full operation in 2018. This voter registration program was its own literacy test as it required information on the voter registration card to be an exact image of that stored in a state database or Social Security office. An accent or hyphen in one better be there in the other. In this election alone, Mr. [Brian] Kemp had trapped 53,000 voter registration cards using exact match, and 70 percent of the applicants kicked into electoral purgatory were African-American, including one of my colleagues, a faculty member at Emory University. Then there [were] the basic election processes that wreaked havoc at

the polls. Voting machines in Snellville in Metro Atlanta arrived with no power cords. People were waiting for hours in a line that was not moving and were finally forced to leave without voting because they had to get to their jobs. This was the same area where absentee ballots were rejected at almost 10 times the state average. Those Neo–Jim Crow barriers were rising up from Georgia's Confederate soil like ghosts." Carol Anderson, "Stacey Abrams, Brian Kemp and Neo–Jim Crow in Georgia," *New York Times*, November 7, 2018, www.nytimes.com, pars. 6–8. As the gubernatorial opponent to then Georgia secretary of state Brian Kemp in that election, and as it builds on so many themes explored in this book, it's also worth quoting Stacey Abrams's insights about that election at length: "Although 'exact match' lacks the explicit racial animus of Jim Crow, its execution nonetheless betrayed its true purpose to disenfranchise voters of color. . . . The state officials behind exact match were well aware, per an earlier lawsuit, that when only a missing hyphen or a typo in a government database can form the basis to withhold the right to vote, people of color will bear the brunt of such trivial mistakes. A particularly egregious example involved a voter whose last name is 'del Rio.' He was affected by the policy merely because the department of motor vehicles office where he registered to vote did not allow spaces in last names. He was 'delRio' there. But the voter rolls do allow spaces. No exact match. Voters like Mr. del Rio faced unnecessary hurdles, and poll workers were not trained properly to make sure that voices like his were heard. Across the country, voter purges employ an easily manipulated 'use it or lose it' rule, under which eligible voters who exercised their First Amendment right to abstain from voting in prior elections can be booted off the rolls. Add to this mix closed or relocated polling places outside the reach of public transit, sometimes as far as 75 miles away, or long lines that force low-income voters to forfeit half a day's pay, and a modern poll tax is revealed." Stacey Abrams, "We Cannot Resign Ourselves to Dismay and Disenfranchisement," *New York Times*, May 15, 2019, www.nytimes.com, pars. 8–12.

41 Shelley de Alth, "ID at the Polls: Assessing the Impact of Recent State Voter ID Laws on Voter Turnout," *Harvard Law & Policy Review* 3 (2009): 198.

42 Marjorie Randon Hershey, "What We Know about Voter-ID Laws, Registration, and Turnout," *PS: Political Science & Politics* 42 (2009): 87.

43 Hajnal, Lajevardi, and Nielson, "Voter Identification Laws," 368.

44 Hajnal, Lajevardi, and Nielson, 375, 372. See also Mark Hoekstra and Vijetha Koppa, "Strict Voter Identification Laws, Turnout, and Election Outcomes," CATO Institute, February 19, 2020, www.cato.org.

45 See Ben Pryor, Rebekah Herrick, and James A. Davis, "Voter ID Laws: The Disenfranchisement of Minority Voters?" *Political Science Quarterly* 134 (2019): 63–83; German Lopez, "A Major Study Finding That Voter ID Laws Hurt Minorities Isn't Standing Up Well under Scrutiny," *Vox*, March 15, 2017, www.vox.com; Justin Grimmer, Eitan Hersh, Marc Meredith, Jonathan Mummolo, and Clayton Nall, "Comment on 'Voter Identification Laws and the Suppression of Minority Votes,'" 2017, http://web.stanford.edu; Justin Grimmer, Eitan Hersh, Marc Meredith,

Jonathan Mummolo, and Clayton Nall, "Obstacles to Estimating Voter ID Laws' Effect on Turnout," *Journal of Politics* 80 (2018): 1045–1051.

46 John Kuk, Zoltan Hajnal, and Nazita Lajevardi, "A Disproportionate Burden: Strict Voter Identification Laws and Minority Turnout," *Politics, Groups, and Identities* 10 (2020): 1.

47 Jennifer Darrah-Okike, Nathalie Rita, and John R. Logan, "The Suppressive Impacts of Voter Identification Requirements," *Sociological Perspectives* 64 (2020): 536–562.

48 Rachael V. Cobb, D. James Greiner, and Kevin M. Quinn, "Can Voter ID Laws Be Administered in a Race-Neutral Manner? Evidence from the City of Boston in 2008," *Quarterly Journal of Political Science* 7 (2010): 1. Pushing this conversation forward, a working paper found that voter ID "laws have no negative effect on registration or turnout, overall or for any group defined by race, gender, age, or party affiliation," but that "the likelihood that non-[W]hite voters were contacted by a campaign increases by 5.4 percentage points, suggesting that parties' mobilization might have offset modest effects of the laws on the participation of ethnic minorities." It also found that "strict ID requirements have no effect on fraud—actual or perceived." Enrico Cantoni and Vincent Pons, "Strict ID Laws Don't Stop Voters: Evidence from a U.S. Nationwide Panel, 2008–2018," National Bureau of Economic Research, March 2020, www.nber.org.

49 Barbara Harris Combs, "Black (and Brown) Bodies Out of Place: Towards a Theoretical Understanding of Systematic Voter Suppression in the United States," *Critical Sociology* 42 (2015): 535.

50 The authors further note, "Among the 5 studies that showed statistically significant effects, 1 of the studies found an increase in voter turnout nationwide of 1.8 percentage points. The other 4 studies that showed statistically significant effects found that voter ID requirements decreased voter turnout, and the estimated decreases ranged from 1.5 to 3.9 percentage points." "Issues Related to State Voter Identification Laws," US Government Accountability Office, February 27, 2015, www.gao.gov.

51 "Issues Related to State Voter Identification Laws."

52 "Issues Related to State Voter Identification Laws."

53 Cassidy, "In Wisconsin, ID Law Proved Insurmountable," pars. 5–6.

54 Lee and Smith, "Everything You've Ever Wanted to Know about Voter ID Laws," par. 6.

55 Tova Andrea Wang, "Got ID? Helping Americans Get Voter Identification," Demos, April 2012, www.demos.org, 11.

56 Kai Brito, "UW Professor Finds More Than 16,000 Wisconsinites Were Deterred from Voting," *Badger Herald*, September 28, 2017, https://badgerherald.com, par. 14.

57 Sara Horwitz, "Getting a Photo ID So You Can Vote Is Easy. Unless You're Poor, Black, Latino or Elderly," *Washington Post*, May 23, 2016, www.washingtonpost.com, par. 35–36.

58 Gaskins and Iyer, "The Challenge of Obtaining Voter Identification," 8.
59 Ariel R. White, Noah L. Nathan, and Julie K. Faller, "What Do I Need to Vote?
    Bureaucratic Discretion and Discrimination by Local Election Officials,"
    American Political Science Review 109 (2015): 129 (emphasis removed). Michael
    Lipsky forwarded this line of thought in arguing that "the decisions of street-level
    bureaucrats, the routines they establish, and the devices they invent to cope with
    uncertainties and work pressures, effectively become the public policies they carry
    out. I argue that public policy is not best understood as made in legislatures or
    top-floor suites of high-ranking administrators, because in important ways it is
    actually made in the crowded offices and daily encounters of street-level workers."
    Michael Lipsky, *Street-Level Bureaucracy: Dilemmas of the Individual in Public
    Services* (New York: Russell Sage Foundation, 1980), xii. For an examination of
    parallel bureaucratic issues in the context of participatory budgeting, see Daniel
    Williams and Don Waisanen, *Real Money, Real Power? The Challenges with Par-
    ticipatory Budgeting in New York City* (New York: Palgrave-Macmillan, 2020).
60 Lonna Rae Atkeson, Lisa Ann Bryant, Thad E. Hall, Kyle Saunders, and Michael
    Alvarez, "A New Barrier to Participation: Heterogeneous Application of Voter
    Identification Policies," *Electoral Studies* 29 (2010): 69–70.
61 Molly McGrath, "The Voter Suppression Diaries: To Save Democracy, We Need to
    Meet Voters Where They Are," ACLU Voting Rights Project, n.d., www.aclu.org,
    pars. 1–2.
62 See Cassidy, "In Wisconsin, ID Law Proved Insurmountable," pars. 14–17.
63 Sobel, "The High Cost," 26. For a look at some of the costs related to passports
    and other issues, see appendix B.
64 Sobel, 2.
65 R. J. Vogt, "Could Fee-Based Voting Restrictions Tilt the 2020 Election?," *Law
    360*, February 9, 2020, www.law360.com. Heather Ann Thompson says that after
    the Civil War the main strategy to disenfranchise four million freed people was
    to criminalize and jail them, while after the Voting Rights Act of 1965 a similar
    movement for mass incarceration took place: "At the very same moment that the
    American Civil Rights Movement had succeeded in newly empowering Afri-
    can Americans in the political sphere by securing passage of the Voting Rights
    Act of 1965, America's [W]hite politicians decided to begin a massive new war
    on crime that would eventually undercut [the] myriad gains of the Civil Rights
    Movement—particularly those promised by the Voting Rights Act itself." This was
    buttressed by the expansive war on drugs, so that "between 1970 and 2010 more
    people ended up in prison in this country than anywhere else in the world. At no
    other point in this nation's recorded past had the economic, social, and political
    institutions of a country become so bound up with the practice of punishment."
    Many laws in the United States' penal system have been engineered to reinforce
    existing power structures, such as the common practice of shipping prisoners to
    rural White areas where prisoners can be counted for census purposes—hence
    receiving federal and state funding and resources to gain political power—

while denying them all their rights, such as voting. This phenomenon draws money away from the poorer areas where many prisoners come from, advancing inequalities from marginalized to privileged communities. It also creates gerrymandered districts that wouldn't even exist if it weren't for the prison population. And without the ability to vote as a felon or former felon, one simply cannot change the system that created these conditions in the first place. By 2006, disenfranchisement laws affected one-fourth of the US population, or forty-seven million Americans, who had criminal records, across forty-eight of the fifty US states. Heather Ann Thompson, "How Prisons Change the Balance of Power in America," *The Atlantic*, October 7, 2013, www.theatlantic.com, pars. 7–8, 20. In Downs, *Voter Suppression*, 71, 50–51.

66 Jeff Stonecash, Mark D. Brewer, and Mack D. Mariani, *Diverging Parties: Social Change, Realignment, and Party Polarization* (New York: Routledge, 2018). See also Eli J. Finkel, Christopher A. Bail, Mina Cikara, Peter H. Ditto, Shanto Iyengar, Samara Klar, Lilliana Mason, Mary C. McGrath, Brendan Nyhan, David G. Rand, Linda J. Skitka, Joshua A. Tucker, Jay J. Van Bavel, Cynthia S. Wang, and James N. Druckman, "Political Sectarianism in America," *Science* 370 (2020): 533–536.

67 John Wihbey, "Voter ID Laws and the Evidence: A Report from the Government Accountability Office," Journalist's Resource, October 16, 2014, https://journalistsresource.org, par. 3. For further history on voter ID laws, see Christina Beeler, "Voter ID Laws: A Solution in Search of a Problem," *Houston Law Review* 55 (2017): 479–510. Supporting the polarization thesis (with some nuances), researchers "find that partisanship shapes respondents' attitudes about the effects of voter ID laws, but in different ways. Democrats, whose opinions vary according to ideology, education, attention to politics, and racial resentment, are divided. Republicans, however, are markedly more united in their support of voter ID laws," demonstrating differences "consistent with an elite-to-mass message transmission reflecting the current context of polarized party politics and the variation in the voter coalitions comprising the Democratic and Republican parties." Paul Gronke, William D. Hicks, Seth C. McKee, Charles Stewart III, and James Dunham, "Voter ID Laws: A View from the Public," *Social Science Quarterly* 100 (2019): 215.

68 Lorraine C. Minnette, *The Myth of Voter Fraud* (Ithaca, NY: Cornell University Press, 2010).

69 Hans von Spakovsky, "New State Voting Laws: Barriers to the Ballot?," Heritage Foundation, September 27, 2011, www.heritage.org, par. 11. Hans von Spakovsky highlights more about the case for voter ID here: "Does the Voter ID Requirement Safeguard the Election Process?," YouTube, April 8, 2020, www.youtube.com/watch?v=6wsIoir9iZU. Of note, the Heritage Foundation has only "found 14 cases of attempted mail fraud out of roughly 15.5 million ballots cast in Oregon since that state started conducting elections by mail in 1998." Andy Sullivan, "Explainer: Fraud Is Rare in U.S. Mail-in Voting: Here Are the Methods That Prevent It," Reuters, July 7, 2020, www.reuters.com, par. 11.

70 Kris Kobach, "The Case for Voter ID," *Wall Street Journal*, May 23, 2011.

71 "Oppose Voter ID Legislation—Fact Sheet."

72 Rich Lowry, "The Poll Tax That Wasn't," *Politico*, October 22, 2014. For Justice Ginsburg's dissent, see *Veasey v. Perry*, 574 U.S. (2014).

73 Alison Durkee, "More Than Half of Republicans Believe Voter Fraud Claims and Most Still Support Trump, Poll Finds," *Forbes*, April 5, 2021, www.forbes.com.

74 Justin Levitt, "A Comprehensive Investigation of Voter Impersonation Finds 31 Credible Incidents Out of One Billion Ballots Cast," *Washington Post*, August 6, 2014, www.washingtonpost.com. One of the participants we spoke to during this project, a founder of a nonpartisan research and election think tank, further claimed that voter fraud is "exceedingly rare. It's not altering the outcome of any elections. It's, it hardly ever occurs intentionally. I mean, it's almost always due to some kind of confusion and we can create a system whereby it's much more . . . unlikely. . . . So it's much less likely that voters would be confused and accidentally cast a ballot they shouldn't be casting. And for those who are truly motivated to commit the dumbest crime in history, and cast a ballot they shouldn't be casting [to begin with], make it difficult for them because they shouldn't be on the list in the first place and receiving a ballot. If we can do those things then voter ID becomes an unnecessary, you know, an unnecessary enterprise to secure the vote."

75 As cited in Sobel, "The High Cost," 7.

76 Kira Learner and Joshua Eaton, "Kansas Secretary of State Seeks to Deliver a Devastating Blow to Voting Rights," *ThinkProgress*, March 6, 2018, https://think progress.org.

77 W. Phillips Davison, "The Third-Person Effect in Communication," *Public Opinion Quarterly* 47 (1983): 1–15.

78 Vandewalker, "Analysis," 5. People must sign off at the polls that they are US citizens, too, under lawful penalties that should and do act as deterrents to non-citizen voting. In light of the massive number of restrictive voter bills introduced after the 2020 US general election across states, we concur with David J. Becker, the executive director of the Center for Election Innovation, who has stated, "It is absolutely legitimate to be concerned about election integrity. . . . Even though fraud isn't widespread, it's good for voters to know there are protections in place against it. What's not OK is to invent fake threats and to ignore the evidence and to act in a way that's clearly designed to result in a partisan outcome." Maggie Astor, "'A Perpetual Motion Machine': How Disinformation Drives Voting Laws," *New York Times*, May 13, 2021, https://advance-lexis-com, par. 25.

79 Charles Stewart III, "Mail Ballot Fraud Case in NJ Illustrates How This Works," Twitter, 07:23 a.m., June 26, 2020, https://twitter.com. For another example of how difficult, isolated, and confined to local elections these cases tend to be, see Stephen Koranda, "Kansas Rep. Steve Watkins Charged with Felonies over Voter Registration at UPS Store," NPR, July 14, 2020, www.npr.org.

80 Josh Lederman writes that "election officials and candidates who have encountered the system up-close say that human and computerized guardrails all along

the journey of a mail-in-ballot create a structure that, while cumbersome and expensive, cannot be breached in any significant way." Josh Lederman, "Guardrails Line the Journey in the Life of a Mail-in Ballot," *NBC News*, July 6, 2020, www .nbcnews.com, par. 2. See also Sullivan, "Explainer." That being said, in contrast to the variety of unsubstantiated, imagined ways fraud is often said to happen, in the past there has been a real issue of people *selling* their votes to others and then using absentee ballots as the mechanism to pull off the scam. David A. Fahrenthold, "Selling Votes Is Common Type of Election Fraud," *Washington Post*, October 1, 2012, www.washingtonpost.com.

81 Andrew Cohen, "How Voter ID Laws Are Being Used to Disenfranchise Minorities and the Poor," *The Atlantic*, March 16, 2012, www.theatlantic.com; see also "Debunking the Myth of Voter Fraud," Brennan Center for Justice, n.d., www.brennancenter.org; Jessica Huseman, "How the Case for Voter Fraud Was Tested—and Utterly Failed," *Propublica*, June 19, 2018, www.propublica.org. See also Shared Goel, Marc Meredith, Michael Morse, David Rothschild, and Houshmand Shirani-Mehr, "One Person, One Vote: Estimating the Prevalence of Double Voting in U.S. Presidential Elections," *American Political Science Review* 114 (2020): 456–469.

82 "Voter ID Rules: A Solution in Search of a Problem," *Washington Post*, March 12, 2012.

83 Shaun Bowler and Todd Donovan, "A Partisan Model of Electoral Reform: Voter Identification Laws and Confidence in State Elections," *State Politics & Policy Quarterly* 16 (2016): 340.

84 Berman, "Why the Voting Rights Act," par. 9. In terms of motivations, Gilda Daniels highlights a critical question: "Consider this: If you could get rid of voters, eligible voters, without violence and within legal means, would you try it? What if the affected voters were predisposed to vote against you, or so you believed? Would you use or propose laws that had this affect?" Daniels, *Uncounted*, 3.

85 Michael Wines, "Some Republicans Acknowledge Leveraging Voter ID Laws for Political Gain," *New York Times*, September 16, 2016, www.nytimes.com.

86 Thanks to our City University of New York colleague Michael Kaplan for pointing this out in a conversation. Kaplan says that on so many counts, from issues of corruption to promiscuity, "the right is all about projecting its own behavior onto its adversaries. . . . it's so consistent and reliable that it's almost parodic." See, for example, Corky Siemaszko, "Republican Official in Ohio Faces Charge for Voting Twice in November Election," *NBC News*, June 22, 2021, www.nbcnews.com.

87 Courtney Coren, "Rasmussen Poll: 78 Percent of Voters Support Voter ID Laws," *Newsmax*, March 25, 2014. For an example of the legal battles taking place on this issue, see Debbie Elliott, "Judge Throws Out Challenge to Alabama Voter ID Law," NPR, January 10, 2018, www.npr.org; Robert A. Pastor, Robert Santos, Alison Prevost, and Vassia Stoilov, "Voting and ID Requirements: A Survey of Registered Voters in Three States," *American Review of Public Administration* 40 (2010): 461–481.

88 Christopher Cooper, "The Voter ID Conversation I Wish We Were Having," *Citizen Times*, June 18, 2018, www.citizen-times.com. A federal court also upheld the ruling. Konstantin Toropin and Caroline Kelly, "Court Affirms Ruling Striking Down Kansas Voter Registration Law," CNN, April 30, 2020, www.cnn.com.

89 Jack Crosbie, "The Supreme Court Just Upheld a Terrible Voter ID Law in North Dakota," *Splinter*, October 9, 2018, https://splinternews.com. As further background: "Amid a nationwide push that advocates have called a voter disenfranchisement tactic disproportionately affecting Black, Latino and Native American citizens, South Dakota passed legislation in 2003 requiring that a photo ID be presented at the polls in order to vote. Acceptable forms include a South Dakota driver's license or nondriver ID card, a passport or other ID issued by the federal government, a student ID from a South Dakota high school or accredited college, or a tribal photo ID. But a tribal ID is not allowed as a valid form of identification to register to vote in the first place, something that advocates say discriminates against Native Americans. Earlier this year, lawmakers rejected legislation that would have allowed it." Matt DeRienzo, "In South Dakota, Native Americans Face Numerous Obstacles to Voting," Center for Public Integrity, October 29, 2020, https://publicintegrity.org, pars. 7–9.

90 Geoff West, "South Dakota Rejects Tribal IDs for Voter Registration," *The Fulcrum*, February 10, 2020, https://thefulcrum.us; "South Dakota Lawmakers Reject Tribal ID Voter Measure, Advance Business ID Use," *Nativeknot*, February 14, 2020, www.nativeknot.com.

91 Jasmine C. Lee, "How States Moved toward Stricter Voter ID Laws," *New York Times*, November 3, 2016, www.nytimes.com.

92 "Election 2016."

93 "Voting Laws Roundup: January 2021," Brennan Center for Justice, January 26, 2021, www.brennancenter.org.

94 Hasen, "Softening Voter ID Laws."

95 Jenée Desmond-Harris, "What Are Voter ID Laws?," *Vox*, February 14, 2016, www.vox.com, par. 1.

96 Gaskins and Iyer, "The Challenge of Obtaining Voter Identification," 14–15.

97 Niki Ludt, "Justice Requires That Legal ID Be Affordable to All," *Legal Intelligence*, January 26, 2015, www.law.com.

98 Vandewalker, "Analysis," 4.

99 Brandi Blessett, "Disenfranchisement: Historical Underpinnings and Contemporary Manifestations," *Public Administration Quarterly* 39 (2015): 3.

100 This story can be found in Horwitz, "Getting a Photo ID," par. 4.

101 Myrna Perez, "Voting after You Move: A Guide," Brennan Center for Justice, June 13, 2009, www.brennancenter.org.

102 "State Voter Identification Requirements: Analysis, Legal Issues, and Policy Considerations," *Congressional Research Service*, October 21, 2016.

103 "The Cost of Voting," Democracy Docket, May 11, 2021, www.democracydocket.com, par. 9. Another analysis underscores that from 1996 to 2016, "Oregon,

which has one of the most progressive automatic voter registration processes and mail-in voting, maintains the first position as the easiest state in which to vote. Texas falls to 50th, in part because it does not keep pace with reforms like online voter registration and no excuse absentee voting." Scot Schraufnagel, Michael J. Pomante II, and Quan Li, "Cost of Voting in the American States: 2020," *Election Law Journal: Rules, Politics, and Policy* 19 (2020): 503.

104 At the time, the report had been updated as of May 2018, with our data collection beginning in June 2018. Wendy Underhill, "Voter Identification Requirements | Voter ID Laws," National Conference of State Legislatures, May 31, 2018, www.ncsl.org. The same site notes that some exceptions to these laws exist; the NCSL explains: "These exceptions may include people who: Have religious objections to being photographed (Arkansas, Indiana, Kansas, Mississippi, South Carolina, Tennessee, Texas, Wisconsin); Are indigent (Indiana, Tennessee); 'Have a reasonable impediment' to getting an ID (South Carolina); Do not have an ID as a result of a recent natural disaster (Texas); People who are victims of domestic abuse, sexual assault or stalking and have a 'confidential listing' (Wisconsin); Additionally, voter ID requirements generally apply to in-person voting, not to absentee ballots or mailed ballots. All voters, regardless of the type of verification required by the states, are subject to perjury charges if they vote under false pretenses." Underhill, "Voter Identification Requirements," pars. 30–37.

105 Some states also allow the use of affidavits and provisional ballots that must generally be brought to a county recorder within a certain number of days since an election.

106 For example, Gaskin and Iyer, "The Challenge of Obtaining Voter Identification," 1–2.

107 Jack Citrin, Donald P. Green, and Morris Levy, "The Effects of Voter ID Notification on Voter Turnout: Results from a Large-Scale Field Experiment," *Election Law Journal* 13 (2014): 228–242; see also Chelsie L. M. Bright and Michael S. Lynch, "Kansas Voter ID Laws: Advertising and Its Effect on Turnout," https://blogs.missouristate.edu, 1–29.

108 Wang, "Got ID?," 2.

109 Wang, 8.

110 "Spread the Vote," n.d., www.spreadthevote.org; Patricia Sullivan, "Voter Access: 'Bringing in People Who Haven't had a Voice," *Washington Post*, October 14, 2018, www.washingtonpost.com. For an interview with Spread the Vote's founder—who underscores the key issues at stake with voter documentation and how the organization is currently tackling the issue—see "'Spread the Vote' Founder, Kat Calvin," The Electorette Podcast, February 19, 2018, www.iheart.com/.

111 "Mr. Thomas Gets an ID," n.d., www.spreadthevote.org.

112 For the problems of simply "educating" citizens toward change, see Jesse Singal, "Awareness Is Overrated," *New York Magazine*, July 17, 2014, http://nymag.com/scienceofus/2014/07/awareness-is-overrated.html; M. D. Hill and

M. Thompson-Hayes, *From Awareness to Commitment in Public Health Campaigns: The Awareness Myth* (Lanham, MD: Lexington, 2017).

113 Nancy Lee, *Policymaking for Citizen Behavior Change: A Social Marketing Approach* (New York: Routledge, 2018).

2. UNDERSTANDING THE PROBLEM

1 In crafting our research design and eventual recommendations based on this book's findings, we were cognizant of the field of social marketing for its alignments with the background and directions of this project. Social marketing, or the use of research and techniques for social impacts, focuses on the everyday, empirical challenges (e.g., beliefs, barriers, and competing factors) that publics face, proposing realistic solutions emerging from wide-ranging evidence. Different from top-down, broadcast-driven public campaigns unmoored from the lives of those they seek to influence, social marketing initiatives stay connected to what stakeholders and participants in communities share about their experiences and struggles, with a particular emphasis on interactions with and dialogue between researchers and priority audiences. Social marketing "principles and techniques are most often used to improve public health, prevent injuries, protect the environment, increase involvement in the community and enhance financial well-being," lending themselves well to a project focused on helping citizens get the resources they need to vote across states where shifting rules and expectations are at play. Social marketing takes a multifaceted approach to change, using applied research and established theories that consider "the multicausality of social problems" to "recommend multilevel interventions." Nancy Lee and Philip Kotler, *Social Marketing: Influencing Behaviors for Good*, 5th ed. (Thousand Oaks, CA: Sage, 2016), 33; R. C. Hornik, "Why Can't We Sell Human Rights Like Soap," in *Public Communication Campaigns*, 4th ed., ed. R. E. Rice C. K. Atkin (Thousand Oaks, CA: Sage, 2013), 148–149; Brenda Dervin and Lois Foreman-Wernet, "Sense-Making Methodology as an Approach to Understanding and Designing for Campaign Audiences," in *Public Communication Campaigns*, 4th ed., ed. R. E. Rice and C. K. Atkin (Thousand Oaks, CA: Sage, 2013), 147–160. See also Robert Smith, Don Waisanen, and Guillermo Yrizar Barbosa, *Immigration and Strategic Public Health Communication: Lessons from the Transnational Seguro Popular Project* (New York: Routledge, 2019).

2 Chip Heath and Dan Heath, *Switch: How to Change Things When Change Is Hard* (New York: Random House, 2010).

3 Mark Sommerhauser, "As Election Nears, Public Campaign Seeks to Help Voters Meet State's Photo ID Requirement," *Wisconsin State Journal*, October 13, 2018, https://madison.com; Wisconsin Elections Commission, "G.A.B. Announces Statewide Voter Photo ID Public Education Campaign," October 9, 2014, https://elections.wi.gov; "Milwaukee County Election Commission 2016 General Election Bring It to the Ballot Campaign," *Declaration of Michael Haas*, October 6, 2016, https://moritzlaw.osu.edu; Jim Malewitz, "Study: Texas Voter Education

Campaign Failed to Prevent ID Confusion," *Texas Tribune*, April 11, 2017, www
.texastribune.org.

4 Jack Citrin, Donald Green, and Morris Levy, "The Effects of Voter ID Notification
on Voter Turnout: Results from a Large-Scale Field Experiment," *Election Law
Journal* 13 (2014): 228–242, www.povertyactionlab.org.

5 Susan Clark, "Community Driven Design Increases Voter Turnout," n.d., http://
ckgroup.org.

6 "A Community Based Approach to Increasing Voter Turnout," adapted from a
May 23, 2000, presentation by Susan S. Clark at the "California Voting in the 21st
Century" conference sponsored by the California Secretary of State, www.litera
cynet.org.

7 Lee and Kotler, *Social Marketing*.

8 Nonprofit VOTE, n.d., www.nonprofitvote.org/.

9 To maintain our participants' privacy, we removed all identifiers from the data
collected. Each part of this research design was reviewed and approved by the
Baruch College, City University of New York Institutional Review Board.

10 "Nonprofit VOTE."

11 "Nonprofit VOTE."

12 There is a slight distinction between Nonprofit VOTE's partners (those groups
listed previously such as the YMCA, Habitat for Humanity, and so forth, on its
national and state partners' pages, as well as its "anchor" partners with whom
it runs a tracked voter engagement program in states), and the broader network it
tapped for this project. Nonprofit VOTE identified individuals who receive their
newsletters and provided an address in the states it was targeting and sent them
emails asking for their participation. Nonprofit VOTE also asked its relevant state
partners to reach out to their networks to drum up additional responses.

13 We were able to offer incentives for participation beyond this first step, however.
Through our research grant, Nonprofit VOTE offered conveners $250 to recruit
ten-plus nonprofit partners to take the surveys, and then small grants to those
nonprofits that would go on to host interviews or focus groups (to help cover any
space costs and staff time to coordinate) and to any community members who
participated. The nonprofits would receive $250 for several interviews with com-
munity members they serve, or $500 for setting up focus groups for members of
our research team to conduct. These relatively small uniform grants to convener
organizations and any other local nonprofits were offered as part of an effort to
join a "research network for the Nonprofit Voter Documentation Project." For the
interviews with community member participants in voter ID states, we offered
$25 to $75 gift cards for participating in an individual interview or a focus group,
depending on the likely length of time for each and budgetary constraints during
our year of data collection.

14 For a report on the use of MTurk for research, see Paul Hitlin, "Research in the
Crowdsourcing Age, a Case Study," Pew Research Center, July 11, 2016, www
.pewinternet.org. MTurk is a service that provides researchers with a population

of customized potential participants. This gave us the advantage of collecting a large amount of data in a short amount of time, at a cost lower than that for traditional surveys. The demographics of MTurk workers are roughly similar to some key characteristics of our research population, with a lower average income and younger skewed age distribution than the US average. Approximately 75 percent of MTurk workers are in the United States. They are almost evenly distributed between men and women (55 percent female). The total worker population is estimated to be 100,000 to 200,000 individuals, with approximately 2,450 active workers available at any given time. Djellel Difallah, Elena Filatova, and Panos Ipeirotis, "Demographics and Dynamics of Mechanical Turk Workers," in *Proceedings of WSDM 2018: The Eleventh ACM International Conference on Web Search and Data Mining*, Marina Del Rey, CA, February 5–9, 2018, www.ipeirotis .com. In terms of identity verification and agreements between MTurk and its workers, Amazon has each worker register on the site using their existing Amazon.com account or a new one, providing a name and address and agreeing to its terms of service. The account is placed under review (although it's not entirely clear what Amazon is checking during this time; see www.quora.com). Once the account is approved, the worker supplies information for the Amazon Payments system, including name, address, and Social Security number (for US workers), which is then verified with the Internal Revenue Service. Workers who have not filed taxes have to submit other proof of identity such as bank account information or a driver's license. There is also a probation period during which the number of HITs (human intelligence tasks) that they can respond to are limited. Beyond signing user participation agreements and Amazon Payments account requirements, the following resource provides comprehensive information about how workers sign up and what Amazon expects: https://turkerhub.com. Although MTurk is composed of a convenience sample, its wide reach, extensive use in current social scientific research, and ability to prequalify participants according to demographic and other characteristics (see below) allowed us to reach potential respondents informed by this study's parameters. Once we connected MTurk to our Qualtrics survey platform, we ran some initial tests to see whether we were on the right track. We offered our survey only to those who met certain criteria, using MTurk's premium qualifications feature. These prequalifying criteria included age (we focused on the 18–30 and 55-plus age groups), income (we started with less than $50,000 household income), and respondents' state of residence (to ensure that only those people who live in the ten strict voter ID states took the survey). Using the MTurk screening qualifications feature, the age qualification added $.50 and the income qualification $.50 per survey, for instance. There's also an interesting screening method that can be used in conjunction with MTurk prequalifications, but after testing the three criteria on MTurk with an initial sample of participants, we concluded that the MTurk prequalifications would be enough to reach our sample size. See http://mturk101.blogspot.com and https://jessicaeblack.wordpress.com. Those who qualified were then invited to take the full survey. The full survey took approximately seven to ten minutes to complete and paid $2.00 after the initial test of the survey with a smaller sample of participants (we took New York's hourly minimum wage and divided by the time it should take to complete the screening; Kim Bartel Sheehan and Matthew Pittman advise paying a percentage of hourly minimum wage, depending on how long the survey or other forms of data collection take to complete). Kim Bartel Sheehan and Matthew Pittman, *Amazon's Mechanical Turk for Academics: The HIT Handbook for Social Science Research* (Irvine, CA: Melvin and Leigh, 2016). We collected completed surveys until we reached a sample size of approximately two hundred qualified respondents over a five-day period.

15 Based on watching a webinar from Qualtrics (www.qualtrics.com), where the researchers tested the effects of the use of different types of control questions on the quality of the resulting data, we were persuaded to move away from an attention check approach (i.e., "tricking" those who are not paying attention) to instead add a question up front securing the respondent's commitment to answering the questions to the best of their ability. In the Qualtrics study, the researchers tested three thousand respondents and found that on just about every indicator, using this kind of question resulted in better outcomes than using attention check questions. In addition, when they used the attention check questions and threw out the ones that failed, it resulted in skewing the age distribution, removing younger respondents. We also instructed participants, "This HIT is periodically re-posted. If you've already completed this HIT previously, please do not complete it a second time. You will not be compensated a second time," based on a recommendation from one of the MTurk advice sites; see item 7 under "Designing a HIT Template" here: https://michaelbuhrmester.wordpress.com. We skimmed several Reddit forums by MTurk workers to understand their motivations and included a question at the end seeking their further comments and feedback after reading the following: "Anyone Ever Write to a Requester to Tell Them How Bad Their Hit Is?," www.reddit.com; "Comments on Survey Hits," www.reddit.com; "Does Anyone Else Try to Motivate the Survey Writers?," www.reddit.com.

16 To sample and provide a manageable number of offices to cover (some states had more than two hundred offices alone), we used the lowest number of counties from our pool of ten strict voter ID states as the target number for the other states. So, for example, if a state with the lowest number of counties had fifteen total, we would be shooting for fifteen counties from every other state as well. In selecting the county offices to call, we contacted elections staff in the five most populous, five least populous, and five other counties that fell within that spectrum. The audit consisted of a short, simple set of questions from which we could easily check off answers, as well as opportunities for providing more open-ended descriptions and impressions of the encounter from our observations (see appendix C).

17 During our research, we were less successful with identifying and interviewing people from religious organizations than the others.

18 "Directory of Charities and Nonprofit Organizations," Guidestar, n.d., www.guid estar.org.

19 Lee and Kotler, *Social Marketing*.

20 Dana Chisnell, "The Epic Journey of American Voters," Center for Civic Design, March 22, 2017, https://civicdesign.org, pars. 4–9, 29–31.

21 Fully attentive to these real types of hurdles that citizens face and the cognitive, affective, and behavioral factors involved in addressing such problems, social marketing invites systematic, holistic thinking in developing interventions, ensuring that all relevant information about the priority audience(s), the social and structural contexts (and the government), and the nature of the issue itself are taken into account in any intervention design. Thus, we kept in mind what's called a "social marketing mix," which includes concepts adapted and extended from commercial marketing practice: *product* (What is the behavior and/or benefit you will offer that most appeals to your priority audience? How is it different and better from the competition?); *price* (What are the "costs" or perceived barriers that prevent your priority audience from adopting the product? How can you lower the costs or remove those barriers?); *place* (What are the times and places at which your priority audience will be the most receptive to your campaign and able to act?); and *promotions* (How can you let your priority audience know about your product via channels they pay attention to and trust?). All these concepts bear on the difficulties that many voters face (inaccessible government offices, costs for official copies, unclear requirements, etc.). Nedra Kline Weinreich provides several concepts for all types of social change efforts. Nedra Kline Weinreich, *Hands-On Social Marketing: A Step-by-Step Guide to Designing Change for Good* (Thousand Oaks, CA: Sage, 2011), 13–22. Additionally, Weinreich provides four more useful concepts that emerged as relevant from our data: *publics* (What internal and external groups do you need to take into account who can either enable or undermine your efforts?); *policy* (What governmental or organizational policies can you work to put into place that will make adoption of the product more likely?); *partnerships* (Which other organizations might you consider working with who have credibility with and access to your priority audience, similar goals, or useful resources?); and *purse strings* (Where will you get the funding for your marketing budget, or how will you distribute the funds to other organizations?). Since most organizations doing social marketing need to figure out where the money to carry out the program is going to come from and how to sustain it, this last item remains particularly important. Given how our research developed, while not that central to our findings and conclusions, some readers may also be interested in four variables that we would add to the original "8ps" that we discussed and were inspired by (via Weinreich) earlier in this project. As an outgrowth of our research, these four concepts include: *Perceptions*—What perception do people have about voting and related process that can be addressed in advance of outreach efforts or used systemically throughout messaging to different audiences (e.g., dealing with perceptions of voter fraud as real

and important)? *Particularity*—What personal and population-based strategies will adapt to the unique local, cultural, and subcultural factors that people must navigate in jurisdictions lacking standardization and consistency in laws and processes (e.g., adapting to unique cultural and subcultural sensitivities—the distinctive difficulties we found with trans populations in Mississippi that we explore in chapter 5 was eye-opening, for instance)? *Prioritization*—How can the most important information be prioritized for different audiences (e.g., putting documents in a hierarchy in our recommendations for making voting processes easier)? Finally, *permanence*—How can we embed and scale more permanent ways of addressing the challenges of voter identification requirements, beyond ad hoc or disconnected efforts (e.g., the need to standardize the experience of working with election offices on these matters)?

3. DIFFERENT PERSPECTIVES

1 "Lawyers Seek Halt to PA's 'False' Voter ID Ads," October 19, 2012, Associated Press State and Local Wire.

2 While our themes cluster around certain areas, we try to retain our participants' phrasings and choice of language as much as possible to let their experiences speak for themselves. Again, for more on this issue we refer readers to Linda Alcoff's extended treatment on the problem of speaking for others. Alcoff, "The Problem of Speaking for Others."

3 The cities covered included Richmond, Milwaukee, Madison, Columbus, Chattanooga, Cleveland, Nashville, Arlington, Durand, Hudson, Atlanta, Augusta, Dayton, Menomonie, Fort Wayne, Lakewood, Phoenix, Topeka, Toledo, Niles, Marysville, Greensboro, Apache Junction, Snow Hill, Akron, Lawrenceville, Riverdale, and Elkhart.

4 Please note that for readability, we have removed many "ums" and "uhs" and some filler words (e.g., "like" and "you know") from our respondents' comments throughout this book.

5 Both participants referred to in this paragraph were from Wisconsin. Both likely meant myvote.wi.gov as, in the latter case, myvote.org is not a site. At the very least, this appears to show how in a multifaceted, not-very-simple or streamlined voting system names can easily get mixed up.

6 Readers can go here for another source on each state's identification requirements: www.usvotefoundation.org.

7 Although we investigated the issue, we are still unsure why none of our participants came from North Dakota, despite specifying this prequalification through MTurk. This may simply have been the luck of the draw, or there could be a lack of participants on the site overall, among other factors. Note that we also decided to retain the seven participants who indicated that they resided in "none of the above" states. When participants sign up as a worker on MTurk, they go through several verification and eligibility requirements, including listing their address at the time they signed up. Apparently MTurk takes the location information

from the address active on the worker's account too, and there is no way for
the workers to update their new location when they move (see https://forums
.aws.amazon.com/thread.jspa?messageID=348725񕈵 https://forums.aws
.amazon.com/thread.jspa?messageID=717096&#717096). We speculated about
a few unanticipated possibilities here: participants may have recently moved
states while not having updated their MTurk address, they could be temporarily residing in another state, and so on. In any case, since MTurk prequalified
these respondents as residents of one of these ten states at some point in time,
we thought that it was reasonable enough to include their responses, considering
the number of scenarios that could be playing out in their clicking "none of the
above."

8 Those clicking "Other" wrote in "Anarchist," "Democratic Socialist," "Liberal/
Middle of the Road," "Libertarian," and "Socialist," respectively.

9 See Table 2, "All Races," from Voting and Registration in the Election of November 2016, United States Census Bureau, April 25, 2018, www.census.gov.

10 This percentage is in terms of total ballots counted. Michael P. McDonald, 2016
November General Election Turnout Rates, United States Election Project, n.d.,
www.electproject.org. While we can only guess as to why this sample had such a
strong showing of registered voters, we think people on MTurk are likely more
tech-savvy than their socioeconomic peers and perhaps more attuned to news
and current events.

11 This finding comports with previous scholarship showing "an overwhelming ma-
jority of Americans support requiring showing photo identification." R. Michael
Alvarez, Thad E. Hall, Ines Levin, and Charles Stewart III, "Voter Opinions about
Election Reform: Do They Support Making Voting More Convenient?," *Election
Law Journal* 10 (2011): 73.

4. BREAKING DOWN THE SYSTEM

1 Lori Dorfman and Lawrence Wallack, "Putting Policy into Health Communication: The Role of Media Advocacy," in *Public Communication Campaigns*, ed.
Ronald E. Rice and Charles K. Atkin (Thousand Oaks, CA: Sage, 2013), 337.

2 We analyzed the data for the frequency and intensity of key insights, clustering
sentences and passages into saturated themes. See Sonja K. Foss, *Rhetorical Criti-
cism: Exploration and Practice* (Long Grove, IL: Waveland Press, 2017); Johnny
Saldaña, *The Coding Manual for Qualitative Researchers* (Thousand Oaks, CA:
Sage, 2015). Recent work underscores that despite decades of claims by researchers that they have reached "theoretical saturation" in their work, in practice it's
impossible to do so. It's far better to cluster data into saturated themes suited to
the task at hand (i.e., with limited but pragmatic applications toward research
questions in mind). We followed this line in our data collection and analysis. See
Benjamin Saunders, Julius Sim, Tom Kingstone, Shula Baker, Jackie Waterfield,
Bernadette Bartlam, Heather Burroughs, and Clare Jinks, "Saturation in Qualitative Research: Exploring Its Conceptualization and Operationalization," *Quality*

& Quantity 52 (2018): 1893–1907; Jacqueline Low, "A Pragmatic Definition of the Concept of Theoretical Saturation," *Sociological Focus* 52 (2019): 131–139.

3 In Tennessee, veterans have also been blocked from access to the ballot by requirements that Veterans Administration cards do not count as approved forms of ID. Daniels, *Uncounted*, 78.

4 Camila Domonoske, "Many Native IDs Won't Be Accepted at North Dakota Polling Places," NPR, October 13, 2018, www.npr.org.

5 Bill Chappell, "Judge Tosses Kansas' Proof-of-Citizenship Voter Law and Rebukes Sec. of State Kobach," NPR, June 19, 2018, www.npr.org.

6 "David Becker," Center for Election Innovation and Research, n.d., https://electioninnovation.org, par. 2. Other groups such as VoteShield have been working on providing "state and local election officials with the most advanced data analysis available to detect unauthorized or improper changes to voter databases." VoteShield, n.d., www.voteshield.us.

7 The guiding premise of the European Union Agency for Fundamental Rights is that "the right to an identity, including a name, surname, date of birth, as well as the right to citizenship are fundamental human rights. Without an identity a person does not officially exist and is invisible to state authorities and crucial private services." "Applying for Birth Registration," European Union Agency for Fundamental Rights, n.d., https://fra.europa.eu, par. 1.

8 What has not helped is "the Presidential Advisory Commission on Election Integrity, also known as the Pence-Kobach Commission, [which] was established to investigate claims that millions of votes were cast illegally in the 2016 election. As an initial act, the vice chair, Kris Kobach, requested voter data from all fifty states. As a result, states witnessed significant increases in voters deregistering to vote in different parts of the country. The commission's actions caused voters to remove themselves from the voter rolls, due to [a] fear that the commission had nefarious goals." After a century of marginalized communities fighting for the right to vote, ironically this set in motion a "self-purging" that would have been unheard of previously. And despite laws such as the US National Voter Registration Act in 1993 (sometimes called the Motor Voter Law due to the use of DMVs and similar locations as places where people can register to vote), overall, voter registration has remained stagnant for decades—a crisis in new registrations. Daniels, *Uncounted*, 112–113, 127.

9 "About Language Minority Voting Rights," United States Department of Justice, March 11, 2020, www.justice.gov.

10 Christine Chung, "State Voter Registration Services in Pandemic Not Working for Multilingual City," *The City*, July 30, 2020, www.thecity.nyc, pars. 3–4.

11 For more on implementation challenges, see the classic work by Jeffrey L. Pressman and Aaron Wildavsk, *Implementation: How Great Expectations in Washington Are Dashed in Oakland; Or, Why It's Amazing That Federal Programs Work at All, This Being a Saga of the Economic Development Administration as Told by*

Two Sympathetic Observers Who Seek to Build Morals on a Foundation (Berkeley: University of California Press, 1984).

12 Among many other factors, this reflects the difference between states that have elected and appointed judges. Many argue that because voters are routinely undereducated about candidates for judgeships, an appointive system is preferable. The question of which is the better system is debated and beyond this book's reach, but it is worth considering how, once again, different state systems translate into so many varying challenges for voters depending on where they happen to live. The number of ballot questions also varies wildly from one state to another. In California, where ballot initiatives are unusually common and numerous, voters receive booklets that are as long as 224 pages to describe the substance of what is on a ballot. Ian Cull, "California's Record-Setting 224-Page Voter Guide Is Costing Taxpayers Nearly $15 Million," *Los Angeles Times*, September 10, 2016, www.latimes.com.

13 "Expansion of Rights and Liberties ~ The Right of Suffrage," The Charters of Freedom, n.d., www.archives.gov/.

14 "Supporting Voters in States with Voter ID Laws," Nonprofit VOTE, April 18, 2019, www.nonprofitvote.org.

15 For further clarification on no-excuse absentee voting: "'Absentee' first came about during the Civil War as a way for soldiers to cast a ballot in their home states. The idea of allowing military voters to cast a ballot 'in absentia' is still one of the driving factors for states allowing absentee ballots. All states, by federal law, are required to send absentee ballots to military and overseas voters for federal elections. For domestic voters wishing to vote absentee or by mail, 16 states require voters to provide an 'excuse' for why they will not be able to vote on Election Day. Some of these states provide early in-person voting. The other 34 states and Washington, D.C., do not require an excuse from those who wish to vote absentee or by mail. Five states conduct elections entirely by mail (Colorado, Hawaii, Oregon, Utah, and Washington), which means voters do not need to request a ballot, and instead automatically receive one." "VOPP: Table 1: States with No-Excuse Absentee Voting," National Conference of State Legislatures, May 1, 2020, www.ncsl.org, pars. 1–3.

16 There is now a centralized voting website to help with this problem, although not everyone has a computer and not everyone might know how to search it. If you enter "Where is my polling place" into Google, you will find www.vote.org/polling-place-locator/.

17 This participant also explained, "I have a personal theory that in a way Ohio gerrymandering has an impact because we live in an area where there is a protected congresswoman who people think is going to win anyways, so 'I don't have to vote.' If there was a contest for her position, then maybe [there would be] more votes."

18 Gus Garcia-Roberts, "Texas Woman Sentenced to Eight Years for Illegal Voting Paroled, Faces Deportation," *USA Today*, February 21, 2020, www.usatoday.com.

19 For those averse to immigrant voting, Daniels reminds us that "noncitizen voting has a significant history [in the United States]. The Founding Fathers allowed noncitizen property owners to vote in elections. The rationale exists that persons who are not citizens live in communities, pay taxes, and contribute to society in many ways." Daniels, *Uncounted*, 189.

20 Anderson, *One Person, No Vote*, 155.

21 Robert Cialdini, *Influence: Science and Practice* (Boston: Pearson, 2009).

22 This doesn't even begin to address the monumental challenges that developed in Georgia during its 2020 primary amid the COVID-19 pandemic, which included major problems with new voting machines, missing primary ballots in majority-minority neighborhoods, and more. Zach Montellaro and Laura Barron Lopez, "'A Hot, Flaming Mess': Georgia Primary Beset by Chaos, Long Lines," *Politico*, June 9, 2020, www.politico.com; Amy Gardner, Michelle Ye Hee Lee, Haisten Willis, and John M. Glionna, "In Georgia, Primary Day Snarled by Long Lines, Problems with Voting Machines—A Potential Preview of November," *Washington Post*, June 9, 2020, www.washingtonpost.

23 Chappell, "Judge Tosses Kansas' Proof-of-Citizenship Voter Law."

24 See Yahya R. Kamalipour, ed., *Global Communication* (Lanham, MD: Rowman and Littlefield, 2020).

25 This site requires candidates to sign on and affirm their positions, so we heard that a "problem is that in our state we had a lot of experience with some candidates not wanting to respond at all because they felt that it gives their opponents some ammunition to work with. The non-response for this online Vote411 has been an issue in our state."

26 Richard A. Lanham, *The Economics of Attention: Style and Substance in the Age of Information* (Chicago: University of Chicago Press, 2006).

27 Daniels pits this established tool against another used for list maintenance procedures, Crosscheck, which was developed by Kris Kobach and is much less reliable, inaccurate, and racially biased. Crosscheck conflates names such as "James Willie Brown" with "James Arthur Brown," and researchers have found that it has a 99 percent error rate via its very selective data gathering and mechanisms. Anderson, *One Person, No Vote*, 137–138, 87.

28 "List Maintenance," ERIC, December 31, 2018, https://ericstates.org.

29 While our general point here stands, we also recognize that there are many legitimate concerns and potentially scary scenarios for completely digital voting systems. Many credible organizations are working on these matters, such as Vote Shield (www.voteshield.org).

30 We should underscore that if Independents want to vote in a party primary, they can register as members of the party to vote in that party's primary. It also happens that, for example, most voters in New York City are Democratic. When people say that Independents and Republicans are not allowed to vote in elections (in this case, speaking only of primaries), they are complaining that only Democrats can vote in a Democratic primary. Open primaries, in which non-party

members are allowed to cast votes for another party's nominee, could be subject to potential abuse. For example, in an open primary, if you're a Republican, you could vote in a Democratic party primary for the candidate least likely to win in the general election, in the hope that the Republican nominee will have a weaker Democratic candidate as an opponent.

31 This is an observation that calls for, among other aspirational changes, reforms that help potentially viable candidates run for office, such as enacting public campaign financing. Attacking these other broad governmental challenges, though vital, is beyond this book's scope.

32 In Indiana, we too heard how "since the 2016 election, there have [been] so many nonprofits that popped up, the last thing we need is another one." But at the same time, "It almost seems like the smart thing to do, something like the Lily foundation here in Indiana, which is totally apolitical and at the same time has money behind it; and the administrative experience behind it to deal effectively with funds like that." An outreach coordinator from a nonprofit group in Kansas further shared, "I think it is good to use a current non-profit. . . . I say go ahead and support the current organizations and then they can become stronger." The executive director of a nonprofit in Wisconsin remarked, "That is a great question. In Wisconsin, we have really strong partnerships. We have an advantage because we have boots on-the-ground and already existing relationships within communities. I guess in Wisconsin, we wouldn't necessarily need additional groups, but there is always a need for funding of the efforts that we are already doing." Support could take various forms, such as helping with infrastructure, developing good resources or materials, or even some processes to help document issues around voter ID requirements. Another executive director of an agency noted: "In our area, the non-profits seem to be doing a good job about it. Based on my narrow vision on a national problem, locally the agencies that work on it do a good job. So, I would say support them." One participant shared that many nonprofits have already developed materials and standard programming for helping with voting in high schools, but there's always an additional need for help when new platforms emerge, such as when states come out with new online voter registration sites without tutorials to navigate the system. Given these realities, "It is always good to find out what is going on in the community before just jumping in and trying to do the work maybe already being done. I believe that there is a way to support it and I believe that there is enough work to go around to help us get more people to the polls."

33 Similarly, the director of a nonprofit working with the Latino community in Wisconsin said that "on the ground [we] are always reluctant for new national organizations to come in and tell us how it's done. So we are, I would say that supporting the work on-the-ground, we had good relationships. We have tables that are set up to do this." Moreover, "If I find somebody who doesn't have ID, we assess. We figure out what the need is and if it's, if it's a bigger lift than what we have the resources for, I have partners that I can send them to to ensure that

it gets done. Things like that. So, so no, I would say [we] have plenty of national groups helping us."

5. TAKING A CLOSER LOOK

1 One prominent example in recent years was the political right's manufactured controversy over critical race theory in the United States, where audiences were whipped up into a frenzy by conservative commentators through rhetoric that did not match the reality of the theory or its virtually nonexistent application in public schools. For more details, see Ibram X. Kendi, "There Is No Debate over Critical Race Theory," *The Atlantic*, July 9, 2021, www.theatlantic.com.

2 We took two voice recorders to the Mississippi focus groups and did everything possible to reconstruct these groups' comments faithfully via transcripts and memory, but we occasionally had pockets of inaudible audio that transcribers found too difficult to translate. In these instances, we went through the audio ourselves and met with the focus group facilitator to clarify and make sure we didn't miss any key points made by the participants.

3 Our focus group participants often communicated about both challenges and ways forward simultaneously in their comments, so we have grouped this chapter's headings in a more integrative manner than in the previous chapter.

4 Michael P. McDonald, United States Elections Project, n.d., www.electproject.org.

5 Thomas Patterson, *The Vanishing Voter: Public Involvement in an Age of Uncertainty* (New York: Alfred A. Knopf, 2002).

6 Ari Berman notes, "Nowhere have hopes for high Democratic turnout collided with the reality of suppressive voting laws more than in Texas. In 2016, there were three million unregistered voters of color in the state, including 2.2 million unregistered Latinos and 750,000 unregistered African-Americans. . . . Texas has the most restrictive voter registration law in the country—to register voters, you must be deputized by a county and can register voters only in the county you're deputized in." Ari Berman, "How Voter Suppression Could Swing the Midterms," *New York Times*, October 27, 2018, www.nytimes.com, par. 10.

7 In addition to a need for election officials to accept broad over narrow forms of documentation for voting, they "can verify the identity of voters without ID through other, time-tested means. For example, if a voter shows up at the polls without necessary ID in Louisiana or Ohio, election officials will verify their identity using other information, such as their date of birth, mother's maiden name, or last four digits of their Social Security number. In Florida, Missouri, and West Virginia, election officials will match the voter's signature with one on file if the voter is unable to show ID. And Iowa and West Virginia will count a ballot if another registered voter verifies the person's identity. In a number of states, voters can cast a regular ballot if they sign a legally binding affidavit attesting to their identity. By asking for voter ID at the polls, but allowing for alternative verification when absolutely necessary, states are able to efficiently and effectively ensure that every person who casts a ballot is eligible to do so, without unnecessarily

turning away registered voters." Liz Avore, "On a Federal Voter ID Law, the Devil Is in the Details," Voting Rights Lab, June 29, 2021, https://votingrightslab.org, pars. 12–14.

8 None of this is helped by the explicit racism of election officials in Mississippi. While we were carrying out our research, a news story emerged about one commissioner who expressed: "I'm concerned about voter registration in Mississippi. . . . The [B]lacks are having lots (of) events for voter registration. People in Mississippi have to get involved, too." Lici Beveridge, "Mississippi Election Commissioner's Social Media Comment about Black Voters Causes Uproar," *Hattiesburg American*, June 30, 2020, www.hattiesburgamerican.com.

9 Samuel Popkin, *The Reasoning Voter: Communication and Persuasion in Presidential Campaigns* (Chicago: University of Chicago Press, 1991), 92.

10 Not incidentally, a change in polling places was the very kind of event that required preclearance by the US Justice Department until the Supreme Court's decision in *Shelby County v. Holder*.

11 We checked the Mississippi website, www.msvoterid.ms.gov, and it appears that a driver's license from another state is enough to get a Mississippi voter ID and possibly to bring as voter ID to vote on Election Day, although we would not be absolutely sure about the latter from the way the page describes what is permissible.

12 Jody L. Herman and Taylor N. T. Brown, "The Potential Impact of Voter Identification Laws on Transgender Voters in the 2018 General Election," Williams Institute, UCLA School of Law, August 2018, https://williamsinstitute.law.ucla.edu, 1.

13 Sandy E. James, Jody L. Herman, Susan Rankin, Mara Keisling, Lisa Mottet, and Ma'ayan Anaf, "The Report of the 2015 U.S. Transgender Survey," National Center for Transgender Equality, December 2016, https://transequality.org, 85.

14 Tova Andrea Wang, "Got ID? Helping Americans Get Voter Identification," Demos, April 2012, www.demos.org, 16.

15 Prepaid postage for mailing absentee ballots should be provided by government so that citizens do not have to bear the cost or make the effort to weigh the mail and calculate and add postage.

16 "Florida's Voting-Rights Fight Could Tip the 2020 Election," *New York Times*, February 21, 2020, www.nytimes.com.

6. HOW TO FIX THE PROBLEM

1 See Douglas Stone, Sheila Heen, and Bruce Patton, *Difficult Conversations: How to Discuss What Matters Most* (New York: Penguin, 2010).

2 See "The Scope of Congressional Authority in Election Administration," US General Accounting Office, March 2001, www.gao.gov. We recognize that two of the most significant national voting rights bills to emerge in years, the For the People Act (House Resolution 1) and the John Lewis Voting Rights Act, would implement many of the recommendations we detail in this section (e.g., universal

automatic voter registration). Peter W. Stevenson, "How Is the John Lewis Voting Rights Act Different than H.R. 1?," *Washington Post*, June 8, 2021, www.washingtonpost.com. Both acts receive our unqualified support. Yet, given our findings in this project, we also propose recommendations beyond what's in these bills. As of 2022, Republican opposition has brought both acts to a standstill, underscoring the need for additional strategies via nonprofits and community organizations to fight the status quo.

3   See Daniels, *Uncounted*; Anderson, *One Person, No Vote*.

4   See the "Registration of Voters Internationally" section in "Voter Registration," Wikipedia, n.d., https://en.wikipedia.org. We provide further details on this proposal relative to the development of REAL ID, which we do not support, in the conclusion to this book.

5   We leave aside the operational question of whether states have the technology to do this currently—the goal would be to move toward every state having a uniform approach, especially given the increasingly advanced election tool technologies available on so many fronts.

6   Allie Bohm, "Yes, the States Really Reject Real ID," ACLU, March 27, 2012, www.aclu.org.

7   We need to highlight that there are some noncitizens who are authorized to work and receive Social Security numbers, so additional safeguards might be necessary to make sure they are not mistakenly registered on the basis of a Social Security number. As we mention, forms of ID such as Social Security, driver's licenses, and more were not created for the purposes of voting. This fact gets to the heart of the challenges identified in this book.

8   We remind readers that proof of citizenship does not necessarily mean having documentation like a birth certificate to vote. Written statements attesting to one's citizenship carry the force of law and have not caused meaningful voter fraud. See Neifeh, "How Do Proof-of-Citizenship Laws Block Legitimate Voters?"

9   We want to recognize that, while some voter roll purges have been done without the purest intent or effect, there is a real administrative reason for doing them. Voting everywhere is done by district. Inactive voters are people who may have moved, changed their names, or passed away—and so the rolls do need to be cleaned. But what we mean here is that, to the greatest extent possible, any new voter ID law should not exclude an already eligible, active voter.

10 It is worth considering, when a state disenfranchises long-time (or even second-ever) voters based on lack of ID, whether that state is violating the due process clause of the US Constitution by taking away a right "without due process." See US Constitution, Amendment 14, Section 1; Anthony Gaughan, "The Due Process Clause and Voting Rights," Jurist, August 27, 2018, www.jurist.org; Edward B. Foley, "Due Process, Fair Play, and Excessive Partisanship: A New Principle for Judicial Review of Election Laws," *University of Chicago Law Review* 84 (2017): 655–756.

11 Location is important on several fronts. For congressional elections, you need to have a location for the district that you are in, and for Senate races the state you are in; even in voting for the president/vice president, location by state will matter for the Electoral College count.

12 Most states tie registration deadlines to election dates. The US Constitution requires that the federal general Election Day is a single day in all states. But many other elections occur at different times, such as primaries and local elections.

13 "Citizenship Evidence," US Department of State Bureau of Consular Affairs, n.d., https://travel.state.gov.

14 See https://ericstates.org.

15 One way to accomplish this is via an agency whose mission is to carry out and continuously improve materials for diverse audiences. One example is the recently formed New York City Civic Engagement Commission, which has been chartered to (among many other, similar goals) "develop a plan to consider the language access needs of limited English proficient New Yorkers with regards to the Commission's programs and services and provide language interpreters at poll sites by the 2020 general election, with advice from a language assistance advisory committee." "About Civic Engagement Commission," 2021, www1.nyc.gov, par. 2.

16 Jonathan Brater, "Automatic Voter Registration in Illinois Is a Landmark Advance," Brennan Center for Justice, August 28, 2017, www.brennancenter.org. See also Rob Griffin, Paul Gronke, Tova Wang, and Liz Kennedy, "Who Votes with Automatic Voter Registration," Center for American Progress, June 7, 2017, www.americanprogress.org; "Automatic Voter Registration," National Council of State Legislatures, February 8, 2021, www.ncsl.org; "Fact Sheet: Voter Registration for the 21st Century," Brennan Center for Justice, July 10, 2015, www.brennancenter.org; "Automatic Voter Registration, a Summary," Brennan Center for Justice, July 10, 2019, www.brennancenter.org; Kevin Morris and Peter Dunphy, "AVR Impact on State Voter Registration," Brennan Center for Justice, April 11, 2019, www.brennancenter.org.

17 Derek Rosenfeld, "Automatic Voter Registration Works Everywhere It's Been Implemented," Brennan Center for Justice, April 11, 2019, www.brennancenter.org. It's worth highlighting at length how this works: "When an eligible citizen gives information to the government—for example, to get a driver's license, receive Social Security benefits, apply for public services, register for classes at a public university, or become a naturalized citizen—she will be automatically registered to vote unless she chooses to opt out. No separate process or paper form is required. Once the voter completes her interaction with the agency, if she doesn't decline, her information is electronically and securely sent to election officials to be added to the rolls. Once registered, election officials would send each eligible voter a confirmation that their registration has been accepted, providing a receipt and confirmation for any electronic voter transaction. Moving to this kind of opt-out system—where eligible voters are registered unless they actively decline the opportunity—is more in line with how our brains work. As behavioral science shows, our brains are

hard-wired to choose the default option. Even those who want to register put it off to the future, when it may be too late. This helps explain why states with Election Day registration have 5 to 7 percent higher turnout. . . . Moreover, having agencies send voter information over to election officials electronically reduces errors and saves money by cutting down on paper forms—which require printing, collecting, completing, mailing, and manual data-entry. An increasing number of states already electronically send voter information collected at motor vehicle offices over to election administrators. These states have reaped substantial benefits." "The Case for Automatic Voter Registration," Brennan Center for Justice, 2016, www.bren nancenter.org, 6. See also "Policy Differences of Automatic Voter Registration," Brennan Center for Justice, June 30, 2021, www.brennancenter.org.

18 Richard H. Thaler and Cass R. Sunstein, *Nudge: Improving Decisions about Health, Wealth, and Happiness* (New York: Penguin, 2009).

19 For more on how US citizenship has been verified for voting, see Amy Sherman, "Fact-Check: Do States Verify U.S. Citizenship as a Condition for Voting?," *Austin-American Statesman*, December 7, 2020, www.statesman.com; Pam Fessler, "Some Noncitizens Do Wind Up Registered to Vote, but Usually Not on Purpose," NPR, February 26, 2019, www.npr.org; "Chapter 4—Automatic Acquisition of Citizenship after Birth (INA 320)," U.S. Citizenship and Immigration Services, current as of August 5, 2021, www.uscis.gov.

20 We recommend going the way of Oregon by providing everyone with a mail-in ballot (among other easy options), which tends to greatly increase voting participation rates.

21 We won't tackle the need for affidavit ballots here, as these may still be helpful for some people in certain situations. But overcoming the need for any kind of provisional ballot except in the rarest of cases through automatic registration and some of the other policies we propose in this section would be a giant step forward for creating less confusion and time, cost, and transportation barriers.

22 We also believe that all policies that prevent felons from voting should be eliminated (with the attendant documentation requirements and voter registration processes that would go along with that). We explore this issue relative to documentation requirements further in the conclusion.

23 Testimony to the Civil Rights Oversight Subcommittee of the US House of Representatives expressed both this need and *desire* for federal intervention into the problems marginalized communities face nationally with voting: "Black people have a sense of hopelessness because they feel they have nowhere to turn for justice. For one fleeting moment, in the sixties, [B]lacks found encouragement and a sense of hope from the intervention of the federal government in support of civil rights and equal opportunity. . . . To continue the passive enforcement level which now exists is to seriously jeopardize the fundamental rights of two-and-a-half million unregistered [B]lacks. To refuse to remove the remaining obstacles is to condemn these people to continuing second class citizenship." Cited in John

Lewis and Archie E. Allen, "Black Voter Registration Efforts in the South," *Notre Dame Law Review* 48 (1972): 123.

24 When the first author's mother passed away several years ago, he was amazed at the rapidity with which many electronic systems in the United States—both governmental and corporate—updated each other to make clear that a person was now deceased. It was like all these systems were having conversations about what had happened without the author's having to do anything beyond pick up a death certificate. This demonstrated that creating such efficient electronic systems is more a matter of political will than anything else.

25 The Brennan Center for Justice argues, "Automatic registration systems will be better than paper-based systems at ensuring that only eligible citizens are registered to vote. The most appropriate agencies for automatic registration already collect citizenship information and the other information needed for voter registration—so the data being used has already been vetted. It is this already-vetted information that will form the basis for voter registration records and updates. A modern system will reduce errors of all types throughout the registration process, including improper registrations. And election officials will continue to review applications for eligibility and errors. Importantly, automatic registration systems can and should be built to enhance security. Since they are more accurate, electronic systems are less vulnerable to manipulation and abuse than their paper-based counterparts. When it comes to the threat of hacking, states can take steps to increase security, like limiting authorized users, monitoring for anomalies, and designing systems to withstand potential breaches. And using a paper backup would eliminate the harm that hacking could render to a registration database. With or without these measures in place, unlike with online voting, no one attempting to hack a voter registration system can change an election's outcome." "The Case for Automatic Voter Registration," 7.

26 For more on the one-click example and its applications, see Heath and Heath, *Switch*.

27 After the fires that ravaged Paradise, California, in 2018, stories of students like Jay Leaird amplify this point: "He's been fixated on trying to obtain a copy of his birth certificate so he can get an ID, so he can get a job, so he can try to get an apartment and have a stable place to apply to college, so he can restart, so he can move forward." Brianna Sacks, "Students Live in Tents, Do Homework under Flashlights, and Deal without Textbooks Months after California's Massive Camp Fire," *Buzzfeed News*, April 25, 2019, www.buzzfeednews.com, par. 20.

28 "Partner Toolkit: Voter ID Chatbot," VoteRiders, 2019, www.voteriders.org.

29 See Cialdini, *Influence*.

30 Lee and Kotler, *Social Marketing*.

31 Longinus once said, "No figure is more excellent than the one which is entirely hidden, so that it is no longer recognized as a figure." Quoted in Chaim Perelman and Lucille Olbrechts-Tyteca, *The New Rhetoric: A Treatise on Argumentation*,

trans. John Wilkinson and Purcell Weaver (Notre Dame, IN: University of Notre Dame Press, 1969), 171.

32 Kenneth Burke, *Language as Symbolic Action: Essays on Life, Literature, and Method* (Berkeley: University of California Press, 1966).

33 We draw the "fair" and "patriotic" constructions from Jonathan Haidt's discussion of the different values underlying liberal and conservative preferences in the United States. Those on the left tend to prioritize fairness and equality as values, while those on the right look to loyalty and similar values in much of their discourse. Jonathan Haidt, *The Righteous Mind: Why Good People Are Divided by Politics and Religion* (New York: Vintage, 2012), 4. Activist and attorney Molly McGrath, who fights against voter ID challenges across the United States, underscores the stakes for building partnerships that help people facing obstacles to voting: "In 2017, at least 99 bills that restrict access to registration and voting were introduced in 31 states. Thirty-two states have some form of voter ID law currently in effect. These ID laws don't affect all people equally: people of color, low-income people, the elderly, students, and people with disabilities disproportionately lack the types of IDs that states deem acceptable. As an attorney and voting rights advocate, I've learned that fighting voter suppression can't be restricted to Congress or the courts—[it] has to take place at every level. Our democracy is diminished every time a disabled voter can't get to the polls, or a voter can't afford to pay for unnecessary or redundant documents that a state requires to prove citizenship before issuing an ID. Every American's voting rights are put at risk when state legislatures enact ID laws that cherry pick the forms of IDs deemed acceptable based on whether a racial or ethnic group is more likely to have them. That's why I've dedicated the last several years to pushing back against restrictive ID laws, one voter at a time. Along with partner organizations like the League of Women Voters and volunteers, I search for would-be voters, document cases of disenfranchisement, and offer the support and resources people need to get IDs and get to the polls. To reach voters where they are, I visit churches, soup kitchens, school campuses, and retirement communities. Every voter's circumstance and needs are different, but with assistance, many can get their right to vote back." McGrath, "The Voter Suppression Diaries," pars. 3–5.

CONCLUSION

1 Cf. *Reynolds v. Simms*, 377 U.S. 533 (1964), cited in H.R. Rep. No. 109-478, at 2. This quote can also be found at www.govinfo.gov. This quotation appears to paraphrase a Supreme Court writing from nearly 150 years ago, from *Yick Wo v. Hopkins* (1886), where the Supreme Court declared that voting is "a fundamental political right, because [it is] preservative of all rights." Cited in Daniel P. Tokaji, "The Right to Vote in an Age of Discontent," American Bar Association, January 7, 2019, www.americanbar.org, 2.

2 See Richard L. Hasen, "Republicans Aren't Done Messing with Elections," *New York Times*, April 23, 2021, www.nytimes.com; Chuck Todd, Mark Murray, Carrie

Dann, and Ben Kamisar, "New GOP Voting Laws Target More Than Just Voter Access," *NBC News*, June 3, 2021, www.nbcnews.com; Nick Corasaniti, "Republicans Aim to Seize More Power over How Elections Are Run," *New York Times*, March 24, 2021, www.nytimes.com; "Voting Laws Roundup: May 2021," Brennan Center for Justice, May 28, 2021, www.brennancenter.org.

3 Adam Harris, "The Voting Disaster Ahead," *The Atlantic*, June 2020, www.the atlantic.com, pars. 1–6.

4 May Wong, "New Research on Voting by Mail Shows Neutral Partisan Effects," Stanford Institute for Economic Policy Research, April 16, 2020, https://siepr. stanford.edu; "Vote-by-Mail Benefits Neither Party and Is Nearly Fraud-Free, New Studies Find," *The Fulcrum*, April 16, 2020, https://thefulcrum.us. Daniel Thompson and colleagues argue that: "1) universal vote-by-mail does not appear to affect either party's share of turnout, 2) universal vote-by-mail does not appear to increase either party's vote share, and 3) universal vote-by-mail modestly increases overall average turnout rates, in line with previous estimates. All three conclusions support the conventional wisdom of election administration experts and contradict many popular claims in the media." Daniel M. Thompson, Jennifer A. Wu, Jesse Yoder, and Andrew B. Hall, "Universal Vote-by-Mail Has No Impact on Partisan Turnout or Vote Share," *Proceedings of the National Academy of Sciences* 117 (2020): 14052. This hasn't prevented lawsuits claiming that vote by mail will lead to partisan advantages, e.g., Musadiq Bidar, "Republicans Sue California Governor Gavin Newsom, Claim His Vote-By-Mail Order Is 'Illegal Power Grab,'" CBS News, May 24, 2020, www .cbsnews.com. A distinction should be made between the rhetoric and reality of this issue; during the coronavirus global pandemic, "The untold story [was] that while the national parties engage in debates, attacks, and counterattacks about the expansion of by-mail voting, state governors and election officials from both parties and in most states have been methodically expanding access to by-mail voting in response to COVID-19." Edward Perez, "The Bipartisan Truth about By-Mail Voting," OSET Institute, May 22, 2020, 1.

5 See, for example, Alexa Ura, "Federal Judge Says All Texas Voters Can Apply to Vote by Mail During Pandemic," *Texas Tribune*, May 19, 2020, www.texas tribune.org.

6 Zach Montellaro, "Coronavirus Threatened to Make a Mess of Kentucky's Primary: It Could Be a Model Instead," *Politico*, July 4, 2020, www.politico.com. Amanda Zoch highlights an important fact, however: "With so many policymakers and election officials encouraging more absentee voting and even debating the value and feasibility of 'going all-mail,' it is worth noting that all elections are hybrid—every state has some combination of mail voting and in-person voting." Even mail-in states such as Oregon have about 7 percent of voters using in-person voting. Amanda Zoch, "Why Elections Need Both Absentee and In-Person Voting," National Conference of State Legislatures, www.ncsl.org, pars. 2, 4.

7 Spencer Overton, *Stealing Democracy: The New Politics of Voter Suppression* (New York: Norton, 2006).

8 "REAL ID Frequently Asked Questions," US Department of Homeland Security, March 20, 2020, www.dhs.gov.

9 "REAL ID Frequently Asked Questions."

10 "REAL ID Frequently Asked Questions."

11 For other critical perspectives on REAL ID, see Joe Mathews, "It's Unreal Just How Awful 'Real ID' Is," Zocalo Public Square, February 11, 2020, www.zocalo publicsquare.org; Hannah Piercey, "Do I Need a REAL ID to Vote?," VoteRiders, 2019, www.voteriders.org; Jacob Mullikan, "Real ID Causing Issues with Voter Registration," *Messenger-Inquirer*, December 27, 2019, www.messenger-inquirer. com; Debra Milberg, "The National Identification Debate: 'REAL ID' and Voter Identification," *I/S: A Journal of Law and Policy for the Information Society* 3 (2007–2008): 443.

12 Milberg, 443.

13 See "DACA Decision at the Supreme Court 2020," Informed Immigrant, 2021, www .informedimmigrant.com; "'The Right Side of History': Professor Robert C. Smith Reacts to the Supreme Court's DACA decision," CUNY Graduate Center, June 18, 2020, www.gc.cuny.edu; Smith, Waisanen, and Yrizar Barbosa, *Immigration and Strategic Public Health Communication*.

14 Steven Rosenfeld, "Tech Glitches Plague an Already Chaotic Primary Season," *National Memo*, July 8, 2020, www.nationalmemo.com.

15 That being said, the Board of Elections in New York permitted online requests for ballots and allowed the potential exposure to the COVID-19 virus as a justi-fication for using an absentee ballot. "Absentee Voting," New York State Board of Elections, June 30, 2020, www.elections.ny.gov; Brigid Bergin, "How to Vote by Absentee Ballot in New York's June 23rd 'Pandemic' Primary," *Gothamist*, May 18, 2020, https://gothamist.com.

16 "Public Health and Political Experts Signers," https://docs.google.com. Liz Avore at the Voting Rights Lab notes that "robust and distinct procedures are already in place to verify mail voters. . . . Most states verify the identity of mail ballot voter via a signature match, while others verify voter identity using basic information, such as date of birth and address. Some states require that voters provide an ID number—such as a driver's license number, state ID number, or the last four digits of a social security number—in order to receive or cast a mail ballot." Yet "Requir-ing voters to provide a copy of an ID with their mail ballot creates an unnecessary and costly burden for voters, especially rural, low income, and elderly voters who rely on mail voting and may not have access to photocopiers, scanners, or print-ers, all while adding no value from an election security standpoint. It also presents privacy concerns for voters who do not want a copy of their ID going through the mail every time they vote." Avore, "On a Federal Voter ID Law," pars. 15, 19.

17 "Voting Outside the Polling Place: Absentee, All-Mail and Other Voting at Home Options," National Conference of State Legislatures, June 22, 2020, www.ncsl .org; "Absentee Ballot Rules," Vote.org, www.vote.org; "Absentee/Mail-in Voting," *Ballotpedia*, July 30, 2019, https://ballotpedia.org. Two other good sources for

absentee and vote-by-mail information by state include the federal government sites www.usa.gov and www.eac.gov.

18   John Hickenlooper, "We've Been Voting at Home for Six Years in Colorado. It's Time to Do It Nationally," *Washington Post*, April 8, 2020, www.washingtonpost. com; Amber McReynolds and Charles Stewart III, "Let's Put the Vote-by-Mail 'Fraud' Myth to Rest," *The Hill*, April 28, 2020, https://thehill.com.

19   Edward J. Moreno, "Here's Where Your State Stands on Mail-In Voting," *The Hill*, June 9, 2020, https://thehill.com.

20   Michael Wines, "Voting by Mail Could Be What States Need. But Can They Pull It Off?," *New York Times*, April 11, 2020, www.nytimes.com; Pam Fessler, "Chaos in Primary Elections Raises Fears for November," NPR, June 15, 2020, www.npr.org.

21   Eddie Burkhalter, "Federal Judge Waives Some Alabama Voting Requirements amid Pandemic," *Alabama Political Reporter*, June 15, 2020, www.alreporter.com.

22   Eddie Burkhalter, "RNC Fighting Nationwide Mail-in Ballots amid COVID-19," *Alabama Political Reporter*, May 18, 2020, www.alreporter.com. A push in Alabama to ban curbside voting, and the state's failure to relax a requirement that those voting by absentee ballot have their mail-in ballot requests notarized or signed in front of two witnesses (for voters over the age of sixty-five) were halted by the Eleventh Circuit Court of Appeals. Potential witnesses were not readily available during the pandemic, much less notaries. "Absentee Voting Information," Alabama Votes, June 28, 2020, www.sos.alabama.gov.

23   The circuit court pointed out that the "state's failure to acknowledge the significant difference between leaving one's home to vote in non-pandemic times and forcing high-risk COVID-19 individuals to breach social-distancing and self-isolation protocols so they can vote reflects a serious lack of understanding of or disregard for the science and facts involved here." Brian Lyman, "Federal Appeals Court Won't Block Ruling Allowing Curbside Voting in Alabama," *Montgomery Advertiser*, June 26, 2020, www.montgomeryadvertiser.com.

24   See Ariane de Vogue and Caroline Kelly, "Supreme Court Temporarily Blocks Court Order That Cleared the Way for Expanded Vote by Mail in Alabama Due to Covid-19," CNN, July 2, 2020, www.cnn.com.

25   Emily Larsen, "Republican Nightmare: Trump Vote-by-Mail Demonizing Driving Down GOP Participation," *Washington Examiner*, June 26, 2020, www.washingtonexaminer.com; Amy Gardner and Josh Dawsey, "Trump's Attacks on Mail Voting Are Turning Republicans Off Absentee Ballots," *Washington Post*, July 7, 2020, www.washingtonpost.com.

26   Astead W. Herndon and Stephanie Saul, "Major Problems with Voting in Atlanta as 5 States Hold Primaries," *New York Times*, June 9, 2020, www.nytimes.com.

27   Dareh Gregorian, "Voter Turnout Soared in Georgia Despite Massive Primary Day Problems," *NBC News*, June 12, 2020, www.nbcnews.com.

28   Linda Blackford, "Voter Suppression Is Enshrined in Kentucky Law, Coronavirus Primary Showed Us a Better Way," *Lexington Herald Leader*, June 24, 2020, www.kentucky.com; Ryland Barton, "Kentucky Primary Turnout Was Up, but Voting

Challenges Remain," WFPL, June 2, 2020, https://wfpl.org; Dan Merica, Eric Brander, and Jeff Zeleny, "Kentucky Braces for Chaotic Primary Election after Cuts to Polling Locations," CNN Politics, June 22, 2020, www.cnn.com; Ryland Barton, "Amy McGrath's Campaign Joins Lawsuit for More Polling Locations," WFPL, June 12, 2020, https://wfpl.org.

29 "All the States That Have Delayed Their Primary Elections," *Axios*, May 8, 2020, www.axios.

30 Alexis Selitz-Wald, "How Do You Know Voting by Mail Works? The U.S. Military's Done It since the Civil War," *NBC News*, April 19, 2020, www.nbcnews .com; Joel Achenbach, "The Election of 1864 and the Last Temptation of Abraham Lincoln," *Washington Post*, September 11, 2014, www.washingtonpost.com. Carol Anderson reminds us, "'How much of a hassle it is to vote is generally a matter of design, not accident. . . . Long lines are deliberate, because they deal with the allo- cation of resources,' . . . it's frustrating to see long lines reported in the news media as evidence of voter enthusiasm: 'What they really show is government ineptness. And oftentimes a deliberate deployment of not enough resources in minority communities.'" Evan Nicole Brown, "What It's Been Like to Vote in 2020 So Far," *New York Times*, July 14, 2020, www.nytimes.com, par. 4; "Should the Supreme Court Be Reformed?," National Constitution Center, December 16, 2021, https:// constitutioncenter.org.

31 "Voter Identification," MIT Election Data and Science Lab, par. 17.

32 Wendy Weiser and Max Feldman, "How to Protect the 2020 Vote from the Coro- navirus," Brennan Center for Justice, March 16, 2020, www.brennancenter.org.

33 Although the following has never been tested in the courts, it's worth noting the power ascribed to Congress in elections via the US Constitution in Article I, Section 4: "The Times, Places and Manner of holding Elections for Senators and Representatives, shall be prescribed in each State by the Legislature thereof; but the Congress may at any time by Law make or alter such Regulations [except as to Senators]." But this may be in contrast with Article II, Section 1, providing that each state shall appoint, "in such Manner as the Legislature thereof may direct, a Number of Electors," without reference to a role for Congress to "make or alter" the way in which the states appoint their electors. What has never been tested is the full meaning of either clause with respect to the limits of state versus congres- sional power with elections.

34 See Latour, *American Government and the Vision of Democrats*.

35 For a helpful listing of options for required documentation and a thoughtful dis- cussion weighing the positive and negative impacts, including increasing burdens on otherwise eligible voters, see the "Voter Identification in Australia" section in Michael Maley, "Election Integrity," Electoral Knowledge Network, 2021, https:// aceproject.org.

36 "When a child is born to a family in Finland, the child is registered in the Population Information System at the hospital." "When a Child Is Born in Finland," n.d., infoFinland.fi; "Registration at Birth in the National Population

Registration System," Ministry of Foreign Affairs for Finland, n.d., https://um..fi. Attempting to create a national registry in the United States would undoubtedly lead to some kinds of political opposition. Although Social Security and the coming effort to institute REAL ID are examples of ways in which the US government already does and might maintain vast lists of US residents and could be recast to support a voter ID, the idea of a national registry has not yet caught on. If it was handled at the local level, the US government could create a program that provides technology and adopts a "best practices" structure for uniform ID, and perhaps even offer funding to the states that are ready to adopt that technology and structure. This might not entice 100 percent of the states, but undoubtedly many would join in, and over time the reluctant states would possibly come along.

37 "Voting in Japan," Becoming Legally Japanese, December 9, 2012, www.turning-japanese.info. See also "How to Vote in Germany," European Elections 2019, n.d., www.european-elections.eu.

38 "ID to Vote," Elections Canada, October 26, 2020, www.elections.ca.

39 Jennifer S. Rosenberg and Margaret Chen, "Expanding Democracy: Voter Registration around the World," Brennan Center for Justice, 2009, www.brennancenter.org, 63.

40 Rosenberg and Chen, 13.

41 The report underscores that because "voting is both a right and a duty, the working group recommends adopting universal civic duty voting for most federal, state, and municipal elections. Requiring citizens to participate, the report authors argue, would survive legal challenges and is 'consistent with our Constitution's guarantees of free speech, robust forms of collective action, and effective government.' The proposal for universal civic duty voting would require mandatory participation in elections, not mandatory voting, allowing voters to choose 'none of the above,' or decline to participate for conscientious objections. The report authors make the case that universal civic duty voting would help ensure increased political participation in communities of color that have long confronted exclusion from our democracy. Coupled with legal and political reforms, universal civic duty voting would drastically undercut voter suppression measures, and strongly encourage election officials and other institutions to work for unimpeded access to the ballot box. Universal voting, the authors write, 'would clarify the priorities of election officials at every point in the process: Their primary task would be to allow citizens to embrace their duties, not to block their participation.'" "New Report by Voting Rights Advocates, Practitioners, and Scholars Details Need for Universal Civic Duty Voting," Harvard Kennedy School of Government Ash Center for Democratic Governance and Innovation, July 20, 2020, https://ash.harvard.edu, pars. 2–4.

42 Jonathan Brater, Kevin Morris, Myrna Perez, and Christopher Deluzio, "Purges: A Growing Threat to the Right to Vote," Brennan Center for Justice, 2018, www.brennancenter.org, 1.

43 Daniels, *Uncounted*, 126. We refer readers to Anderson's painstaking analysis on all the undercover tactics at play in voter purges across the United States, especially for how they violate the requirements of the National Voter Registration Act on procedures for updating voter rolls. Anderson, *One Person, No Vote*, 72–95.

44 See Daniels, *Uncounted*, 94–121. Daniels cites the real-life examples of politicians telling voters that Democrats vote on Wednesday while Republicans should vote on Tuesday (the actual Election Day) and deceptive robocalls telling voters their polling places have changed or that voting wouldn't be necessary because the election had already taken place.

45 Daniel Schleifer, "Unlocking the Vote: Activists and Disenfranchised Former Felons Restore Voting Rights in Rhode Island," *The Nation*, December 18, 2006, www.thenation.com. For a listing of the voting status for ex-felons in different states, see "Felon Voting Rights," National Conference of State Legislatures, June 28, 2021, www.ncsl.org; "Felony Disenfranchisement Laws in The United States," The Sentencing Project, April 28, 2014, www.sentencingproject.org.

46 Abrams, "We Cannot Resign"; Berman, "How Voter Suppression Could Swing the Midterms."

47 "Voting Rights Restoration Efforts in Florida," Brennan Center for Justice, May 31, 2019, www.brennancenter.org; Alex Pickett, "11th Circuit Blocks Order Allowing Felon Voting in Florida," Court House News Service, July 1, 2020, www.court housenews.com.

48 Nina Totenberg, "Supreme Court Deals Major Blow to Felons' Right to Vote in Florida," NPR, July 17, 2020, www.npr.org; Lawrence Mower, "Florida Felons Lose Voting Rights Case in Federal Appeals Court," *Tampa Bay Times*, September 11, 2020, www.tampabay.com. We must remember that people have paid their debt to society by serving their sentences. They then return to the outside world that should be treating them as regular civilians. Plenty of law-abiding citizens are in debt in some way or another, and they are allowed to vote. Yet someone who must readjust to society (and has no immediate way to pay for fines or costs or for anything else) and find a job and housing (which can be extremely difficult) is the one who is prevented from being allowed to reenter and participate in society by voting.

49 Heather K. Gerken, *The Democracy Index: Why Our Election System Is Failing and How to Fix It* (Princeton, NJ: Princeton University Press, 2009). For other interesting ideas, see Jack H. Nagel and Rogers M. Smith, eds., *Representation: Elections and Beyond* (Philadelphia: University of Pennsylvania Press, 2013).

50 Joshua Geltzer, "The Lost 110 Words of Our Constitution," *Politico*, February 24, 2020, www.politico.com, pars. 1–2, 7, 6.

51 Geltzer, pars. 33–34.

52 Daniels, *Uncounted*, 60, 87.

53 There are deeper issues at hand in terms of what is happening within and between states in the United States. While this topic is beyond the scope of this book, we would feel remiss without pointing readers toward what other scholars have

revealed, such as James Gardner, who writes, "In light of the recent turn, globally and nationally, toward authoritarianism, and the concurrent sharp decline in public support not merely for democracy but for the philosophical liberalism on which democracy rests, it is necessary to discard or to substantially revise prior accounts of the nature of state-to-state variation in the U.S. All such accounts implicitly presuppose a common commitment, across the political spectrum, to the core tenets of democratic liberalism, and consequently that subnational variations in policy preferences and modes of self-governance reflect nothing more than disagreements within the shared American liberal tradition. That assumption, if it was ever valid, may be no longer. As in other federal states in which subnational 'illiberal enclaves' have persisted over time, the United States may be witnessing a replication at the subnational level of what appears to be happening at the national level: a growing chasm along a cleavage between democratic liberalism and illiberal authoritarianism, in which some states remain committed to inherited forms of democratic liberalism while others cling to (or develop, or resurrect) patterns of illiberal authoritarianism." James A. Gardner, "Illiberalism and Authoritarianism in the American States," University at Buffalo School of Law Legal Studies Research Paper No. 2020-001, https://ssrn.com, 1.

54 Weiser and Feldman, "How to Protect the 2020 Vote from the Coronavirus," par. 21.

55 And if citizens find one polling place closed or underresourced and must travel to another, all that time off from work or standing in lines effectively constitutes a poll tax. Stacey Abrams in Downs, *Voter Suppression*, 25. On a satirical note, David Blight urges Republicans to simply offer those whose votes they are already suppressing through voter ID laws a check not to vote: "Give people a choice: take the money and just not vote, or travel miles without easy transportation to obtain a driver's license they do not need. It's their 'liberty'; let them decide how best to use it. Perhaps they will forget their history as much as the Republican Party seems to wish the nation would. Such an offer would be only a marginal expense for a 'super PAC'—plus a bit more to cover the lawyers needed to prove it legal under federal election law—and no one would have to know who paid for this generous effort to stop fraud. Once and for all, the right can honestly declare what the Supreme Court has allowed it to practice: that voters are commodities, not citizens." David W. Blight, "Voter Suppression, Then and Now," *New York Times*, September 7, 2012, www.nytimes.com, pars. 15–16.

56 "US Elections—Is the Fox Guarding the Henhouse?," YouTube, 2008, www .youtube.com/watch?v=BydnlXBkT9E. Highlighting the graver challenges of this overall issue, Joshua Cohen suggests that typical forms of voter suppression in Georgia's elections bill created after the 2020 US general election are actually not as alarming as "the real purpose of SB 202: sweeping reforms to electoral administration that have dramatically changed who runs Georgia's elections. . . . these provisions create wholesale changes to Georgia's electoral administration, all aimed at increasing the power of Georgia's Republican Party. This has

been done through a reshaping of the State Election Board, which has been transformed overnight into one of the most powerful agencies in the state. This once-esoteric body now has nothing less than the absolute authority to suspend county elections officials and replace them with handpicked appointees. These appointees could have tremendous power over the post-election certification process, a crucial aspect of the peaceful transfer of power. While this power can theoretically only be exercised if the State Election Board feels that local boards are engaging in 'nonfeasance, malfeasance or gross negligence,' there are no standards or guidelines for this judgment, allowing it to be enforced arbitrarily. . . . In effect, the state legislature took an obscure bureaucratic appendage, annexed it, gave it sweeping powers and made it accountable only to their own appointees. They did this because they know they can't keep enough people from voting to truly stop the state's leftward political trend. Rather than even try to make a case for themselves, they are consolidating power, transferring authority away from elected officials to the hyper-gerrymandered state legislature and its new pocket institutions. . . . While Democrats carried both Senate run-offs and the Presidential race, state offices are still awash with Republicans. Rather than waiting for Democrats to win state offices before usurping their authority, Republicans are taking it now—and positioning themselves to overturn results they don't like." Joshua Cohen, "The Most Important Yet Unheard of Parts of Georgia's Election Bill," *The Red&Black*, June 18, 2021, www.redandblack.com, pars. 5–8, 10, 12. We'd add that this is one of the most important antivoting situations that has emerged in US history other than the exclusion of Blacks and women from the vote and, while beyond this book's immediate scope, needs to be given prominence. Previously in Georgia "election board members were selected by both political parties, county commissioners and the three biggest municipalities in Troup County. Now, the G.O.P.-controlled county commission has the sole authority to restructure the board and appoint all the new members." Rick Hasen, "Must-Read NYT: 'How Republican States Are Expanding Their Power over Elections,'" *Election Law Blog*, June 19, 2021, https://electionlawblog.org, par. 3. As an example of some immediate effects, Republican Baoky Vu and Democrat Helen Butler, who opposed President Trump's lies about the election, were both let go from their election board roles in Georgia "after Gov. Brian Kemp signed a law that allows the GOP to appoint members to local election boards." "They Stood Up to Trump's Lies and Now Are Losing Their Jobs," CNN, 2021, www.cnn.com.

57 Waldman, "Voter Suppression's Death by a Thousand Cuts."

58 Tim Wu, "The Oppression of the Supermajority," *New York Times*, March 5, 2019, www.nytimes.com.

59 Joseph Biden, "Remarks by President Biden on Protecting the Sacred, Constitutional Right to Vote," White House, July 13, 2021, www.whitehouse.gov, par. 75.

60 Biden, par. 85.

APPENDIX B

1 "Passports," USPS, n.d., www.usps.com.
2 "Vital Records," Arizona Department of Health Services, 2018, http://azdhs.gov.
3 "Ordering Birth Certificates by Regular/Priority Mail," Kansas Department of Health and Environment, 2018, www.kdheks.gov.
4 "How to Apply for a Kansas Identification Card," Department of Motor Vehicles, 2018, www.dmv.com.
5 "Identification Cards in Arizona," 2018, www.dmv.org.

INDEX

Abrams, Stacy, 8

absentee, 76, 160, 162–165, 171; addressing challenges as, 8; address changes, moving and matching, 121–122; serving clientele in, 43–52; unclear differences in ballots, provisional and otherwise, 132; variations in requirements, state and county, 74–75

American Civil Liberties Union: and advocating voting rights, 117; and combating voter suppression, 132; inability to find mass voter fraud, 23; and violations of the VRA, 13; working with public and nonprofit institutions in, 153

Andrew Goodman Foundation, 153

audience passivity, 96

azsos.gov, 55

Biden, Joseph, 172

birth certificate, 3, 12, 15–16, 60–61, 74, 79, 85, 96, 100, 121, 136, 147–148, 150; blanket policy solution, 141; circular traps, 70; current state of voter ID laws regarding, 25–26; and destroyed documents, 2; disabled populations lacking access in, 11; election official responses, 56; financial costs in, 20; receiving personal help with voter documentation, 135; solutions for lacking documentation, 145; survey responses and nonprofit collaboration, 44, 47–48; voter registration drive challenges, 68–69

Board of Elections: difficulties with runoff elections in, 132; lack of other language

speakers in, 80; letting voters know documentation needs in, 146; working on ID issues in off-election years, 151

Brennan Center for Justice, 17; advocacy for same-day registration in, 170; funding challenges for, 116; interactive maps of, showing increase in voter ID states and laws, 25; lack of government-issued photo identification among US citizens revealed in study, 15; positive results of automatic voter registration study, 149

Bush v. Gore, 13; Florida's hotly contested vote counts in, 129; interest in inadequate and unfair voting practices awakened nationwide, 13; lack of uniformity in voter ID, registration, and balloting identified as source of chaos, 165

campaign finance reform, 170

circular trap, 70–71; variation across states' voter documentation requirements, 143

citizen service experience, 53

citizenship: access difficulties of time, money and transportation identified, 67–68; Arizona proof of citizenship requirements, 84; citizenship misinformation, 77–79; citizenship/naturalization delays in, 73; Kansas proof of citizenship requirements in, 105

conservative, 14, 22–24, 164

convenience sampling, 59, 65

Don Waisanen is Professor at the Baruch College, CUNY Marxe School of Public and International Affairs, where he teaches courses and workshops in public communication—including executive speech training; strategic communication; and seminars on leadership, storytelling, and improvisation. All his research seeks to understand how communication works to promote or hinder the force of citizens' voices. Since "every human advancement or reversal can be understood through communication" (Walter Annenberg), he has written six books and close to fifty scholarly publications on the subject, covering topics from strategies in public speaking to the ways that organizations and governments can better communicate with different stakeholders. He is the author of *Leadership Standpoints: A Practical Framework for the Next Generation of Nonprofit Leaders*; *Improv for Democracy: How to Bridge Differences and Develop the Communication and Leadership Skills Our World Needs*; *Political Conversion: Personal Transformation as Strategic Public Communication*; and co-author of *Immigration and Strategic Public Health Communication: Lessons from the Transnational Seguro Popular Healthcare Project*; and *Real Money, Real Power? The Challenges with Participatory Budgeting in New York City*. Previously, Don worked in broadcast journalism, as a speechwriter, and on political campaigns. He is the founder of Communication Upward (www.commupward .com) and an adjunct lecturer at Columbia University's School of Professional Studies and New York University's Wagner Graduate School of Public Service. He received a PhD in communication from the University of Southern California's Annenberg School.

Sonia R. Jarvis is Distinguished Lecturer at the Baruch College, CUNY Marxe School of Public and International Affairs, and an accomplished scholar whose research and teaching focus on race, politics, and the media. She has written several book chapters and policy papers and is currently completing a book entitled *Through a Prism, Darkly: The Media's Impact on Race and Politics in America since the Civil Rights Act of 1964.* She is an active member of several professional associations and academic organizations. In addition to her scholastic work, she has served in a number of administrative positions, including most notably as the executive director of the National Coalition on Black Voter Participation and as managing director of the Center for National Policy Review Clinic formerly based at Catholic University of America's Columbus Law School. A frequent commentator on public issues, she has been interviewed by almost every major media outlet in the country, such as National Public Radio, the *Washington Post*, and CNN. She has taught undergraduate and graduate courses on race, media, and politics, and she brings a wealth of practical and theoretical knowledge to the courses she teaches. She graduated with a degree in political science (with honors and distinction) and a degree in psychology, both from Stanford University, followed by a JD from Yale University.

NICOLE A. GORDON is Faculty Director of the CUNY Baruch College Executive MPA program and Distinguished Lecturer at the Baruch College, CUNY Marxe School of Public and International Affairs. She was the founding Executive Director of New York City's pioneer Campaign Finance Board, building it into a nationally and internationally recognized model. She was the Vice President of the JEHT Foundation, whose focus included elections, and where she worked closely with government officials, academics, not-for-profit institutions, and other foundations to effect change in policy and practice. Ms. Gordon served as counsel to the chairman of the New York State Commission on Government Integrity and has practiced law in the public and private sectors. She is a past president of the Council on Governmental Ethics Laws; has taught at the Fordham University School of Law, Cardozo Law School, and NYU/ Wagner; and has written academic articles on campaign finance, ethics in government, public policy, and public administration. She holds an AB from Barnard College with honors in classical Greek and a JD from Columbia Law School.